Au Revoir, Europe

Au Revoir, Europe
What if Britain left the EU?

David Charter

Biteback Publishing

First published in Great Britain in 2012 by
Biteback Publishing Ltd
Westminster Tower
3 Albert Embankment
London SE1 7SP
Copyright © David Charter 2012

ISBN 978-1-84954-121-3

10 9 8 7 6 5 4 3 2 1

A CIP catalogue record for this book is available from the
British Library.

Set in Sabon and Bulmer

Printed and bound in Great Britain by
CPI Group (UK) Ltd, Croydon CR0 4YY

For Michelle and Leo, with love

Contents

Acknowledgements

When Iain Dale proposed a book on Britain's fraught forty-year relationship with the European Union, it fitted in perfectly with my own plans to write a Brussels valediction after spending five years working there for *The Times*. I would like to thank Iain for the opportunity to write the story of Britain's detachment from the EU and Hollie Teague at Biteback for her judicious editing.

I am grateful to James Harding, editor of *The Times*, Robert Thomson, former editor, and Richard Beeston, foreign editor, for providing me with the opportunity to spend so much time with the European Union, and my other colleagues in *The Times* foreign news department for their support.

I have many other people to thank for their kind assistance with this book, including: Dennis Abbott, Eva Baumann, Pervenche Berès MEP, Stephen Booth, Elmar Brok MEP, Anthony Browne, Martin Callanan MEP, Brent Cameron, David Campbell Bannerman MEP, Richard Corbett, Neil Corlett, Chris Cummings, Andrew Duff MEP, Senator Alan Eggleston, George Eustice MP, Nigel Farage MEP, Patrizio Fiorilli, Chris Fretwell, Phil Goff MP, Antony Gravili, Mark Gray, Chris Heaton-Harris MP, Tom Hind, James Holtum, Baron Howard of Lympne, Syed Kamall MEP, Sony Kapoor, Mohan Kaul, Helen Kearns, Maja Kocijancic, Philippe Legrain, Edward McMillan-Scott MEP, Denis MacShane MP, Paul Moore, Mats Persson, David Poyser, Konrad Schiemann, Fredrik Sejersted,

Eleanor Sharpston, Ransford Smith, Martin Sorrell, Philip Souta, Struan Stevenson MEP, Ulf Sverdrup, Jonathan Todd, Gawain Towler, Marjory Van Den Broeke, Ton Van Lierop, Guy Verhofstadt MEP, Roger Waite, Simon Walker, Baroness Williams of Crosby, and those who talked to me off the record, as well as my brilliant Brussels colleagues Stephen Castle, Geoff Meade, Ian Traynor, Bruno Waterfield and the incomparable Jacki Davis for her generous advice.

Special thanks are due to Stephen Cave for wise words and numerous suggestions of improvements. Needless to say, all mistakes, omissions and misunderstandings are mine. Last, but not least, I am eternally grateful to my family and especially to Michelle for making it all possible.

Berlin, October 2012.

Glossary

Common Agricultural Policy (CAP) – An EU system of subsidies for farmers.

Council of the European Union – Forum for national ministers to meet and take policy and legislative decisions.

Economic and Monetary Union (EMU) – The system underpinning the single currency.

Enlargement – Policy of expanding the EU to include more countries.

Euro – The European single currency shared by seventeen nations.

European Central Bank (ECB) – Administers monetary policy for the seventeen countries in the single currency.

European Commission – Executive body of the European Union, responsible for administration, oversight and proposing legislation.

European Commissioner – Member of the European Commission cabinet (known as the college, comprising one representative from each of the twenty-seven EU member states).

European Council – EU institution where leaders from the member states meet to set policy.

European Court of Human Rights (ECHR) – Court in Strasbourg that upholds the European Convention on Human Rights. It is not part of the European Union.

European Court of Justice (ECJ) – Court based in Luxembourg that upholds and interprets EU law, comprising one judge from each member state.

European Economic Area (EEA) – Thirty countries (EU plus Iceland, Liechtenstein and Norway) that take part in the single market and adopt all relevant EU laws.

European Economic Community (EEC) – Former name of the EU, which changed under the Maastricht Treaty of 1993.

European External Action Service (EEAS) – Diplomatic corps and overseas representation of the EU.

European Free Trade Association (EFTA) – Four-country group (Iceland, Liechtenstein, Norway and Switzerland) originally set up with more countries, including the UK, in 1960 as an alternative to the EEC.

European Parliament – Elected legislative body of the EU, composed of 754 Members of the European Parliament (MEPs) including seventy-three from the UK.

European Union (EU) – Economic and political alliance of twenty-seven nations synonymous with its main location in Brussels and built upon a series of treaties starting with the Treaty of Rome in 1957.

Four freedoms – The basis of the single market: the free movement of capital, goods, people and services.

Multi-annual financial framework – Seven-year EU budget programme.

Qualified majority voting (QMV) – Method of deciding matters between ministers in the Council of the EU that attaches extra weight to bigger countries in a complicated formula.

Schengen – Name taken from a border town in Luxembourg for the common visa-free travel zone in continental Europe joined by twenty-six countries.

Single market – EU internal tariff-free trading area established by the Single European Act of 1986.

Structural funds – EU system of internal aid for infrastructure projects in poorer areas.

Introduction

And finally, the United Kingdom...

A parade of Prime Ministers and Presidents from twenty-six European nations had signed the Lisbon Treaty. Each country was represented by its leader and Foreign Secretary at the grand ceremony staged in the magnificent sixteenth-century Jerónimos Monastery in the Portuguese capital. For France, the trio of President, Prime Minister and Foreign Minister all gathered at the podium to autograph the European Union's latest set of rule changes and then congratulate each other. When the turn of the twenty-seventh and final EU member (alphabetically) was announced, David Miliband, the Foreign Secretary, approached the signing table. He was alone. Instead of celebrating with his Prime Minister after the historic moment of signature, Miliband shook hands with the usher who handed him the pen. The commemorative photo of smiling leaders taken in front of the monastery in the sunshine shortly afterwards shows Miliband standing rather sheepishly at the end of the back row, grinning like a naughty schoolboy.

Gordon Brown stayed behind in London that morning to attend a routine session of the House of Commons Liaison Committee and then, ludicrously, jumped on a plane to Lisbon. He arrived more than three hours late while everyone else was finishing a sumptuous banquet lunch at the National Coach Museum. It was here, in front of a display of gilded carriages which once carried papal envoys and Portuguese kings, that the British Prime Minister filled in the gap left for his name on the treaty.

The manner of the signing of the Lisbon Treaty spoke volumes about Britain's relationship with the EU. It was awkward, it was half-hearted and it was late. It seemed to symbolise the way that, while special treatment is often demanded by the British, Europe rarely receives our full attention. Of course, if they had really wanted to, Downing Street could have rescheduled Brown's appearance at the committee of MPs, which was announced some time after the date was set for the grandiose European gathering. Perhaps it was intended to convey a proper focus on domestic affairs during Europe's hour of self-congratulation, perhaps it was a genuine attempt to keep everyone happy, but in the event the Prime Minister's performance pleased no one, not the eurosceptics who wanted a referendum and the chance to reject the document, nor the europhiles who hoped to see Britain playing a more central role in Europe. It was a gift to the newspaper sketch-writers – the backroom deal, the bungled snub, the very British embarrassment.

Fast forward four years almost to the day and the British Prime Minister was once again standing alone. David Cameron ensured that he would not have to face any lavish signing ceremony for the Fiscal Compact, a German-inspired set of new rules for national budgets, by the simple expedient of using his veto to prevent it from becoming a fully fledged EU treaty. Back in Britain, Cameron's gesture was hailed as a triumph by his backbenchers and rewarded with a leap in support for the Conservatives in the opinion polls. It was a surge that lasted all of three weeks. He and George Osborne, the Chancellor of the Exchequer, then spent the next year telling the eurozone countries to hurry up and get on with their integrationist reforms to save the struggling single currency, which by this time was having a serious impact on Britain's economic prospects. The veto had prevented an EU treaty, from which the UK would have been granted an opt-out, cheered British eurosceptics and annoyed almost every political leader in Europe, twenty-five of whom went ahead anyway with their new rules in an inter-governmental agreement.

Like Gordon Brown's graceless dash to Portugal, Cameron's own Brussels snub fitted a pattern of British ambivalence that dated all the way back to the founding years of the European project. The hesitancy and reluctance of most Prime Ministers – as well as the zealous enthusiasm of the two genuinely pro-European leaders, Edward Heath and Tony Blair – have contributed to a wider British mistrust of all things Brussels. The UK has never come to terms with a system that requires its sovereignty to be shared and its national interest to be compro-mised in the name of continental harmony and a place on the world stage. By 2013, the fortieth anniversary of joining the European club, Britain finds itself heading firmly in the opposite direction to the federation of nations foreseen for those partici-pating in the single currency. As the 'new European Union' takes shape, a British referendum on continued membership seems inevitable. This book looks at how we got to the point of departure from the EU, what Britain's options are now and what it would mean to say 'au revoir, Europe'.

The UK's original application to join came in 1961, four years after Belgium, France, Italy, Luxembourg, the Netherlands and West Germany signed the Treaty of Rome to launch the European Economic Community. The overriding ambition of the six was summed up in the very first sentence of the treaty, which stated that they were 'determined to lay the foundations of an ever closer union among the peoples of Europe'.[1] This sounded grand and rather daring, not to say noble, coming so soon after yet another war between these countries had ripped the continent to shreds. It was not a goal that Britain ever fully accepted. Nor was the UK made particularly welcome, with Charles de Gaulle using his veto to block British entry for twelve years, fearing – rightly – that France's key controlling role would be diluted by London. West Germany was in no position to call the shots in those formative years, leaving Paris to dominate the gang of six and turn the club into a lucrative support system for its farmers.

When British membership finally came in 1973, the UK and fellow joiners Denmark and Ireland had no choice but to swallow whole 13,000 pages of established rules, regulations, objectives and court judgments. These papers stood in a metre-high pile (wrapped neatly, presumably with no sense of irony, in red tape) as Edward Heath signed on the dotted line in a Brussels ceremony. In a telling move that did not bode well for future cooperation, the new members were cynically lumbered with the blueprint of a disastrous Common Fisheries Policy cooked up between the six as soon as they learnt of the formal application of the sea-faring nations.

From the first post-war British Prime Minister, Clement Attlee – who dismissed 'the so-called Common Market of six nations' by declaring: 'Know them all well. Very recently this country spent a great deal of blood and treasure rescuing four of 'em from attacks by the other two' – all the way to David Cameron, Britain has not only been a reluctant participant but has never lost the feeling of being an outsider.[2] Sir Winston Churchill himself, in the Zurich speech of 1946 in which he called for a United States of Europe and gave the idea such important momentum, was clear: 'Great Britain, the British Commonwealth of Nations, mighty America, and I trust Soviet Russia – for then indeed all would be well – must be the friends and sponsors of the new Europe and must champion its right to live and shine.'[3] Churchill believed that Britain should remain a friendly supporter and neighbour of the new Europe, not part of it.

As a reporter for *The Times* with five years' service as Chief Political Correspondent in London, I came to Brussels in 2006 knowing precious little about how the EU really worked and its true impact on Britain. I was not alone in my ignorance, for the day-to-day deeds of commissioners, eurocrats and MEPs were not much covered in the British media, nor were they a prominent feature of life as a Westminster journalist. MPs and ministers preferred to talk up their own deeds in the areas of national life that remained under their control, notably fiscal policy, defence, education, law and order, the NHS and welfare. Nevertheless 'Brussels' (a common shorthand label for anything involving the EU) has full power over international trading agreements and enforcing the rules of Europe's single market, and its tentacles reach deep into agriculture, the environment, industry, health and safety, employment law, justice and home affairs, transport, international aid and development and even sport.

Moreover, there was little public awareness of how the EU worked and what it did. It was a topic hardly mentioned at school, as far as I can remember, and rarely, if ever, did an MEP appear on *Question Time* or the *Today* programme to explain what they were up to. So I came to Brussels keen to find out more about this European Union. After all, it seemed like such a good idea. Who could argue with a system that had guaranteed peace and stability for nearly seventy years in a region which had suffered so many regular and terrible wars? Of course Brussels is also home to NATO, the North Atlantic Treaty Organization, the military alliance of twenty-eight nations founded in 1949 which also deserves much acclaim for preserving the precious Pax Europaea. NATO's mission was, after all, as a former Secretary-General once said, to 'keep the Russians out, the Americans in and the Germans down'.[4] But if NATO had provided a military framework for uniting old enemies, the EU had undeniably found a political and economic way of binding together France and Germany, the origin of so much continental strife over the centuries.

Beyond peace, Brussels was also given much credit, back in 2006 when I first arrived, for providing the conditions for the remarkable prosperity of the continent. It was all the more

impressive given that the good times were also being enjoyed
by new member states in the east that had only recently thrown
off Communism. Such was the confidence of the Europeans at
the turn of the millennium that books were written with titles
like *Why Europe Will Run the 21st Century.* The EU adopted
a bold plan called the Lisbon Agenda which aimed to 'make
Europe, by 2010, the most competitive and the most dynamic
knowledge-based economy in the world capable of sustainable economic growth with more and better jobs and greater
social cohesion'.[5] The strategy was 'designed to enable the
Union to regain the conditions for full employment'. There was
also a new common currency and, to cap it all, a constitution
to codify all the aims and laws in one handy document.

Things did not quite turn out as planned. Instead of consolidating its considerable achievements, the EU over-reached
itself. And here we get to one of the fundamental irritations
that many in Britain have with the whole project. Key figures in
European positions of power, be they in the member states or
the Brussels institutions themselves, simply cannot rest in their
pursuit of the Treaty of Rome's call for 'ever closer union'. The
EU was always more than a system of rules for facilitating
trade; it was and is a political project. It has been compared to
a shark constantly moving to stay alive or, more benignly, to a
bicycle that will fall over without forward motion. Even while
the economies of Europe were thriving, its political leaders were
looking for yet more ways to advance the European project.
British voices were among those calling for a timely pause to
consolidate existing goals, notably entrenching Europe's single
market, which is still very far from being completed. And yet
it was not the Brits but voters in two founding member states,
France and the Netherlands, who decided in 2005 that they
needed a grand constitution, well, like a fish needs a bicycle.

The EU could not rest and found a fresh policy mission –
combating climate change. Emissions targets were seized upon
in Brussels as a galvanising force with which Europe could

rediscover its purpose in a new century and lead the world out of carbon darkness and into the renewable light. But on 18 December 2009, the USA and China stitched up an ineffectual deal with Brazil, South Africa and India at the Copenhagen climate change summit without any Europeans even in the room. There would be no binding targets to supersede the Kyoto Protocol and there was to be no more sobering example of the EU's place in the emerging world order during my time in Brussels.

President Obama was by this time refocusing his foreign policy on Asia, where he had spent four days just before Copenhagen getting to know President Hu and Premier Wen. The economic crisis which started in the US detonated an atomic bomb under the European single currency and led to widening divisions between the two continents. José Manuel Barroso, President of the European Commission, told *The Times* in July 2010 that the Obama presidency was in danger of being a missed opportunity for the transatlantic relationship. It was a diplomatic understatement. The US had already moved on.

As the debt crisis deepened in Europe, the battle to save the euro overshadowed my own final two years in Brussels. It was an exhausting time of seemingly endless summits, rescue packages and austerity plans, each billed as more crucial and hard-hitting than the last, until eventually Greece was forced into the largest private debt restructuring ever attempted. The solution? Why, further European integration of course. A common monetary system that began idealistically with the notion of the voluntary pooling of powers ended up requiring ever greater surrender of sovereignty as well as sanctions in order to survive as a common economic system. Along the way, a whole generation of young Europeans were left out of work. Misery and penury of a kind not seen for generations returned to countries cruelly labelled 'peripheral' despite having been fully paid-up members of the EU club for years. Democracy was shoved to one side in Greece and Italy as technocrats took control in collaboration with EU officials and the International Monetary Fund. Somewhere along the road, the twin founding goals of the European project, peace and prosperity, were replaced with pain and austerity. My final weeks in Brussels were indeed depressing. It felt like I was witnessing the slow death of the European dream I came in search of.

In my new post as Berlin Correspondent for *The Times*, I have been able to see how the Germans want to guide the European Union into its next phase – economic and political union. They just don't want to pay for it. Of course, other member states have firm views on the level of integration that is necessary and desirable. Polish leaders, for example, have been outspoken in calling for the European Commission and European Parliament to become the true government of the EU. Herman Van Rompuy, the President of the European Council, claimed in September 2012 that

> there is a genuine willingness amongst EU leaders to address the systemic nature of the crisis. To finish a house half-built... the leaders commit themselves to bringing the Economic and Monetary Union to its solid and stable end-state in the years ahead. And having talked with many of them in the past weeks and even days, I can confirm their political will is unyielding.[6]

Even the more sceptical Finns want a stronger European Commission to monitor budgetary discipline. The UK finds itself not just on the fringes of this debate, but unwilling to participate in any of the resulting reforms. In fact, Britain has been distancing itself from the core activity of the EU ever since the single currency was devised and now finds itself, I believe, in the process of leaving a European project that it never firmly embraced.

From 1961 until 1973 the UK was in its joining phase as it sought and won accession to the European club. The next twenty years or so after that could be called the integration phase, when Britain tied its future trajectory to Europe by helping to formulate the single market. This deep level of commitment could not survive the triple shocks of Margaret Thatcher's fatal battle with Jacques Delors, Black Wednesday and the Maastricht Treaty that created the euro and the European Union. John Major declared that he had won 'game, set and match' by securing an opt-out from the single currency, putting Britain firmly on a divergent path from the rest of the EU. His analogy showed how Europe was now viewed by the UK as a zero sum game which could only be won or lost. Denmark is the only other country with a formal opt-out from the single currency – all the others not yet in the euro have signed up to binding treaty agreements to work towards joining, even if the crisis has put some of them off for the time being. But even in Denmark some senior politicians are waiting for their moment to reverse the single currency opt-out despite public opinion hardening against the idea during the euro crisis. The other member states are on a diametrically opposed trajectory to Britain.

Despite Tony Blair's best efforts, the UK entered into a new phase of growing alienation from the EU as successive treaties claimed more national sovereignty. While integration also still took place under New Labour thanks to the remorseless continental drive towards 'ever closer union', it was increasingly reluctantly undertaken by Britain. Antagonism became the dominant mood. This was an era dominated by arguments over red lines that the UK refused to cross into deeper federation, making it the least Europeanised member state. David Cameron's veto, although less effective than John Major's opt-out two decades earlier, was only the latest in a long series of separatist British actions, such as the refusal to join the Schengen borderless travel zone, steadfast opposition to regulation of the financial services industry and rejection of deeper coordination of fiscal policy.

With our continental allies planning even deeper cooperation in a banking union leading to more common
economic governance and a new form of political union, Britain
finds itself being forced towards the EU exit door. The actual
point of departure will come when the eurozone countries press
on to create the 'real European Union', leaving the non-euro
nations with a choice. They will have to commit to adopting the
single currency and join the real EU, devise a comfortable form
of second-tier membership or withdraw altogether. Of course
Britain will try to muddle through for as long as possible – it is
a tactic that has served for more than twenty years. But in 2012
even the arch-europhile Lord Mandelson observed:

> I believe there will be an inevitable gravitational pull of decision
> making towards the inner eurozone core. Britain will be invited
> to support this evolution but if we refuse, we will be ignored...
> It is certainly not inconceivable – indeed I think it is likely –
> that Britain will find itself a decade from now the only state
> in the EU, certainly the only large state, outside the eurozone.
> Effectively the EU will have been rebooted, with the UK on the
> outside. We must not delude ourselves about this.[7]

As Mandelson himself identified, the dice have been cast and,
barring a dramatic change of heart, Britain seems to be heading
out of the EU.

Future historians may one day date the terminal phase of
Britain's relationship with the 'real EU' from as far back as
'game, set and match' at Maastricht, or from Gordon Brown's
decisive ruling out of euro entry in June 2003, or perhaps from
David Cameron's EU Act of 2011. Before the Act, none of the
various British opt-outs and no-thank-yous were, constitution-
ally, deal-breakers. But the EU Act, which received Royal Assent
in July 2011, meant that any further sharing of power with
Brussels must be put to a referendum. Any British plebiscite on
new proposals or a treaty would be conducted against a hostile

background of frustration that the wider question of membership remained unput – and a 'No' vote on a specific measure
would propel the UK further into the sidelines. A 'Yes' vote on
a particular measure, while extremely unlikely, would not lay
to rest the fundamental question, what Sir John Major called
'one of the long-running sores of British politics, which is the
nature of our relationship with Europe'.[8]

Given the years of tabloid hostility, growing discontent among
MPs and declining popular support expressed in opinion polls,
a referendum on a new treaty to enhance EU powers would
also be exhausting and distracting politically for the government of the day. A lost vote would lead to irresistible pressure
for a more fundamental say about the UK's future relationship
with its nearest neighbours. If the choice was simply between
in or out, who would bet against a so-called Brexit as the most
likely result?

A third way could still be found, a formal second tier of
membership, perhaps along the lines of a wider community
of less integrated nations beside the core union of euro states,
as proposed by Lord Owen in a book in June 2012. In fact,
there are federalist thinkers in Brussels plotting such a fate
for the UK. A move to some kind of secondary or associate
membership would formalise a disentangling process which is
already under way – the government is conducting a Review
of the Balance of EU Competences, due to report in 2014, to
see where it can take back powers from Brussels. With most
of the other members simultaneously moving to centralise
power – proposals for a new treaty to entrench economic coordination are promised in 2014 by the European Commission
– it almost seems like they are leaving us as surely as we are
leaving them.

Of course, other countries have their own complaints and
ambitions, but they usually start from the same premise – the
idea that 'more Europe' is the answer. Often the UK really did
not want what was on offer but our gallant officials gamely

sought to make the best of it anyway. As one senior UK civil
servant told me:

> If you ask British negotiators in Brussels what is the single most
> frequent question they will pass to their colleagues in London, it
> is 'can we live with this?' Not 'do we like it?' or 'is it any good?'
> That is the level that negotiations happen at across the board.
> You are rarely making a really positive case.

Should Labour win the next election, it may be less confron-
tational with Brussels and less intent on taking powers back
than a Conservative-led administration, but Britain will still be
faced, sooner or later, with a new treaty that seeks to deepen
integration and triggers the inevitable referendum.

There is yet another key reason why the fortieth anniversary of UK accession on 1 January 2013 marks a watershed
in the relationship with Europe. Britain's europhiles have been
defeated. Never before, in the four decades of membership, have
those arguing for deeper ties with Europe been more muted or
less able to make a positive case for deeper federation. Largely
this is the result of missteps by the EU, notably the horrendous
spectacle of the prolonged economic crisis fuelled by the rigid-
ity of the single currency in countries like Ireland and Spain,
where property bubbles were encouraged by inappropriate
one-size-fits-all interest rates. But Britain's pro-Europeans have
failed to make the argument for 'ever closer union'; they
have failed to prevent an overbearing bureaucracy from giving
Brussels a bad name; they have failed to win popular approval
for the European Union, or win the argument for its ultimate
goals – philosophically, economically or politically; they have
failed to follow the dream of Europe's founding fathers with a
convincing vision for the future. While there was a 'brave new
world' moment when it could have been possible to join the
euro in the late 1990s and turn Britain decisively back towards
a European destiny, the window of opportunity was missed by

Tony Blair. It is impossible to believe now that British voters will ever agree to share the same currency as Estonia, Greece, Slovakia and Spain. A Populus poll in May 2012 for Lord Mandelson's own think tank, Policy Network, showed that 80 per cent of British people were against ever joining the single currency.[9] For Britain's pro-Europeans, only the scale of their defeat remains to be settled. Their ambitions to play a full role in the future of the European Union lie in ruins, but will Britain have any part to play?

The longer I stayed in Brussels, the more I wanted to think through what lies ahead for Britain in Europe and its options beyond the European Union. This book starts from the premise that the status quo is not on offer to the UK, with the EU moving rapidly in another direction as it seeks to salvage its core project – the euro. As a journalist, there is no greater stimulus than being constantly told 'there is no alternative'. It is axiomatic in Brussels that the EU is not only the best hope for Europe's future but in fact the only possible way of ensuring peace, prosperity and global influence for its member states. The Brussels believers might be right – but that does not mean that their case should not be examined and compared with the alternatives. Nor does it automatically follow that Britain needs to be a fully paid-up member of the EU for both to succeed.

I approached this journey of inquiry with – I hope – an open mind, and found answers and arguments that genuinely surprised me and, I believe, should challenge entrenched beliefs on both sides of this crucial debate. This is not a campaigning book. Nor is it about the continental struggle to save the single currency, the intricate details of which will doubtless fill many academic and technical volumes. This book is an attempt to take stock of the perpetual evolution of the EU and its impact on British life since we joined forty years ago and, given our inexorable drift towards the exit, to see what it might mean to say *au revoir*.

ONE

Sovereignty Shared

There is no question of any erosion of essential national sovereignty.
– White Paper on the United Kingdom and the European Communities, July 1971

Heinrich Himmler's handshake was soft, wet and flabby. But it left an indelible impression on the 21-year-old Oxford scholar on the receiving end. Edward Heath was on a student exchange trip to Nuremberg in 1937 when he encountered the chief of the feared SS paramilitary, as well as the German Propaganda Minister, Joseph Goebbels, 'his pinched face white and sweating – evil personified'.[10] But of all the Nazi high command, it was Adolf Hitler who most struck the young undergraduate. After witnessing the crowd rise as one and raise their right arms in salute, Heath described 'the mob orator, the demagogue, playing on every evil emotion in his audience'.[11] Just a few years after meeting the men who would destroy Europe in a conflict that cost more than fifty million lives, Heath took part in the Normandy landings with the Royal Artillery, helped to destroy Caen and liberate Antwerp, and even commanded a firing squad that executed a Polish prisoner for rape.

These searing first-hand experiences motivated the future Prime Minister's life's work. 'My generation could not live in the past; we had to work for the future. We were surrounded by destruction, homelessness, hunger and despair. Only by working together had we any hope of creating a society which would uphold the true values of European civilisation.'[12] Heath's dream was the creation of a continental community of interdependent nations that would bring an end to war for good. When he took his own country into this community, it was 'one of the greatest moments' of his life.

The organisation that Britain joined in 1973 was very different from the European Union of today. For a start, it was then called the European Economic Community, the name chosen by the original six member nations to reflect the organisation's primary focus. In British popular debate, as accession became a reality, it was referred to by a term plucked from the founding Treaty of Rome – the Common Market. It made the EEC sound disarmingly like a simple trading deal for cheaper Liebfraumilch and Golden Delicious – and masked the true political and constitutional implications of membership.

The name change to European Union brought about by the Maastricht Treaty twenty years later only confirmed what was by then abundantly clear – control over large areas of national jurisdiction had been ceded to a supranational organisation. Back in 1971, after France's President Pompidou had finally reversed his predecessor's opposition to Britain's application, Heath's White Paper addressed the sovereignty issue in the least hair-raising way it possibly could. It introduced the concept of preserving 'essential national sovereignty', a phrase designed to reassure while tacitly conceding that areas of non-essential national sovereignty would indeed be sacrificed.

This was the start of a pattern of disingenuous political rhetoric about Britain's European adventure which would characterise and poison debate as the full implications of membership became clear. By the time of Heath's death in 2005, his carefully constructed reassurances had become fetishised by the eurosceptic movement and even portrayed as treachery. The UK Independence Party had to be dissuaded from hanging his effigy from Traitor's Gate, after a reminder that he was actually a decorated war veteran.[13] But Heath was far from alone among leading British politicians over the years in seeking to play down the constitutional implications of European participation. This reluctance, no doubt born out of concern for the greater prize of a seat at Europe's top table, led to wider mistrust of the motivations of Britain's europhiles and contributed to their ultimate failure to sell the European dream.

The logic of pooling sovereignty was established for many years before Britain joined the continental club. The primacy of EEC law, for example, was first claimed by a ruling of the European Court of Justice in 1963. It was a fundamental guiding principle of the European project. This was the idea that a supreme court based in Luxembourg, with one judge drawn from each member state, would have ultimate legal authority over disputes between the members on matters covered by the European treaties. A true community of nations needed an arbitrator so that the strong could not push around the weak. It was a logical guarantee of fairness and order.

But British leaders were reluctant from the start to spell out to the British public that national legislators and courts would necessarily be subject to a higher authority. 'What is proposed is a sharing and an enlargement of individual national sovereignties in the general interest,' Heath's 1971 White Paper added. Britain would hand authority over some areas of its national life to the EEC in exchange for the privilege of taking part in decisions which would hold sway over all nine member states. The deal came with a guarantee, spelt out in the government's own leaflet for the 1975 referendum on the EEC, that 'the minister representing Britain can veto any proposal for a new law or a new tax'.[14] In those early days, it was explained that sovereignty would be shared only when Britain explicitly consented. It was not a guarantee that lasted long.

For the government ministers and civil servants who took Britain into the EEC, the whole point of joining was to give up a little power to gain a lot of influence. In the precarious post-Empire world of opposing superpowers, membership would have the double benefit of expanding neighbourly trade and increasing Britain's clout on the world stage. No Prime Minister set this out more clearly than Harold Macmillan in 1962, in a pamphlet explaining his decision to apply for membership:

> It is true of course that political unity is the central aim of those European countries and we would naturally accept that ultimate goal. But the effects on our position of joining Europe have been much exaggerated by the critics. Accession to the Treaty of Rome would not involve a one-sided surrender of sovereignty on our part but a pooling of sovereignty by all concerned, mainly in economic and social fields.[15]

With this clear explanation of the sovereignty question, Macmillan seemed to belong to a golden age of candour. But although he went further than Heath and any of his successors in admitting what was at stake, Macmillan, too, was capable of giving comforting – some would say misleading – guarantees:

> In renouncing some of our own sovereignty we would receive in return a share of the sovereignty renounced by other members. Our obligations would not alter the position of the Crown, nor rob our Parliament of its essential powers, nor deprive our Law Courts of their authority in our domestic life.[16]

Here was the exact same formula later used by Heath and others – that the 'essential' powers of Parliament would be preserved, whatever the ultimate ambitions were among the other members and in Brussels for political union. Macmillan's guarantee over court supremacy covered only 'our domestic life' because he must have known that the areas where Europe had a stake would be claimed by the judges based in Luxembourg.

The carefully crafted reasoning of Macmillan and Heath raised a new question – which areas of sovereignty were 'essential' and which were non-essential? This would only be answered more fully in the years that followed, and in ways that even Britain's most pro-European Prime Minister could only dream of. Ordinary voters could not have anticipated the dramatic developments to come, leading to accusations of deception or, at least, sleight of hand, as the UK and the other member nations would agree to share more and more of their traditional domestic powers. The growing size and scope of the European project meant that it could only avoid becoming bogged down if national capitals agreed to abide by majority decisions, rather than always insisting upon unanimity. No progress could be made if everyone insisted upon getting their own way all the time. As this new Europe took shape, national sovereignty would not be so much shared as bartered in fraught Brussels battles, unleashing powerful forces that brought successive governments to the brink of disaster.

During the British accession process, the government chose to emphasise the economic case and play down the constitutional implications. But far-reaching developments were already being planned elsewhere. The principle of direct elections to the European Parliament, which at this point was called an Assembly and composed of national appointees, was already widely accepted in Brussels circles. Just two days after the European Communities Act 1972 received its Royal Assent, the six original member nations met for the first time with the three accession states at a Paris summit where they agreed to pursue economic and monetary union and to form a European Union by 1980. Not for the first time, as soon as one step was taken towards a federal Europe, several more were immediately lined up.

This process was even awarded its own academic theory: neofunctionalism. The theory, espoused by one of the EEC's founders, the French diplomat Jean Monnet, was that advances involving the sharing of powers would automatically trigger further integration as 'positive spill-over effects' became obvious or unavoidable. It just goes to show that there was a philosophical method behind the sometimes baffling European obsession with continual integration. The starkest example would come at the turn of the century when monetary union was introduced with no effective common economic system. No matter, this would surely follow. This process was not really made clear to MPs, let alone voters, for fear that they would not agree to the first step.

Heath's treatment of the sovereignty question has been assailed on all sides. Writing in the second volume of her memoirs five years after she was ousted from Downing Street, Margaret Thatcher called his White Paper 'an extraordinary example of artful confusion to conceal fundamental issues'.[17] Roy Hattersley, the former Labour deputy leader and firm advocate of the European project throughout this period, wrote: 'Nothing has more injured the idea of Britain in Europe than Edward Heath's foolish assurance (given at the time of our entry into the Common Market) that membership would involve no loss of sovereignty.'[18]

But it was not just his political adversaries who accused Heath of being misleading about the true implications of membership and contributing to public suspicion of the project dearest to his heart. Hugo Young, former senior political commentator at *The Guardian* and paramount chronicler of Britain's entry into the EEC, put it like this:

> The White Paper phrases, however explicable, and even defensible, were a hostage to anyone who later desired to mount a case for saying there had been a crucial element of dissimulation in what the world was told. If nothing else, they lowered the guard of a nation supposedly on watch for any fundamental change that entry into Europe was about to impose upon it.[19]

Even Heath's election manifesto was beguiling – it pledged that his government would seek to negotiate with the EEC 'no more, no less'.[20] In 1970, he also seemed to promise a referendum on accession, pledging that Britain would only join with 'the full-hearted consent of parliament and the people'.[21] But Heath never delivered a referendum, later calling the idea 'abhorrent'.

Britain's europhiles maintain that those who complain about Heath's handling of the accession process and the conduct of the 1975 British referendum under the Labour government of Harold Wilson have misremembered events and that they were, in fact, told the unvarnished truth about what Britain was in for. But here is what the pro-European Hugo Young, who studied the former Prime Minister closely and often at first hand for many years, had to say: 'Heath himself seldom talked about sovereignty being surrendered. He was not prepared to concede, in cold fact, that although there might be a gain in power, there would be a loss of independence.'[22]

In his definitive analysis of the passage of the 1972 Act into British law, Young added:

> Ministers did not lie, but they avoided telling the full truth. They refrained from stating categorically that the law of the European Community would have supremacy over British law... The Bill did not contain, as it might have done, a clause stating in terms the general rule that Community law was to be supreme... This disguising was part of an intensely political process. Only by sweetening the truth about national sovereignty, apparently, could popular support be kept in line.[23]

Thus the British foundations of the European project were laid on sands that would shift political and public opinion resentfully against it as the true extent of the Brussels superstructure was revealed.

Even Hattersley, who so sharply condemned Heath's double-dealing, has offered his own *mea culpa*:

> What we did throughout all those years, all the Europeans, was

say, let's not risk trying to make fundamental changes by telling the whole truth, let's do it through public relations rather than real proselytising... spin the argument rather than expose the argument. Not only was it wrong for us to deal superficially with what Europe involved, but we've paid the price for it ever since... Joining the European Community did involve significant loss of sovereignty but by telling the British people that was not involved, I think the rest of the argument was prejudiced for the next twenty or thirty years.[24]

At best the pro-Europeans were coy about sovereignty and at worst they were downright deceptive. It would come back to haunt them by contributing to public mistrust and, eventually, outright hostility to further European integration, even where logic suggested that European countries were better off cooperating.

Of course there were some contrary voices – Hugh Gaitskell had dramatically warned as far back as 1962 that joining the European project would mean 'the end of a thousand years of history' for an independent Britain. Tony Benn on the left and Enoch Powell on the right raised fears about adverse constitutional effects. Lord Denning, the Master of the Rolls, stated in a Court of Appeal judgment of 1974 that

when we come to matters with a European element, the Treaty is like an incoming tide. It flows into the estuaries and up the rivers. It cannot be held back. Parliament has decreed that the Treaty is henceforward to be part of our law. It is equal in force to any statute.[25]

Twenty years later, Denning would give an even more robust verdict on the overwhelming impact of EU law.

But in the wider national debate that culminated in the in/out EEC referendum of June 1975, the sovereignty argument did not become a central issue on either side. The far more immediate concerns were over jobs, prices and industry, for in the troubled British economy of the 1970s unemployment and inflation loomed large. The extra costs of membership versus benefits for consumers and companies, including the effect of higher EEC tariffs on trade with Britain's traditional Commonwealth partners, were subject to the fiercest arguments.

UK inflation spiralled from 9.2 per cent in 1973 to 24.2 per cent in 1975 and the country was in recession for months leading up to the referendum. From 1950 to 1973, the UK economy had grown by an average of 2.9 per cent a year, compared to 6 per cent a year for West Germany, 5.1 per cent for both France and Italy, 4.5 per cent for Belgium and 4.4 per cent for the Netherlands – all founder members of the EEC. These figures alone made a compelling economic case for membership. The ailing Britain of the 1970s was fertile ground for politicians promising a brighter future.

British voters cast a resounding 'Yes' vote in the 1975 poll to the question 'Do you think the UK should stay in the European Community (*Common Market*)?' Neither in the question nor in the sixteen-page government leaflet sent to every British household was the goal of 'ever closer union' mentioned as an aim of the EEC. Two pages in the leaflet were given over to the topic 'Will Parliament lose its power?'[26] This acknowledged that 'another anxiety expressed about Britain's membership of the Common Market is that Parliament could lose its supremacy, and we would have to obey laws passed by unelected "faceless bureaucrats" sitting in their headquarters in Brussels'. For voters of a nervous disposition, the leaflet went on to offer considerable reassurance under the sub-heading 'What are the facts?'

Fact No. 1 played upon the same fears of isolation used to make the case for continued membership today.

In the modern world even the Super Powers like America and Russia do not have complete freedom of action... Since we cannot go it alone in the modern world, Britain has for years been a member of international groupings like the United Nations, NATO and the International Monetary Fund. Membership of such groupings imposes both rights and duties, but has not deprived us of our national identity, or changed our way of life.

At the time, the EEC was essentially an agricultural support and cross-border trade organisation. But neither the membership fees nor the obligations of any other international body are remotely comparable to those demanded by the European Union.

In contrast with today's reassurance that Britain is still able to use its veto to protect several important areas such as taxation, Fact No. 2 in 1975 stated categorically:

> No important new policy can be decided in Brussels or anywhere else without the consent of a British Minister answerable to a British Government and British Parliament. The top decision-making body in the Market is the Council of Ministers, which is composed of senior Ministers representing each of the nine member governments. It is the Council of Ministers, and not the market's officials, who take the important decisions. These decisions can be taken only if all the members of the Council agree. The Minister representing Britain can veto any proposal for a new law or a new tax if he considers it to be against British interests.

Much has changed since these key facts were used to persuade the British electorate to cast their 'Yes' vote (67.2 to 32.8 per cent). Most strikingly, the national veto has long been negotiated away in many policy areas to facilitate decision-making, something that was simply not foreseen at the time. A minister representing Britain now has to work hard to build up a number of allies if he or she wants to block measures under the majority voting rules used for most decisions.

For good measure, the 1975 leaflet added Fact No. 3:

The White Paper on the new Market terms recently presented to Parliament by the Prime Minister declares that through membership of the Market we are better able to advance and protect our national interests. This is the essence of sovereignty.

Here again was the same reassurance as Macmillan and Heath, this time repeated by a Labour government, that the 'essence' of sovereignty would be preserved. In this case, sovereignty was defined as the ability to advance and protect national interests. With the Cold War at its height, the extra reassurance of closer alliance with democratic western neighbours was implicit in the benefits to UK as a sovereign nation.

Sovereignty would only become a more contentious point as the EU accrued more powers in successive treaties that at the same time reduced member states' ability to stand in the way of decisions taken by the majority. At every turn, the British government of the day negotiated hard before accepting these changes, often participating actively in their formulation. An intense period of integration was about to take place, largely encouraged by Britain. Even the question put in the referendum of 1975, with its references to the Community and Common Market, would become obsolete within two decades as the terms were replaced by the Union and single market.

Five major treaties would revise the founding Treaty of Rome and transfer more powers from the member states. But first came a change to the European Assembly which showed dramatically how Brussels was acquiring attributes more akin to a government than an alliance. On 7 June 1979, a month after Margaret Thatcher's first election victory, British voters went back to the polls to choose eighty-one directly elected members of the European Assembly. Until then, members had been seconded from the House of Commons and the House of Lords.

The impression of a new and significant European experience was enhanced by voting being held more or less simultaneously in the eight other countries. The European Assembly only had limited powers but the greater democratic legitimacy conferred on it by a direct election gave its members ambitions to wield ever more influence over the legislation proposed by the European Commission (the civil service of the European project, which formulates all its new laws and regulates the internal market). All the treaties that followed British accession extended the European Assembly's powers to change legislation.

The first of these treaties, the Single European Act, came along in the mid-1980s when Thatcher was at the peak of her domestic powers. She was fresh from a notable victory in Europe – the Fontainebleau Summit of 1984, at which she had secured the British rebate, an annual cashback deal to compensate for the rising contributions that taxpayers were being asked to make to the EEC budget. Yet while a strong Prime Minister with a solid parliamentary majority was reshaping her nation, the process of the Single European Act showed that in Europe not even the Iron Lady could call the shots.

The fact that there was to be a treaty at all came as a rather nasty surprise to Thatcher and illustrated how by 1985 Britain was unable to get its way on the biggest reform yet contemplated to the EEC. Up until then, major changes such as the European Assembly direct elections were introduced by specific Acts. There had been no tradition of new wide-ranging power-building treaties. The Thatcher government thought that the blueprint for turning the Common Market into a single market, largely drawn up by a Conservative former Cabinet minister and European Commissioner, Arthur Cockfield, would simply be adopted and implemented by the member states.

But Thatcher was ambushed at a European Council meeting in Milan when the Italian Prime Minister proposed a formal intergovernmental conference to write a new legally binding treaty to enforce the single market – and much more besides.

Britain, joined in its opposition to such a conference only by Denmark and new member Greece, was outvoted. Although treaties themselves required unanimity, calling a conference to debate a treaty only needed a majority vote. It was the first time that the UK had been overruled in this way and a sign of things to come. British officials, not for the last time, were ordered by their Prime Minister to 'search for minimal, acceptable treaty change, avoiding risky isolation for Britain'.[27] This would become a familiar refrain as treaty followed treaty, establishing a pattern of British resistance to the idea of 'more Europe' beloved of Brussels and politicians in some member states.

To get the single market that Britain coveted, Thatcher would have to consent to a whole raft of European social and political powers that were shovelled into the new treaty. The momentum towards 'ever closer union' was back. Although angry at what she saw as the Italian betrayal, Thatcher went along with the treaty as the price of progress. That was because the Single European Act set out the conditions for creating 'the free movement of goods, persons, services and capital' – the so-called four freedoms – by the end of 1992. This was the part of the treaty that Thatcher approved of, although Europe is still waiting for the completion of this goal, most notably in services such as banking, healthcare, insurance, maintenance and training. In the trade-off, the treaty also laid the ground for the coordination of foreign and security policy, for economic and monetary union, and for the Europeanisation of social and employment rights. It renamed the European Assembly the European Parliament.

The treaty also, crucially, ended the right of national veto in a dozen key policy areas in order to push through the reforms needed for the single market by switching from the unanimity rule to qualified majority voting (QMV). This meant that one or two recalcitrant nations could no longer stop a reforming measure, unless they gathered a 'blocking minority' of several allies around the table. Thatcher was initially reluctant to concede the formal loss of the British veto. She thought that there could simply be a general agreement not to insist upon unanimity for the adoption of European-wide standards. As Stephen Wall, then a Foreign Office adviser on Europe and later Britain's ambassador to the EU, said: 'We wanted improved decision-making but saw it happening by making better use of the existing rules.'[28] But once the draft treaty emerged from the European Commission with proposals for QMV that would even extend to tax harmonisation, British officials concentrated on limiting it to the technical measures needed for the single market.

While QMV would eventually become a three-letter acronym synonymous with the erosion of national sovereignty, Thatcher accepted the concept, as she later explained to the House of Lords:

> Yes, we wanted a common or single market but it was a long time before the Community got down to it. Eventually in 1985 we started to prepare for this single or common market and to get rid of the massive number of both tariff and non-tariff barriers that were needed. I was at the forefront of that campaign because I believed that we wanted it. At first, I thought that we could get it without any changes in legislation. I thought that if there was reasonable goodwill, we could have it. But there was not reasonable goodwill and we had to have an intergovernmental conference. And the point is this: we would never have got the single market without an extension – not the beginning, but an extension – of majority voting. We could never have got our insurance into Germany – where they promptly kept it out – unless we had majority voting. We could never have got a fair deal for our ships in picking up goods from other ports as others could pick up from ours. We could never have got a fair deal for our lorry and transport business because our lorries had to go over there full and come back empty as they were not allowed to pick up on the way back. Yes, we wanted a single market and we had, in fact, to have some majority voting.[29]

The potent combination of the single market, QMV and Margaret Thatcher kick-started some spectacular commercial successes taken very much for granted by consumers today. In May 2012, a leading eurosceptic commentator wrote: 'Mine was the generation that was taught that Europe would be our oyster in a post-Soviet world. And it came to pass – not thanks to the European Union but to 1p Ryanair flights, email and text messages.'[30] Yet the first of these owes its existence entirely to the EU, thanks to air transport liberalisation measures taken through the single market between 1987 and 1992, while the third has been facilitated by Brussels using its powers to limit the cost of texting.

Before EU intervention, it was impossible for private airline companies to offer cheap flights between European countries because of the carefully guarded and price-controlled monopolies of national flag-carriers. Ryanair is a case in point, as it was only able to start flights from Ireland to the UK under the EU's market-opening 'double disapproval' regime, which stated that the governments of both countries had to object to prevent the service. The Irish government refused permission in order to protect Aer Lingus, but Ryanair got the go-ahead from the Thatcher government. It is now Europe's largest low-cost carrier. The second-largest, easyJet, also used the EU framework to grow from humble beginnings to become not just a major employer but also a key supporter of European industry, buying more than 200 Airbus aircraft to date.

'EasyJet is a child of the EU,' said Paul Moore, its communications director.[31] European open competition laws developed for the single market helped upstart new companies find their feet against national champions.

In the old days, if you were a British airline and wanted to fly between Britain and France, you had to rely on agreement between those countries. The flag-carriers represented their countries and until relatively recently were bankrolled by their countries. Essentially aviation was controlled by each sovereign state and easyJet broke down historic sovereignty-based aviation agreements.

Following liberalisation, the number of routes flown in Europe has increased by more than 60 per cent.[32] This was one aspect of national sovereignty progressively dismantled by the EU – and, as it was done in the name of consumer-friendly commercial competition, the British government was behind it all the way.

But when it came to control over traditionally national levers of political power, the UK was far more defensive. Still today in the British popular imagination, fears of the federal European ambition to make the UK a vassal of Brussels are embodied by one man – Jacques Delors. The Socialist former finance minister served as President of the European Commission from 1985 to 1994. At the start of his tenure, Thatcher and Delors collaborated to fashion the Single European Act despite his political add-ons to the treaty. But the Frenchman became increasingly demonised in much of the British press as battles over Europe largely stemming from the ground-breaking treaty eventually proved fatal for Thatcher.

The Act included an aspirational clause on economic and monetary union (EMU), signed up to reluctantly by Thatcher, following a personal assurance from Helmut Kohl, the German Chancellor, that he was also against the idea of a single currency. Thatcher relied on the obvious economic fact that the countries of Europe were far away from the kind of economic convergence necessary for sharing a common currency. But she underestimated the political imperative. EMU became the cause célèbre of Delors. He would later be lampooned for his obsession in *The Sun* newspaper with its classic headline 'Up Yours Delors'. But in early 1988, with Thatcher growing weary of the federal agenda in Brussels, she could do nothing to prevent her fellow leaders from reappointing Delors to his job as European Commission President and even tamely seconded his nomination. Any favour curried by this act of submission was soon destroyed, however, as the battle of wills between the two intensified dramatically over a familiar battleground – the fate of national sovereignty.

In July 1988 Delors told the European Parliament that within ten years he expected 80 per cent of economic legislation, and perhaps social and taxation legislation, would be made by the European Community. He called for the beginnings of a 'true European government'. In September, Delors spoke at the Trades Union Congress – the hotbed of resistance to Thatcher's domestic reforms – and promised social protections at a European level. Whatever one's view of Thatcher and the direction she was taking the country, there was now a direct ideological challenge to the elected UK government from an alternative political powerbase in Brussels – one with the ability to affect the direction of policy in Britain. The sovereignty question vis-à-vis Europe had ceased to be something rather academic and suddenly assumed central importance in British political life.

Thatcher's response was her infamous speech at the College of Bruges in September 1988 with its most quoted sentence: 'We have not successfully rolled back the frontiers of the state in Britain only to see them reimposed at a European level, with a European superstate exercising a new dominance from Brussels.'[33] The Bruges speech was not a statement of intent for Britain to withdraw from Europe – far from it. It was an appeal for a limited and practical British vision of Europe, based primarily on cooperating sovereign nation states rather than the giant protectionist social construct that Thatcher now feared. She also said:

On many great issues the countries of Europe should try to speak with a single voice. I want to see us work more closely on the things we can do better together than alone. Europe is stronger when we do so, whether it be in trade, in defence, or in our relations with the rest of the world.

The speech marked a Rubicon in the UK's relationship with Europe. It set out an alternative vision of a more cooperative and less coordinated Europe that showed how the British approach differed from the mainstream continental view. This divergence was not yet irreversible, but the UK was now battling to prevent a superstate and the prevailing national mindset irrevocably shifted from cooperation to confrontation.

The impact on the Conservative Party of the Bruges speech was summed up by the Margaret Thatcher Foundation:

> The speech began the transition by which the Conservatives ceased to be 'the party of Europe' in British politics, moving fitfully, by lurches, lunges and sidesteps, to a position now known as Euroscepticism. The term itself was invented in the process. These events proved deeply divisive within the party and did more than anything else to destroy the relationship between Margaret Thatcher and Geoffrey Howe, her Foreign Secretary. That, in turn, ended her premiership a little over two years later.[34]

Not for the first time or the last, Europe was driving the tectonic plates of national politics, to the point where it became a key factor in the downfall of the century's longest-serving Prime Minister.

Thatcher's final confrontation with Delors before her defenestration led to her most often quoted riposte to the Frenchman's vision. Speaking in the House of Commons about a summit in Rome which focused on preparing for a treaty to follow the Single European Act, she said:

> The President of the Commission, Monsieur Delors, said at a press conference the other day that he wanted the European Parliament to be the democratic body of the Community, he wanted the Commission to be the Executive and he wanted the Council of Ministers to be the Senate. No. No. No.[35]

While these three noes have not yet been overturned, subsequent treaties would greatly enhance the European Parliament's powers and, across Europe, there are still plenty of cheerleaders in powerful positions calling for the completion of Delors's European government dream.

The Single European Act acted like a slow-burning incendiary device at the heart of the British government, even as it boosted the economy by opening up the European market. In the rush to achieve economies of scale across Europe, there were 300 major company mergers in 1987 compared to just sixty-eight the year before.[36] But all this was soon to be overshadowed by the destructive force of the European Exchange Rate Mechanism (ERM) on the pound during Britain's short-lived membership of the precursor scheme to monetary union. The ERM was a system that linked European currency exchange rates in bands with the aim of reducing volatile fluctuations. Thatcher resisted joining until the last weeks of her premiership, against the wishes of the Treasury and senior Cabinet members, as well as almost all of Fleet Street. She did not want the British currency restricted by being pegged to the Deutschmark. In the end, the pressure from Brussels and from within her Cabinet was irresistible – her Chancellor and Foreign Secretary both threatened to resign in the summer of 1989 if she did not set a date for entry – but by the time this happened the Deutschmark was too strong and the rate at which sterling joined sowed the seeds of disaster. The currency crisis would detonate under her successor, John Major, just as the second European treaty to amend the original Rome document was causing another existential fight in Westminster.

The Maastricht Treaty contained even more measures towards the goal of 'ever closer union' and made further claims on British sovereignty at the very moment when the ERM debacle completely undermined confidence in grand European schemes. Maastricht, the treaty that changed the name of the EEC to European Union, also made all Britons 'Citizens of the Union' with the formal right to live and work in any EU country. In historical terms, citizenship implied belonging to a state along with the democratic rights and responsibilities that the nation conferred, such as direct elections and taxation. No wonder it was seen in Britain as another step along the continuum to a European superstate and as a further grab for national sovereignty.

Suspicions were raised further by the introduction of EU citizenship coincidentally just as the traditional dark blue British passport was being phased out. In use since 1920, these distinctive hard-backed booklets declared on the front 'British Passport' and 'United Kingdom of Great Britain and Northern Ireland'. The new, smaller, red travel document began to be issued in 1988 under a standardising measure signed off by EEC foreign ministers in 1981.[37] The new passport had the phrase 'European Community' at the top of the front cover, soon to be superseded by 'European Union'. The word 'British' was removed from in front of 'Passport'. It was the most tangible example many people had yet had that British sovereignty was, literally, being erased.

Once again with Maastricht, as with the Single European Act, the UK government did not want a treaty but could not stop the momentum from its continental allies. Once again, Delors was behind it. Born out of a report by the Frenchman on monetary union, the initial draft of Maastricht caused a furore in the British press over the inclusion of the 'f-word' – the treaty proposed 'leading gradually to a Union with a federal goal'. To the British government, federalism stood for the surrender of national sovereignty and rule from Brussels. To the continental mind, it was simply a description of the way in which functions of government were apportioned to the relevant level – local, regional, national or supranational. To the bemusement of some continental negotiators, British diplomats fought tooth and nail to replace the offensive word with the Treaty of Rome's familiar 'ever closer union among the peoples of Europe'.[38]

The Maastricht draft was also modified by an alliance of Britain and France to spell out the two distinct ways of doing business in Europe. Despite Delors's fervour for federalism, France has generally always fought to protect its own national sovereignty and, like all member states, to advance its core interests in European negotiations. One way of doing business in Europe was the so-called Community method, which meant truly supranational control by the European Commission in consultation with the European Parliament, with ultimate arbitration by the European Court of Justice. This was used for policy areas such as the single market and agriculture. Other areas of European coordination, such as the new field of common foreign and security policy, would remain inter-governmental – essentially a matter for cooperation at European level between sovereign governments under the auspices of their own forum, the European Council, where ministers would meet and take the main decisions.

A third field of policy, in justice and home affairs, would remain primarily intergovernmental with decisions on asylum, immigration and visa issues, for example, based on consensus of national ministers. These three areas became the three 'pillars' of the Maastricht Treaty. The European project was getting more complicated and more far-reaching. The pillars, it turned out, would eventually crumble as federal forces exerted their gravitational pull on the intergovernmental policy areas. But that would be a few years down the road. Britain was enthusiastic about Maastricht's rather confusing pillar system because it seemed to draw firm lines around certain areas of national sovereignty to protect it.

In all, national vetoes were reduced in the treaty by extending QMV in thirty policy areas. A trade-off here was to increase the powers of the European Parliament by giving MEPs the responsibility of signing off new EU laws in tandem with the European Council in some policy fields, known as the right of 'co-decision'. Aware of fears of a European superstate, Delors also introduced the principle of subsidiarity into Maastricht, which declared that

> in areas which do not fall within its exclusive competence, the Union shall act only if and in so far as the objectives of the proposed action cannot be sufficiently achieved by the Member States, either at central level or at regional and local level, but can rather, by reason of the scale or effects of the proposed action, be better achieved at Union level.[39]

But at the same time, the treaty also wanted to take further the EU's responsibility, inherited from the founding Treaty of Rome, 'to promote improved working conditions and an improved standard of living for workers, so as to make possible their harmonisation'. The Single European Act had committed the EEC to developing the 'dialogue between management and labour at European level'. Delors believed that the Common Market should go hand-in-hand with a European Social Area that protected workers' rights. After all, a completely open market could lead companies to relocate to cheaper areas, with uncompetitive firms going bust, leading to job losses.

'The creation of a vast economic area, based on market and business cooperation, is inconceivable – I would say unattainable – without some harmonisation of social legislation. Our ultimate aim must be the creation of a European Social Area,' Delors said in 1986. To this end he drew up a Community Charter of Fundamental Social Rights, signed by all members except Britain in 1989. It was a significant moment – the UK was starting to peel away from the European pack. While the British were still prepared to integrate with the others, the Thatcher government wanted the boundaries of the single market to be drawn some way to the right of those desired by its European allies. But the charter, which called for enhanced rights for workers and greater social protection, would not go away. It became the Social Chapter of the Maastricht Treaty and only stubborn resistance by John Major relegated it to an optional clause – again signed by every member except Britain.

Major had vowed in his first big foreign policy speech as Prime Minister, delivered in Bonn in March 1991, to put Britain back 'at the very heart of Europe' following the distance and suspicion that developed during the Thatcher years.[40] However, rows about the f-word, the Social Chapter and the central goal of the Maastricht Treaty – the procedure for establishing Economic and Monetary Union – proved steps too far. EMU became the latest three-letter abbreviation to torture British governments.

Britain was at first treated as a special case with its own opt-out from the proposed currency union, although Denmark later also received an opt-out following its initial rejection of Maastricht in a referendum. A plebiscite was passed in Ireland and narrowly in France (the '*Petit Oui*') but British voters were not polled. The Major government argued that parliamentary approval was sufficient, as indeed it had been for every other constitutional measure apart from the EEC vote called by Harold Wilson.

The Conservative Party was against referenda. Thatcher had counselled against one in 1975, saying that 'perhaps the late Lord Attlee was right when he said that the referendum was a device of dictators and demagogues'.[41] A year out of office, she reversed ferret and demanded a referendum on Maastricht. 'We should let the people speak,' she said in November 1991, after warning:

> The history of our dealings with the European Community seems to consist of our conceding powers, of reassurances being given about their limits, of those limits being breached and then of the EC coming back with a new set of demands for a more powerful Commission. That is the conveyor belt to federalism.[42]

It took even Thatcher a while, but when she finally grasped that the Brussels machine was in perpetual motion towards ever closer union (the neofunctionalism adopted as far back as the 1950s by Jean Monnet), she turned on it bitterly.

But even without a referendum on his hands, the ratification process for Maastricht was debilitating and divisive for John Major's government with a series of rebellions by backbench MPs that wrecked his authority. A second European treaty helped to break a second Conservative Prime Minister and he was not helped by another Brussels hurricane, in the form of Britain's messy exit from the ERM on Black Wednesday, 16 September 1992. It was Major, as Chancellor of the Exchequer, who had finally persuaded Thatcher to take sterling into the Exchange Rate Mechanism. It was Major as Prime Minister who had to pull Britain out after a frantic government buy-up of the currency in a vain attempt to keep it in its narrow band with the Deutschmark. Treasury papers released in 2005 showed that the cost to the national reserves alone of devaluing sterling was £3.3 billion. Conservative poll ratings never recovered and the ERM debacle contributed to their huge election loss of 1997 – even though Labour had fully backed the government's policy of joining in the first place.

It is tempting to see the ERM episode as a microcosm of Britain's engagement with the EU as a whole. The UK joined late, rancorously and half-heartedly, on terms largely dictated by others. Membership was always divisive and controversial, and powerful forces drove the country to the exit door against the wishes of its political leaders. Although expensive at the time, departure sowed the seeds of a remarkable period of economic recovery and stability which lasted for years. Could there be a lesson there on the wide question of EU membership?

Maastricht came into force on 1 November 1993 and was undeniably a great advance for the European project. It marked a turning point in the process of integration, superseding the original goal of building a common market with the objective of political union. It was a turning point for Britain too. British voters had not signed up to political union or the removal of the national veto, which was being used in ever more policy areas. The era of the cuddly Common Market was over. The EU was now about so much more than its original mission to facilitate and regulate food production and commerce (even if the definitive regulation 2257/94 that banned 'abnormal curvature' in bananas would not be introduced for a couple more years).

In April 1992, Helmut Kohl, the federalist German Chancellor, who was fond of bombastic rhetorical claims for Europe, declared:

> In Maastricht we laid the foundation stone for the completion of the European Union. The European Union treaty introduces a new and decisive stage in the process of European union which within a few years will lead to the creation of what the founding fathers of modern Europe dreamed of after the last war: the United States of Europe.[43]

Except that Maastricht did not create a superstate. It undeniably concentrated and enhanced the European Union's powers. But its awkward pillar structure set down those areas of European policy decided supranationally and those decided by co-operating governments. Its inclusion of the principle of subsidiarity meant, at least in theory, that the EU would not take decisions best made nationally.

Maastricht also highlighted growing resistance to the European project in several national parliaments and among the EU's newly claimed citizens – at least the minority who were directly consulted (three of the twelve member states, amounting to 20 per cent by population). The Danes ratified the treaty at the second attempt after being given four opt-outs from policies including monetary union and EU citizenship; the French supported it with just 51.05 per cent in favour; and even in Ireland, which had voted with 83.1 per cent in favour of joining the EEC in 1972, support for Maastricht was down to 68.7 per cent. These were early signs that the ultimate ambitions of the grand federalists epitomised by Kohl would never be realised – at least, not with popular consent.

By 1993, Europe was a very different place to the devastated post-war wasteland that gave the idea of the United States of Europe its real impetus. Most of the so-called Founding Fathers (a term deliberately chosen to echo that used in the USA), men like Schuman, Monnet, Spaak and De Gasperi, names barely known in Britain but celebrated above numerous door mantels and statue plinths in Brussels, were long since dead. The fall of the Iron Curtain in 1989 had created a dozen potential new member nations looking forward to running at least some of their own affairs themselves for a change. Jacques Delors, unquestionably the most aggressively federalist European Commission President to date, retired at the end of 1994. The twelve member nations were joined by Austria, Finland and Sweden in 1995 and the bigger membership made deeper integration more difficult.

This was a moment when a pause to consolidate the real achievements of the single market and Economic and Monetary Union would have benefited the European project, especially for its acceptance in the UK. Deep suspicions in a country where two Prime Ministers had been mortally wounded by their battles to hold back European centralisation had created an indelible impression that a superstate was indeed the ultimate goal. It is an impression that has never been shaken off. Die-hard opposition movements sprang up like the Bruges Group, a dedicated band of anti-federalists inspired by Thatcher's 1988 speech.

It was in 1990 that Lord Denning wrote a paper for the Bruges Group on the progress of EU law following his famous 1974 judgment. He concluded:

Our sovereignty has been taken away by the European Court of Justice... Our courts must no longer enforce our national laws. They must enforce Community law... No longer is European law an incoming tide flowing up the estuaries of England. It is now like a tidal wave bringing down our sea walls and flowing inland over our fields and houses – to the dismay of all.[44]

In 1994, the very same metaphor chosen by Denning was also deployed by Kohl to emphasise the new order created in Brussels. 'The process of Union is like the Rhine flowing to the sea. Anyone who stands in its way is crushed against the river bank.' Britain and the EU were becoming entrenched in opposing dynamics. One was trying to ward off a 'tidal wave' while the other was trying to expand a system where dissent would be 'crushed'. The rhetoric was increasingly aggressive. The pro-European movement in Britain has never recovered from the treaty battles of the 1980s and 1990s because it never managed to allay fears of a superstate, even as the expansion of the EU and growing wariness in many member nations meant that there would be no such thing, let alone one that Britain could acquiesce to. This spectre, kept alive by a hostile media, would not die because pro-European politicians had never clearly explained what membership truly meant. As Thatcher's experience showed, even she did not realise what it entailed at first.

The Maastricht Treaty also spurred the formation of the UK Independence Party (UKIP) in 1993, which campaigns for unconditional unilateral British withdrawal from the European Union. It has grown in support at every European Parliament and general election since, although it stands little chance of winning a Westminster seat in the first-past-the-post system and has been hampered by infighting. Notwithstanding a motley cast of maverick candidates, UKIP came second at the European Parliament elections of 2009 and threatens to do just as well, if not better, in the 2014 election. At both the 2005 and 2010 general elections, the Conservative Party blamed UKIP for taking votes that prevented more than a dozen Tory hopefuls from winning seats. Ironically, UKIP was even blamed by some for denying the Conservatives an outright majority in 2010, obliging the party to form a coalition with the pro-European

Liberal Democrats in which manifesto pledges to repatriate powers from Brussels were dropped.[45] Among Labour MPs whose winning margin was far lower than the UKIP vote in their constituencies were former senior ministers like Ed Balls and John Denham. It put the Conservative leadership under huge pressure to concede an in/out referendum on EU membership to neutralise the UKIP threat at the next general election.

John Major fought hard to ensure that the Maastricht Treaty could not force employment or social legislation onto Britain. But the sense of British indignation with the Brussels process was heightened when Delors simply bypassed the need for the Social Chapter by using a legal sleight of hand to propose the working time directive. Since the legal basis he used was health-and-safety policy, and not the Social Chapter, it was therefore applicable in the UK and subject to majority voting. It was duly passed in the European Council with eleven of the twelve votes in favour.

Not every European issue was a case of Britain versus The Rest, of course. Far from it. Most measures were subject to shifting alliances as each nation sought to defend its own red lines and win the best deal within the proposals on offer. But the working time directive was a clear-cut case where Britain felt hoodwinked. David Hunt, the Employment Secretary, fumed:

> The UK strongly opposes any attempt to tell people that they can no longer work the hours they want. This measure is not about health and not about safety, it is a flagrant abuse of Community rules. It has been brought forward as such simply to allow majority voting – a ploy to smuggle through part of the Social Chapter by the back door.[46]

Britain had been bounced into a new era of involuntary integration with its EU partners. It added to suspicions that the QMV principle, advanced by Thatcher and consolidated by Major, would erode national sovereignty without British consent.

In Brussels, there was a sense of powerful momentum following the two significant treaties of the Delors years and this immediately spawned a third, the Treaty of Amsterdam. Its goal was ostensibly to respond to the perceived need for greater democratic accountability in Brussels by enhancing the powers of the European Parliament. MEPs would be given more 'co-decision' with the European Council on legislation, meaning that ministers and officials from the member states would need to thrash out the final wording of new laws with the parliament. The Amsterdam Treaty would also grab some more chunks of national sovereignty, notably from Britain on social legislation, thanks to a new Prime Minister who was keen to change the country's approach to Europe. To the astonishment of his Conservative opponents, Labour's new leader, Tony Blair, was making a virtue of his willingness to agree to more majority voting.

As the 1997 general election approached, Europe became a clear dividing line between the two main parties. In February of that year, Malcolm Rifkind, the Foreign Secretary, gave a speech in Bonn that showed how deeply the British distrusted the EU and feared for their sovereignty. 'Part of what disturbs people in Britain, and many elsewhere, is that they see a constant transfer of power in one direction only,' he said.

> They see all the footsteps leading into the cave and none of them coming out. So they doubt whether it is wise to go any further inside themselves. Where does it end? The conclusion that many draw is that, logically, this process will end in a European state. Mistaken or not, that is a political fact. And this is associated especially with Germany. We hear political leaders in Germany tell us that after Maastricht II we should look forward to Maastrichts III, IV and V.

The German government was at the time proposing more QMV, more co-decision with the European Parliament and the creation of a European police authority and a common defence policy. 'People in Britain ask: how does a United States of Europe differ from the proposals made by Germany and others for closer integration?' Rifkind added. 'All of these proposals seem to point the same way – a transfer of power from the member states to the European institutions.' The Germans were furious. The *Frankfurter Allgemeine Zeitung* created a diplomatic incident by dismissively referring to 'the Jew Rifkind'. This had nasty echoes of the kind of xenophobic attitude witnessed first-hand by the young Edward Heath, the fear of which impelled him to take Britain into the European Community in the first place. Anglo-German relations were soon patched up after the unfortunate phrase was blamed on a junior reporter. And in the next two decades, all of the German proposals would come to pass.

Maastrichts II, III, IV and V turned out to be called the treaties of Amsterdam, Nice, the Constitution and Lisbon. None would be as far-reaching as the first two treaties negotiated under Thatcher but they would see further calls on national sovereignty to strengthen this unique and expanding European alliance. Formerly oppressed nations were queuing up to join the club, seeing it as a bastion of western democracy. The twin goals of peace and prosperity were still widely accepted across Europe as ample reward for the sharing of sovereignty that enabled barriers to trade and travel to be demolished in a continent renowned for its nationalistic protectionism and border squabbles.

But a different dynamic had developed in Britain. The European dream still had many champions but the British trajectory was defined by opposition and exceptionalism. Britain was already on another path, one that led away from its continental allies. All but one of the member states were committed to adopting the same currency in a giant experiment in shared sovereignty that was hard to imagine Britain joining even though it remained a live issue in domestic politics for another decade. The pace of European centralisation would falter with the ill-judged EU Constitution and growing public discontent in a number of member states, but the general direction towards ever closer union continued nevertheless. While it was welcomed by Tony Blair, who tried to set out a completely different tone on Europe, even he could not persuade the British to follow him into the embrace of the European Union.

TWO

Towards a Referendum

There are three choices open to Britain. The first is leaving. The second is in but impotent. The third is remaining in but leading... It is misguided to make perpetual isolation the aim of our policy... I want Britain to be one of the leading countries in Europe.
– Tony Blair

As he greeted voters in well-to-do Beaconsfield with a winning smile, the fresh-faced candidate with the private school education seemed like perfect Tory material. He even produced a leaflet for the 1982 by-election, in the true blue heartland of stockbroker belt Buckinghamshire, entitled *Why Conservatives are Voting for Tony Blair*. Not many of them did, at that time. That was partly because the 29-year-old barrister's policies were vintage Old Labour. Included among them in his election material was the explanation that 'the EEC takes away Britain's freedom to follow the economic policies we need'. This, together with the expensive Common Agricultural Policy, were 'just two of the reasons for coming out. Only a Labour government will do it.'[47] Labour voted against the European Communities Act that took Britain into the EEC and against the Single European Act that created the single market. The party, and Blair, would change a lot in the next fifteen years. Labour had never truly loved Europe but the Conservatives were becoming increasingly hostile and their rivals sensed an opportunity. Labour swung in favour.

Blair inherited a country that had benefited economically from the European Union's single market but was intensely wary of its other grand schemes. He would try and talk the country into a closer relationship but was unable to take it much further towards accepting one. He struggled to reconcile Britain's feelings of otherness from Europe with the inevitability of a world of superpowers and large multi-national blocs. Ultimately he did not manage the tricky manoeuvre of steering Britain towards the full-hearted European destiny that he personally believed in. Blair delivered some of the most pro-European speeches heard from a British Prime Minister since Edward Heath and unlike his predecessor could not be accused of concealing his intentions. He wanted the euro and he wanted a constitution for Europe, one that made clear that the EU was primarily an alliance of nation states. But the ambivalence and antagonism of the two decades before him ultimately proved too entrenched to deflect. The familiar pattern was firmly re-established under Gordon Brown and David Cameron after him, and Britain resumed its inexorable drift towards the door marked exit.

It could conceivably have been different. If Europe had been Tony Blair's absolute top priority, above his fear of moving Gordon Brown from the Treasury and above his commitment to war in Iraq, Britain would have plunged into the euro and Blair himself would probably have ended up as the first full-time President of the European Council. To many British voters, both of these may seem like terrifying thoughts. Perhaps the ultimate outcome in terms of Britain's relationship with the EU would, then, have been the same – a deep distrust of the European project, to the point where the outcome of the next EU referendum, either on a new treaty, a new deal for Britain or a straight in/out vote, is pre-determined by years of frustration finally finding an outlet into the ballot box.

By the time he tried to win a second general election victory, John Major's own vow to put Britain at the 'very heart of Europe' was long forgotten. He was too battered by the pain of Black Wednesday and the battle to pass the Maastricht Treaty to talk up Europe any more. Blair's pledge on the 1997 campaign trail to be 'one of the leading countries' was not quite as exuberant as his predecessor's but the soon-to-be Prime Minister was only reflecting the reality that Britain had begun to distance itself from the core of the European project.

Blair mustered some of his most heartfelt words about the EU for his speech to the European Parliament during Britain's tenure of the rotating six-month presidency:

> I am a passionate pro-European. I always have been. My first vote was in 1975 in the British referendum on membership and I voted yes. In 1983, when I was the last candidate in the UK to be selected shortly before that election and when my party had a policy of withdrawing from Europe, I told the selection conference that I disagreed with the policy. Some thought I had lost the selection. Some perhaps wish I had. I then helped change our policy in the 1980s and was proud of that change.[48]

But he could not change his country's view. The benefits of the EU struggled to be heard in an increasingly eurosceptic media environment that often focused relentlessly on its faults. In a new century, the central prize of peace in Europe came to be taken for granted while the other key target of prosperity went spectacularly awry due to the design faults of the euro. As Blair would himself later acknowledge, the European Union needed to find modern reasons to excite existential passions.

Benefits of the EU (according to the European Movement)

Safer and cheaper flights
Regulation to open up competition has led to cheaper flights and coordinated safety procedures.

Student exchange programmes
Different educational programmes 'give students the possibility to experience different national cultures and broaden their personal horizon'.

The single market
Guarantees free movement of people, goods, services and capital. Enables people 'to live, work, study and do business throughout the EU, enjoying a wide choice of competitively priced goods and services'.

Protection of intellectual property
'EU efforts in this area have resulted in laws aiming at protecting company's or individual's knowledge.'

Peace
The EU has established a lasting peace among its member states.

The euro
The single currency 'is now part of our everyday life but not all of its benefits are well known. From the practical advantages of travelling with a single currency, to the benefits of economic growth, to the strengthening of... political integration, the introduction of the euro has achieved much more than people expected'.

Regional funds
'Unity and solidarity are some of the most significant aims for

the EU. One important reason why the European regional policies have been created is because the EU is of the opinion that
equal standards and rights should be provided to all citizens.'

Cheaper and better phone calls
Liberalisation of telecommunication markets in 1998 and tech-
nological developments have resulted in a steady decrease in
prices within the EU.

Consumer protection
'Consumer protection and the safety of food in the European
Union are two issues that have always gone hand in hand.'

A healthier Europe
Besides many public health regulations, the EU has introduced
the European health insurance card 'that is your guarantee if
you should fall ill when going abroad'.

Environmental protection
'The EU is leading the "Kyoto" drive to reduce the air pollution
that causes global warming.'

Equal opportunities
'Many directives have been put in place to combat inequalities
that occur in the member states.'

External trade
'The EU accounts for 20 per cent of global imports and exports
and is now the world's biggest trader.'

Source: http://www.whathaseuropedone.eu/index.php

The Labour government increasingly set 'red lines' that it would not cross in EU negotiations on sharing sovereignty over matters as diverse as political asylum, freedom to travel and workers' rights. Continental hopes of a truly common foreign policy were destroyed by the Iraq war, to the dismay of France and Germany. Gordon Brown as Chancellor made occasional trips to Brussels to resist financial regulation and as Prime Minister seemed to have little interest in the European dimension. New Labour's initial enthusiasm for the EU slipped into traditional British behaviour of fighting to deflect or deter the forces of integration.

Blair's main foreign policy speech of the 1997 campaign was designed to show his deeper personal commitment – including a pledge to abandon the national veto in some policy areas to help advance the European project. It ended up in an unwitting echo of the dubious reassurance given by Heath in his White Paper back in 1971. 'We will consider the extension of QMV in areas where it is in Britain's interest to do so whilst retaining the veto in areas where it is essential.' Once again this tacitly conceded that further areas of sovereignty governed by Westminster and the British courts were to be considered non-essential.

Much to the delight of his continental partners, Blair began by showing his exuberance for the EU when one of his first acts in office was to reverse Major's Maastricht opt-out from the Social Chapter. Robin Cook, the Foreign Secretary, said: 'We do not accept that the British people should be second-class citizens with less rights [sic] than employees on the Continent.'[49] With Britain now on board, the Social Chapter was included in the Amsterdam Treaty, agreed just six weeks after Labour came to power. It would soon give workers extra maternity and paternity benefits, as well as the right of formal dialogue with managers through works councils. The treaty also introduced or moved twenty-four more policy areas from decision by unanimity to QMV.

Despite Blair's grand rhetoric, however, there were to be two huge exceptions to his aim of leading in Europe – monetary union and the scrapping of internal EU borders known as Schengen. Instead of joining the first wave of countries binding their economies to the single currency in October 1997, the Treasury set out five economic tests for sterling to join the euro bandwagon. Gordon Brown and his lieutenant Ed Balls, who allegedly wrote the five tests in the back of a taxi, kept a grip on the currency issue, despite sympathy to the euro cause from Blair himself and key advisers like Peter Mandelson. The tests covered the convergence of the economic cycle, the impact on the City, growth and jobs as well as more general considerations such as 'flexibility' and the effect on long-term investment in Britain. But the real significance of the five tests was the fact that the decision was firmly anchored in Brown's Treasury.

Blair remained keen on the single currency, telling the Labour Party conference in his keynote speech in 2002 that 'the euro is not just about our economy but about our destiny'.[50] Frustrated with the Chancellor's intransigence, Blair was even said to have considered leaving office early in return for Brown's agreement to join the euro. Clare Short, the former International Development Secretary, wrote that Blair told her in February 2002: 'I really wish Gordon would let me join the euro. If he would... I don't want a third term, I would hand over to him.'[51] Her recollection of the exact words is disputed but the destiny of a British Prime Minister again hung on a key European decision.

It was Brown who ensured that Britain would not be among the first twelve nations to introduce euro notes and coins in 2002. But when the Chancellor ruled Britain out of this first wave in October 1997, he was not able to kill the idea completely because of Blair's fervour and conceded that 'to give ourselves a genuine choice in the future, it is essential that government and business prepare intensively during this parliament so that Britain will be in a position to join a single currency, should we wish to, early in the next parliament'.[52]

Blair and Brown approached the euro from two different mindsets. Anthony Seldon's *Blair Unbound* summed up the Blair view: 'He fundamentally could not see how Britain could be Europe's leader if it was not a member of the euro. He had a fifty-year view, it was Britain's destiny.'[53] The political case ranked highest with Blair: 'He did not worry about the economics, which he never fully grasped. Brown in contrast saw the political advantages too, but became increasingly concerned about the economics.' The duo encapsulated British government ambivalence towards grand European projects that had been evident from the start – Macmillan's deputy Rab Butler told him in 1962 that joining the EEC would split the Conservative Party, while the 1975 Labour Cabinet was divided sixteen to seven on recommending a 'Yes' vote in the referendum and Thatcher's disagreements with senior ministers in 1990 over Europe precipitated her downfall.[54]

By Christmas 2002, a team of twenty-five working full time in the Treasury had completed eighteen background studies on the five tests at a cost of £5 million. Things came to a head in April 2003 after the Treasury reported negatively on their studies to No. 10, leading to one of the most furious rows between Blair and Brown of the second New Labour term. It ended with Blair telling Brown that if he did not keep open the possibility of joining in the near future, Brown would have to consider his position. Just as with the previous Conservative administrations, Europe was again at risk of tearing the government apart.

When Brown made his announcement to Parliament in June 2003, despite a pledge to review the issue in the following year's Budget and to bring forward an enabling Bill for a referendum on the euro, the Chancellor's message was clear. David Blunkett, then Home Secretary, wrote in his diary: 'I think the issue is dead for some years to come.'[55] With Brown in control of the five tests, they would never be passed.

Nor did Blair's pledge shortly before his 1997 landslide to make Britain one of the leading countries in Europe apply to another project enthusiastically adopted by the continentals. The Schengen agreement had first been signed by five nations back in 1985 near the town of that name in Luxembourg. A ceremony took place on a boat in the Moselle River at the symbolic meeting point of France, West Germany and Luxembourg. This truly ground-breaking measure abolished internal border controls so that, once inside the group of countries, travellers could move freely without having to show passports. Anyone driving through mainland Europe can simply carry on cruising on the motorway from one nation to the next past abandoned frontier posts.

When the Labour government came to power, negotiations were well under way to include Schengen in the Amsterdam Treaty. Blair decided not to stand in the way of it becoming part of the EU's body of law but secured an opt-out for Britain, which was joined by Ireland because of its close geographical relationship to the UK, and the two countries also won the ability to opt into any of the frontier and migration measures that the Schengen states would take in the future. Despite all of Blair's grand rhetoric, it was another example of Britain detaching itself from the core European project.

Blair presented his own views about the sovereignty question in a speech in Birmingham in 2001, in the clearest exposition of the subject from a Prime Minister since Macmillan.

> I see sovereignty not merely as the ability of a single country to say no, but as the power to maximise our national strength and capacity in business, trade, foreign policy, defence and the fight against crime. Sovereignty has to be deployed for national advantage. When we isolated ourselves in the past, we squandered our sovereignty – leaving us sole masters of a shrinking sphere of influence.[56]

This went further than Edward Heath, who shared the notion of 'deploying' sovereignty for national advantage but rarely articulated it so openly. In classic Blair 'Third Way' style, he then jumped to a bit of Thatcheresque defiance. 'It is true that British governments have shared sovereignty over some decisions. But we have retained control over our immigration policy and national border controls, our tax, defence and foreign policies – and will continue to do so.' Blair the shape-shifter was at work here, trying to have his cake and eat it at home and in Brussels. He mentioned defence both in the section on deploying sovereignty and the section on retaining control.

Blair felt that he had to make up for the opt-outs from monetary union and Schengen if Britain was to remain a credible leader in Europe – and this would involve one of the crown jewels on his protected list. The Amsterdam Treaty had barely advanced the Maastricht Treaty's call for the 'eventual framing of a common defence policy'. Territorial defence would remain the domain of NATO, while the treaty gave the central leadership role for non-NATO European military activity to the Western European Union (WEU), the Cold War self-defence organisation created in 1954 and the forum for joint European humanitarian, rescue and peacekeeping missions. Blair decided this was the area where he would seize the initiative.

Britain had long been hostile to the idea of creating a common European defence capability – let alone the federalist dream of a European army – but Blair reversed direction in a joint declaration with French President Jacques Chirac after a meeting at St Malo in December 1998. Europe's two nuclear military powers announced:

The European Union needs to be in a position to play its full role on the international stage... This includes the responsibility of the European Council to decide on the progressive framing of a common defence policy in the framework of Common Foreign and Security Policy. The Union must have the capacity for autonomous action, backed up by credible military forces, the means to decide to use them and a readiness to do so, in order to respond to international crises. In order for the European Union to take decisions and approve military action where the Alliance [NATO] as a whole is not engaged, the Union must be given appropriate structures and a capacity for analysis of situations, sources of intelligence and a capability for relevant strategic planning, without unnecessary duplication.

This was a key British contribution to a potentially huge change in European coordination. It led directly to the transfer of the crisis management capabilities of the WEU to the EU under the Nice Treaty of 2003, paving the way for the eventual abolition of the WEU as the EU took over its remaining military functions. The creation of the European Defence Agency followed in 2004 to promote European armaments cooperation and defence research. A Franco-German-British plan in 2004 would go on to create, in some eyes, the prototype European army with the formation of EU battlegroups. Since 2007, two of the eighteen battlegroups, each composed of 1,500 troops, have been constantly on standby, the nationality of the soldiers rotating every six months.

'European defence is the principal area of European policy where the Labour government moved British policy,' wrote Stephen Wall, Blair's former EU adviser.[57]

Today there is greater integration of European forces, a rapid reaction capability, coordinated planning at European level and an embryonic headquarters arrangement. EU forces are involved in significant peacekeeping operations in the Balkans and beyond Europe's frontiers. This has, not without difficulty, been achieved with the consent of the United States, and Tony Blair played a decisive part in assuring that consent.

The UK provided a battlegroup in the second half of 2008 and the first half of 2010 and will do so with Sweden in the second half of 2013. Northwood in Hertfordshire is one of five military headquarters for the battlegroup programme.

St Malo and the establishment of a nascent European defence programme were to be the high-water mark of Blair's co-operation with Chirac and Schroeder, the French and German leaders at the time. He had corralled them into support of the Afghanistan campaign after 9/11 but the Iraq war of 2003 set them at loggerheads when France helped to ensure that there would be no second UN Security Council resolution sanctioning the attack. Blair sided with the United States against France and Germany, and Schroeder never forgave him. The war split the EU, with around half of member states, old and new, supporting the invasion, including the Czech Republic, Hungary, Italy, Netherlands, Poland, Slovakia and Spain. If nothing else, it showed the difficulty of coordinating a single European foreign policy although this did not stop the later creation of the EU's External Action Service to do just this. But when push came to shove, after 9/11 and over Iraq, Britain looked across the Atlantic for its key global partner, rather than to its immediate neighbours.

In this rancorous post-Iraq period, Blair himself was said to regard his greatest single diplomatic EU achievement as the blocking of Chirac and Schroeder's pick for European Commission President, Guy Verhofstadt, the ultra-federalist former Prime Minister of Belgium, in 2004. Instead, Blair pushed for, and got, the more liberal-minded José Manuel Barroso, the centre-right Portuguese Prime Minister. It was a triumph for 'new Europe', corralled by Britain, and a defeat for the traditional Franco-German 'motor' which so often calls the shots in the EU. It showed that, in an enlarged club, Britain could work effectively to build winning coalitions of diverse states with skilful leadership and diplomacy.

Aside from the impetus given to EU defence, the Nice Treaty also attempted to pave the way for the impending enlargement of the EU to include ten former Communist nations after the fall of the Iron Curtain. It drew up a complicated new method of working out qualified majority votes and managed to end the national veto in a further forty-six areas. But in general it was seen as a missed opportunity by European leaders who dreamt of a more streamlined EU, the adoption of a Charter of Fundamental Rights and greater coordination in foreign policy. Germany and Italy in particular were not satisfied and called for a wide-ranging debate on a further, more comprehensive treaty. The goals were stated in the EU's Laeken Declaration of 2001: 'What citizens understand by good governance is opening up fresh opportunities, not imposing further red tape. What they expect is more results, better responses to practical issues and not a European superstate or European institutions inveigling their way into every nook and cranny of life.'[58] It all sounded very sensible.

To further these laudable aims, a Convention on the Future of Europe with 105 members, including six from Britain, was set up under the chairmanship of former French President Valéry Giscard d'Estaing. It sat for eighteen months at a cost of more than €10 million and it produced the draft EU constitution. Its aim was to consolidate and update the five main treaties of Rome, the Single European Act, Maastricht, Amsterdam and Nice, replacing their legalese with a simple, readable text. But for a process intended to reconcile the EU to its citizens and disavow them of fears of a European superstate, some very grand claims were made. Never one for false modesty, Giscard said that his convention 'recalls, in some respects, the famous convention of Philadelphia in 1787'.[59] In other words, it was preparing a constitution much in the same way as the Founding Fathers wrote the constitution for the United States of America. Giscard added: 'We will have a structure in which we will have federalistic functions and still some pieces of national sovereignty. And how this will be integrated at the end into a single system will certainly take time. We will have a sort of government in the making.'[60]

No wonder that many in Britain saw the spectre of a super-state looming again. Popular distrust of government intentions was only heightened by reassurances that the constitution was a 'tidying-up' exercise. Peter Hain, the Europe Minister and government representative in the negotiations, argued against a referendum on the document by declaring that the constitution was not as significant as the Single European Act or Maastricht: 'Those were big constitutional treaties. This is more of a tidying up exercise,' he said.[61] Following a media outcry that he was seeking to downplay the treaty's significant advances, Hain finessed this claim a few days later by calling the constitution 'a combination of a tidying-up exercise, because more than three-quarters of the clauses in the new Constitutional Treaty are just transposed from previous treaties, and modernisation, and reform, because Europe has outgrown its structure designed for six member states, now it's got to have twenty-five'. But it still did not merit a referendum, he argued.

> Look at the single market treaty that Mrs Thatcher signed in the mid-1980s. She gave up more vetoes, more British sovereignty than any, all the other treaties that have been signed by both party governments, in the entire history of our membership with the European Union. So if there was a referendum to be had, it was on that.[62]

Thatcher, of course, opposed referenda in office and never considered calling one on the Single European Act less than a dozen years after the 1975 vote that so emphatically confirmed British membership of the EEC. But the country had moved on considerably by the time of the constitution debate, not least because of a backlog in public consultation over the treaties of Maastricht, Amsterdam and Nice. Clearly there was also a good case for a public vote on something billed as the constitution of Europe with all the implications that had for British sovereignty. The Blair government had also established something of a tradition for referenda, holding them for devolution in Scotland, Wales, Northern Ireland, London and the North East. In the end, Hain's arguments were shoved aside in the name of political expediency.

Blair's principles were called into question when he conceded a referendum under party pressure to shore up Labour's chances in the 2004 European Parliament elections. It was a U-turn that led John Bruton, the former Irish Prime Minister and member of the convention that drafted the treaty, to accuse Blair of showing 'no leadership' on European issues. 'This is an example of him wanting to hand this problem over to the public, rather than take responsibility himself,' Bruton said.[63] Blair had always wanted to guide Europe's destiny but lost his pre-eminent role following Iraq. Now he helped to steer it into unforeseen territory – his referendum decision also helped to push the French into calling their fateful vote on the constitution.

As intended, the EU constitution was indeed easier to read than the previous five treaties. However, it was far longer than originally envisaged and proposed yet further integrationist leaps such as a European Foreign Minister and a permanent President of the European Council to replace the system where responsibility for organising the agenda rotated among member state Prime Ministers every six months. It would hand the European Parliament more powers, such as co-decision over the EU budget for the first time, and give the EU 'single legal personality', meaning that, rather like a sovereign state, it could sign international treaties. It stated formally that the anthem of the EU was Beethoven's *Ode to Joy*. But Giscard was to be thwarted. His constitution was decisively rejected in referenda in summer 2005 in two founding member states – the Netherlands and Giscard's very own France, where he had been President for seven years.

The two votes showed how far the European project had lost touch with the people whose interests it was meant to serve. A similar outcome could have been expected in the UK, a trauma Blair was spared by the double continental rejection. Despite the expensive and long-winded convention held in public, the constitution seemed more and more like the grand design of a European elite out of touch with the real lives of citizens. Appointing Giscard to oversee the project at the age of seventy-six turned out to be a massive missed opportunity to modernise the European Union. But while the constitution format was sunk, much of the substance would be revived in the next update of the EU's rule book. It was an episode that further fuelled public cynicism, a feeling compounded when ministers explained that, despite the similarities of substance between the constitution and the Lisbon Treaty, there would be no referendum because of the style of the new document.

Named after the Portuguese capital, where it was adopted, the Lisbon Treaty amended the earlier treaties rather than standing alone like the constitution. This different technical arrangement was an unconvincing reason for avoiding the burden of a referendum on essentially the same practical measures. It was argued that having a constitution would have fundamentally reformed the Union into something more akin to a country. But there was no escaping the fact that, whether it was called the constitution or the Lisbon Treaty, it would have been difficult for the government to pass a referendum. The UK was not alone – six other countries that planned or held referenda on the constitution decided not to do so on Lisbon, including France and the Netherlands. The impression that Europe's political leaders were now afraid to put changes to the EU to voters contributed to growing dissatisfaction in many countries.

A new treaty was also needed because of the enlargement of 1 May 2004 when ten nations joined to bring the total membership to twenty-five, with Bulgaria and Romania to follow in 2007 and Croatia also on the way. Blair lobbied hard for the swift and inclusive admission of the ex-Communist countries and it is regarded as one of Britain's greatest achievements in forty years of EU membership, alongside the creation of the single market, even if both came at the cost of dramatic extensions of majority voting. Enlargement also meant a diminishing influence for the existing members in terms of voting power and key jobs.

The unavoidable logic of the expanded union has seen Britain's mathematical ability to block unwelcome measures steadily fall and likely to continue to ebb as both the EU and the eurozone carry on growing in size. With ever more decisions taken by majority voting, Britain's voting weight in the European Council has fallen from ten out of fifty-eight votes in 1973 (17.2 per cent) to twenty-nine out of 345 (8.4 per cent).

Europe by numbers 1973/2012

EEC 1973
Member nations: 9
Commissioners: 13 (UK 2 or 15.4 per cent)
MEPs: 198 (UK 36 or 18.2 per cent)
UK votes in European Council: 10 out of 58 votes (17.2 per cent)
EEC budget: 4,588 million (euro equivalent)
UK gross contribution: £181 million (9.33 per cent)
UK net contribution: £102 million

EU 2012
Member nations: 27
Commissioners: 27 (UK 1 or 3.7 per cent)
MEPs: 754 (UK 73 or 9.7 per cent)
UK votes in European Council: 29 out of 345 (8.4 per cent)
EU budget: €129,088 million
UK gross contribution: £11,849 million (11.61 per cent after rebate)
UK net contribution: £6,895 million

In the European Commission Britain's influence has declined from two in thirteen commissioners (15.4 per cent) to one in twenty-seven (3.7 per cent) and in the European Parliament from eighty-one out of 410 MEPs in 1979 (19.8 per cent) to seventy-three out of 754 (9.7 per cent). In practice, British officials remain extremely good at putting together voting alliances and negotiating to have the most hair-raising bits of egregious proposals removed. No country can have it all its own way, which is why Britain, as one of the 'big four' with France, Germany and Italy, still carries significant weight where it engages with the EU. After all, most issues are decided by consensus after endless negotiations.

Blair viewed enlargement as an opportunity to take the EU in a new direction. When Britain held the rotating presidency of the EU in 2005, he urged a move away from traditional concerns of 'old' member states such as agricultural support and social regulation towards fresh challenges of the new century such as globalisation, energy security and – his one-time mantra – education. He put his new ideas on the agenda of a summit at Hampton Court and slowly momentum began to return to the European project. Under the German EU presidency of 2007, Blair and Chancellor Angela Merkel drove through the EU's 20–20–20 targets, for 20 per cent emission cuts and 20 per cent of fuel to come from renewable sources by 2020. This achievement moved David Cameron, after formally thanking Blair for his Commons statement on the summit, to say: 'May I also do something that he is perhaps not always used to from the Leader of the Opposition after European statements, and congratulate him on the outcome to the European Council?'[64] It showed that Cameron believed in the potential of the EU to contribute to British policy goals when facing global challenges such as climate change.

Blair and the newly elected Nicolas Sarkozy of France were among those who ensured that the c-word was not associated with the next treaty, which was duly named after the

Portuguese capital, where it was signed. The many measures in the Lisbon Treaty included the permanent post of the President of the European Council, a job which Blair had his eye on. Sarkozy did his best to support his friend for it – at least for a while until Angela Merkel ruled Blair out. The Foreign Minister for Europe was renamed at British insistence and became the High Representative of the Union for Foreign Affairs and Security Policy, to serve as a Vice President of the European Commission as well as head of the European External Action Service (EEAS). This new service combined the overseas offices of the Commission and the European Council into 136 EU delegations worldwide which, according to the EEAS website, 'have a similar function to those of an embassy'.

The new treaty made the Charter of Fundamental Rights legally binding although Britain and Poland secured a protocol ensuring that it did not overrule their domestic law. Qualified majority voting was made the general rule of voting in the European Council with the national veto ended in fifty-one further areas including justice and home affairs matters – demolishing the third 'pillar' of the Maastricht Treaty, which Britain had so welcomed as a way of preserving national sovereignty. The change meant that the European Court of Justice gained jurisdiction over justice and home affairs, with Britain continuing to enjoy exemption from this until 2014, by when it had to decide whether to accept ECJ dominion over those areas where it opted in, such as the European Arrest Warrant.

Giscard d'Estaing, the man who oversaw the drafting of the constitution, recognised straight away what had happened with the Lisbon Treaty, declaring: 'This text is, in fact, a rerun of a great part of the substance of the Constitutional Treaty.'[65] José Luis Rodríguez Zapatero, Prime Minister of Spain, confessed: 'We have not let a single substantial point of the Constitutional Treaty go. It is, without a doubt, much more than a treaty. This is a project of foundational character, a treaty for a new Europe.'[66] Despite all this, and his party's 2005 manifesto pledge for a referendum on the constitution, Gordon Brown, newly installed as Prime Minister, steadfastly refused a popular vote on Lisbon.

David Cameron, the new Leader of the Opposition, sought to capitalise on Labour's discomfort by telling *Sun* readers in September 2007: 'Today, I will give this cast-iron guarantee: If I become PM a Conservative government will hold a referendum on any EU treaty that emerges from these negotiations. No treaty should be ratified without consulting the British people in a referendum.'[67] With its vague echo of the 'Iron' Lady who stood up to Brussels, it sounded like a refreshingly unambiguous political commitment on Europe. But, as with the government Cameron would replace, it proved not to be. The cast-iron guarantee ended up in yet another avoidance of a referendum that enraged Britain's eurosceptic media and saw public disenchantment with the EU deepen. The political class were making a bad habit of bandying around referendum promises primarily to meet short-term party needs. 'Cast-iron' became redefined in Britain's political lexicon as 'expedient and expendable'.

Brown's Foreign Secretary, David Miliband, brushed aside Conservative demands for a public vote, telling William Hague in the Commons that Hague had 'voted against a referendum on the Maastricht Treaty, which involved a smaller transfer of power [than Lisbon]'.[68] It was a strange argument to choose against holding a referendum, accusing the shadow Foreign Secretary of opposing a vote fourteen years earlier on a lesser treaty. Unsurprisingly, the admission that Lisbon was more substantial than the notorious Maastricht Treaty that ushered in the single currency – and the EU itself – only increased the calls for the public to have their say.

Miliband would hone his arguments in the coming months and the government mantra became that the Lisbon Treaty did not merit a referendum because it was a traditional 'amending treaty', in that it updated the previous treaties, rather than acting as a stand-alone EU constitution that replaced all of them with a single text. The plain truth was that a referendum with unpredictable consequences, with the Conservatives campaigning for a 'No' and gaining in the opinion polls by the week, would have destabilised the Brown government even more than the Prime Minister managed to do all by himself.

Following the referendum row, the European Commission's twice-yearly Eurobarometer survey in spring 2008 showed the extent of public alienation from the EU, registering that just 30 per cent of Britons agreed with the phrase 'Our country's membership of the EU is a good thing'. This was down four points on the autumn 2007 figure and the second lowest among the twenty-seven member states after Latvia. The EU's image in Britain was being irreversibly damaged by the endless bickering over institutional structures, the revival of complicated changes from the unloved constitution and the growing impression that there would never be a chance to express a view in a referendum despite repeated pledges from the main parties.

The longer it wore on, the more the Labour government seemed to give up on the EU. It was taking its lead from the top. Brown had never been particularly bothered with Brussels and the feeling was becoming mutual. As Chancellor, he had the worst attendance record of any European Finance Minister at their monthly gatherings, going to barely half of the meetings.[69] The whole tone of the EU debate in the UK was poisoned not just by public mistrust with their politicians' flexible promises but by aggressive coverage of 'barmy Brussels' from sections of the media. While the *Guardian* and *Independent* remained broadly supportive of the EU, newspapers from News International as well as the *Daily Mail* and *Daily Express* were strongly eurosceptic, with the *Express* becoming the first national title to start campaigning for British withdrawal in November 2010. The campaign is accompanied by regular stories, such as 'Now EU bans plastic bags', which point the finger at 'meddling EU bureaucrats' who in this case 'sparked fury over a plan to ban plastic shopping bags in Britain'.[70] By way of illustrating the contrasting tone used in other EU countries, the same topic a few days earlier was given the headline 'EU wants to reduce plastic shopping bag use' on German website *Spiegel Online International*, which explained that a bag ban had been considered but ruled out as 'a blunt instrument that gives little flexibility to producers, retailers or consumers'.

At the same time as support in Britain for the European project was waning under the weight of incessant treaty-making and media hostility, official British engagement with the EU was weakening from top to bottom. In the summer before Brown's half-hearted signing of the Lisbon Treaty, ministers suspended the 'fast stream' Foreign Office training programme that prepared civil service high-flyers for working in Brussels. Started by the Conservatives in 1991, from a peak of thirty graduates a year there were just three in 2007. Although restored with ten a year from 2009, it fitted a pattern of dramatic decline in British recruitment to the European institutions. While the UK makes up 12.4 per cent of the EU population, it has just 4.7 per cent of the jobs in the European Commission and only 1.8 per cent at the entry level.[71] The pay and perks are excellent but the problem seems to be twofold – the poor image of working in Brussels and the woeful level of language-learning in British schools, especially after the Labour government in 2004 made foreign languages optional from the age of fourteen.[72]

The concours, the annual examination to find new blood to work at the European institutions, is taken in an applicant's second language, while a good third language is essential for the young eurocrat to rise up through the ranks. In the 2011 round of exams, just 2 per cent of the 41,708 applications to take the concours were from the UK and of the 282 successful candidates from across Europe, just seven were British (2.5 per cent), the same number as the year before.[73] The most accomplished nationalities were the Italians with forty-four selected candidates, Belgians (forty-two), Germans (thirty-two), Dutch (twenty-five) and Spanish (twenty-one). As a European Commission spokesman put it: 'We continue to struggle to attract sufficient numbers of the brightest and best from the UK.' The government was so concerned at low British participation that it asked José Manuel Barroso, the European Commission President, whether the exam could be taken just in English. This was one opt-out that Britain failed to win. 'It would be purely and simply illegal,' said a spokesperson.

Britain has excelled in the past in placing high-quality recruits into the European Commission, a policy that saw the number of British eurocrats in the most senior jobs peak in 2011 following the steady rise of the 1970s generation, with Brits holding six director-general posts at the European Commission, more than any other country (although this dropped to four in 2012 following retirements). But what also matters is having a presence throughout the system. Why? *The Economist* recounted one tiny example that spoke volumes:

> Britain was seeking to ease emissions rules for tractors that haul lifeboats up British beaches. Buoyancy aids leave no room for fitting catalytic converters, and there are only thirty tractors, Britain's man at the table pleaded. The commission representative opposite him was also a Briton – the exemption went through.[74]

David Cameron sought to establish his eurosceptic credentials early on, pledging during the Conservative leadership contest in 2005 to remove his party's MEPs from the European Parliament group of conservatives, the European People's Party, because of its founding charter's commitment to create a federal Europe. It was hard to tell how much of this arose from heartfelt eurosceptic conviction and how much it owed to a desire to neutralise rivals for the party leadership, particularly Liam Fox, who had already made the same promise. But much to the annoyance of President Sarkozy and Chancellor Merkel, Cameron went through with the split after the 2009

European Parliament election and formed an eclectic new group, the European Conservatives and Reformists, with right-wing Czech and Polish parties and assorted misfits from Latvia, Lithuania and Hungary. Both Merkel and Sarkozy tried hard to persuade Cameron to change his mind, arguing that this took Britain out of the European family of centre-right parties. 'I look forward to good and intensive co-operation with you, in particular within the framework of the EPP as a clear base for our bilateral dialogue as partners,' Chancellor Merkel wrote to him in December 2005.[75] The decision still rankles to this day in Berlin. Whether born of conviction or pragmatic domestic politics, it marked another key moment in continental eyes when Britain took a further step away from a European destiny.

Even before the 2010 election, Cameron's 'cast-iron guarantee' of a referendum on the Lisbon Treaty had been dropped. Hague explained that, after the Czech Republic became the last country to ratify the treaty in November 2009,

> the treaty is going to become European law and is going to enter into force, that means a referendum can no longer prevent the creation of the President of the European Council, the loss of British national vetoes... These things will already have happened and a referendum cannot unwind them or prevent them.[76]

For some on the Tory right, this represented a familiar betrayal of principle by politicians unwilling to commit to a real fight with Brussels. The Bruges Group called it 'a dark day for the Tory Party but a worse one for Britain' and threw Cameron's own words back at him:

> When David Cameron made his pledge to readers of The Sun to hold a referendum on Lisbon, he said this about the Prime Minister: 'The final reason we must have a vote is trust. Gordon Brown talks about new politics. But there's nothing new about

breaking your promises to the British public... Small wonder that so many people don't believe a word politicians ever say if they break their promises so casually.' The Tory leader stands condemned by his own words.[77]

For Cameron, there could only be one way of responding. It was back to *The Sun* to explain that Brown was the one who had gone back on a guarantee, not him, given that Labour had promised a referendum on the constitution back in 2005. As its successor, the Lisbon Treaty, was now 'set in legal cement... sadly our battle to stop this EU Treaty has come to an end'.[78] But after listing some of the failings of the Brown government ('biggest debt in our peacetime history... society blighted by crime and poverty... war in Afghanistan') Cameron said something very revealing about why a Prime Minister-in-waiting could not afford to provoke a fight with the EU. 'The to-do list for the next government is long and daunting. That is why I know that if we win that election, we cannot afford to waste time having a row with Europe.' That one sentence spoke volumes about Cameron's thinking on the Europe question and the likelihood of him ever agreeing to a referendum that would substantially change Britain's relationship. Compared to all the other things he wanted to do in government, disagreements with Europe were simply a waste of time.

After 'Brown's betrayal', Cameron went on, voters 'deserve to know exactly where we stand on Europe' because giving up on the Lisbon Treaty 'does not mean we are going to meekly surrender to some new European order'. A Cameron government would legislate for 'a referendum lock to which only you – the voters – have the key' before any more powers were handed over to Brussels. The 2010 Conservative Party manifesto pledged to reverse the history of Britain's one-way transfer of sovereignty to Brussels by taking, in Malcolm Rifkind's memorable image from 1997, several steps back out of the cave. The manifesto stated:

A Conservative government will negotiate for three specific guarantees – on the Charter of Fundamental Rights, on criminal justice, and on social and employment legislation – with our European partners to return powers that we believe should reside with the UK, not the EU. We seek a mandate to negotiate the return of these powers from the EU to the UK.[79]

'In future, the British people must have their say on any transfer of powers to the European Union' in a referendum, it added. For the first time since the 1975 referendum, the party that won the general election had a manifesto commitment to take specific powers back from Brussels.

In victory, however, the repatriation pledges were ditched by Cameron during negotiations with his new pro-European partners, the Liberal Democrats. Nor could room be found in the coalition agreement for the Lib Dems' own manifesto commitment to offer 'an in/out referendum the next time the British government signs up for fundamental change'. This showed that the repatriation pledge was not felt to be a core part of Cameron's plan for government. It may have been in the manifesto mainly to shore up his restive right wing and tempt those to whom it really mattered not to vote for the UK Independence Party. 'Protecting our national sovereignty' was instead set out as the guiding principle of Britain's approach to Europe in the coalition programme for government, along with that familiar refrain 'the government believes that Britain should play a leading role in an enlarged European Union'.[80]

Yet while promises to take back powers were dropped, there was a clear pledge that there would be no further loss of sovereignty on Cameron's watch. The coalition agreement included the striking pledge that 'we will ensure that there is no further transfer of sovereignty or powers over the course of the next Parliament'.[81] This went even further than the 'referendum lock' to give the people the final say over a bigger role for Brussels. It sounded like an easy guarantee to give in 2010, with the EU still suffering from 'treaty fatigue' after the struggle to pass Lisbon when Ireland at first voted against in a referendum and only swung in favour sixteen months later after various guarantees. But it was another promise that would provide Cameron with a European-sized headache once the rapidly developing debt crisis in the eurozone provoked fresh calls to boost the role of Brussels little more than a year later.

Nailing down the right to a referendum on the EU would become the central focus of the European Union Act 2011. With the exception of changes brought by further enlargement of the EU, the Act made any substantial future transfers of powers from Westminster to Brussels subject to a plebiscite. Dismissed as a sop to eurosceptic backbenchers at the time, it fundamentally changed Britain's relationship with the EU. The Act marked a line in the sand that effectively halted British participation in any new integrating moves. Within months of it gaining Royal Assent in July 2011, its impact was felt for the first time.

Pressure on the government for a fundamental rethink of Britain's European deal grew steadily, with eighty-one Conservative backbenchers defying party orders in October 2011 by supporting a referendum on EU membership. The motion was the first of its kind to be drawn from a 100,000-signature petition as part of the government's Big Society initiative, showing the strength of popular feeling for a rethink on Europe. But even more telling was the fact that so many backbenchers were prepared to vote against a three-line whip, supposedly the strictest order that a Prime Minister can issue. It showed that the centre of gravity within Cameron's party had shifted firmly against deeper participation in Europe.

Matters came to a head when Cameron was faced with German-driven demands to sign up to the Fiscal Compact, a set of rules to harmonise and enforce budget discipline in the euro-zone, including the introduction of a national law to limit the structural deficit. The compact gave the European Commission the legal right to vet annual national budgets. Angela Merkel began to sound like her federalist mentor Helmut Kohl, promising her party conference in November 2011 that 'the challenge of our generation is to complete economic and monetary union, and build political union in Europe, step by step. That does not mean less Europe, it means more Europe. If the euro fails, then Europe will fail.'[82]

On the very same day, Cameron was pulling in the other direction in his Lord Mayor's Banquet speech:

> The EU's achievements are dramatically overshadowed by its problems. It's not just the crisis in the eurozone – urgent and all-consuming though that is. It's how out of touch the EU has become when its institutions are demanding budget increases while Europe's citizens tighten their belts. It's the pointless interference, rules and regulations that stifle growth, not unleash it.[83]

His attitude towards Europe could not have been more different to its most powerful national leader. For Merkel, the solution was 'more Europe', for Cameron, it was less. For Merkel, the challenge was to build political union, for Cameron, it was to avoid it at all costs. Merkel placed absolute central importance on the euro as the core European project, while for Cameron the single currency's shortcomings were 'all-consuming'. At least they were agreed on one thing – the failure of the euro would be very bad indeed. Again, the trajectory of Britain, in the opposite direction to the undisputed leading nation of Europe, was starkly clear.

Before Cameron's showdown with his European allies over the Fiscal Compact, a fresh threat to British sovereignty became apparent. Open Europe, the increasingly influential eurosceptic think tank, published an analysis warning that, under voting arrangements due to start in 2014, the seventeen eurozone nations would be able to form an unbeatable caucus to push through any EU measures to suit themselves. New voting weights agreed in the Lisbon Treaty meant that Britain would be unable to form a blocking minority in majority vote show-downs in European Council meetings, where national ministers sign off legislation.

Only time would tell if the 'caucusing' would become a real-ity. Much less discussed was that the same risk had applied since 2009 from the dominant members of the European People's Party – the pan-European conservatives abandoned by Cameron – who always convene a meeting the day before EU summits in Brussels to discuss issues of mutual importance. This centre-right caucus had stitched up an agreement for Herman Van Rompuy of Belgium to become the first permanent President of the European Council, for example (albeit while Gordon Brown was still Prime Minister, although Cameron would still have been invited to attend the meetings as an oppo-sition leader had he not broken with the group).

Merkel hoped to bring in the Fiscal Compact as a full EU treaty enforced by the European Court of Justice. She viewed it as an essential piece in the jigsaw to saving the euro. But not only were rebellious backbenchers on Cameron's mind, he was now under pressure from a potential leadership rival. Boris Johnson, the London Mayor, urged him 'to use Britain's author-ity to prevent the EU from making fundamental mistakes and from exacerbating the mistakes of Maastricht' by rejecting a new treaty.[84] Two Cabinet members were also openly agitat-ing for a referendum from the right wing of the party. Owen Paterson, the Northern Ireland Secretary, for example, said that extra powers for the eurozone would make it 'effectively a new country from which we were excluded', leading to 'huge pressure for a referendum'.[85] Moreover, there was the coalition agreement lurking in the background and its pledge to 'ensure that there is no further transfer of sovereignty or powers over the course of the next Parliament'. Yet another British Prime Minister was caught in a vice on Europe.

At the EU's December summit, Cameron used his veto to

stop the Fiscal Compact becoming an EU treaty after attempting to barter his agreement in exchange for several safeguards for the City against financial services legislation. It was a first stab at repatriating powers. It failed. There had not been any doubt for weeks that President Sarkozy, in particular, would reject British calls for a special deal. The fact that Cameron went ahead and pushed the repatriation case during the meeting anyway showed how limited his options had become. For some, the tactic was evidence of Cameron's desire to avoid triggering a referendum under the Act. As one law expert put it:

> Because of the EU Act 2011, Cameron may have been faced... with the prospect of a mandatory referendum. While the treaty changes regarding fiscal discipline did not apply to Britain, signing the summit agreement would have set in motion a process that could result in extension of EU regulatory power... The EU Act 2011, for better or worse, limits the power of leaders and diplomats in such a situation to make decisions and the promises that may be needed to secure concessions, and delegates authority to the people acting through a referendum.[86]

This episode showed how ineffective the power of the British veto had become. On the face of it, British sovereignty was safeguarded. But Cameron had torpedoed an EU treaty that would not actually have applied to Britain – and then watched on as most of the other nations just went ahead in a slightly different legal form anyway. Acting on the basis of intergovernmental cooperation, they drew up their new document, the Treaty for Stability, Co-ordination and Governance (TSCG), and twenty-five states (only the Czechs joined the British on the outside) signed up in January 2012. Cameron's own fears about this were relayed by one EU diplomat who said that the British Prime Minister 'could be heard arguing with his fellow leaders that when members of the new club hold their planned monthly summits, they should not be allowed to use the buildings and meeting rooms of the European Council'.[87] If true, this was a rather desperate last-gasp attempt to assert some authority, which again failed.

In June 2012, nearly a hundred Tory MPs wrote to the Prime Minister urging him to give a clear legal commitment to hold a referendum before 2015. Cameron's old rival from the Conservative leadership battle, the former Cabinet minister Liam Fox, followed up with a high-profile call 'to negotiate a new, looser and largely economic relationship with our continental neighbours'. Fox added: 'If we succeed, a referendum should be held and formal acceptance advocated. If, on the other hand, this approach is rejected outright or falls short of necessary red lines, then we would have no alternative but to recommend rejection and consider departure from the EU.'[88] Fox was articulating widely held anti-EU feelings among the party's grassroots, among whom discussion on leaving the club was becoming more commonplace.

Fox's speech bounced Cameron into changing his implacable opposition to a public vote by declaring that he was 'not against referendums on Europe' but that the timing was wrong while the eurozone was still deciding what measures to take to save the currency.[89] Instead, he said that a Foreign Office analysis of EU powers would determine which could be subject to renegotiation. But it soon became clear that the government was in no rush to repatriate. Within days Hague announced that the comprehensive assessment, the Review of the Balance of Competences, would take two years to 'provide a constructive and serious British contribution to the public debate across Europe about how the EU can be reformed, modernised and improved'.[90] The long grass beckoned.

Cameron's response to Fox also called into question whether he was ever prepared to call a referendum. Although his words were spun by his team as opening the door to a plebiscite, they actually pointed towards a different kind of vote. 'There is more to come – further moves, probably further treaties – where we can take forward our interests, safeguard the single market and stay out of a federal Europe,' the Prime Minister wrote, little knowing that plans for the next EU treaty would be announced in Brussels less than three months later. 'As we get closer to the end point we will need to consider how best to get the full-hearted support of the British people, whether it is in a general election or a referendum.'

This was a phrase that resonated across the years back to Edward Heath's pledge in 1970 that Britain would only join the EEC with 'the full-hearted consent of Parliament and the people'. The significance was that, with Heath, this type of full-hearted consent turned out not to mean a referendum at all but a vote for their representatives in Parliament at a general election (which he lost). Cameron's words seemed to reveal his true desire never to call a referendum on Europe.

The timetable looked like this: a two-year government review of EU powers reporting back in 2014, followed by an attempt to retrieve some of those powers possibly lasting a year, followed by a vote on the result – a vote that could coincide with the 2015 general election or come soon afterwards in the event of Conservative victory. Despite this emerging plan, many of Cameron's backbenchers were dismayed at the Prime Minister's personal commitment to staying in the EU. They claimed that he had undermined his own chances at repatriating powers because he would never be able to use the ultimate negotiating tactic – the threat of leaving.

'When I look at what is in our national interest, we are not some country that looks in on ourself or retreats from the world,' Cameron said in a newspaper interview later in July 2012.

Britain's interest – trading a vast share of our GDP – is to be in those markets. Not just buying, selling, investing, receiving investment but also helping to write the rules. If we were outside, we would not be able to do that. It comes back to this, who are going to be the winning nations for the twenty-first century? If your vision of Britain was that we should just withdraw and become a sort of greater Switzerland, I think that would be a complete denial of our national interests.[91]

Cameron's own commitment to staying in the EU should not necessarily ruin any attempt to redraw Britain's relationship. After all, the final say will not be in his hands. The real threat to the EU is that if Britain does not get a convincing new deal, the UK population will vote to leave in a referendum.

Would leaving really amount to a retreat from the world, as Cameron, like Blair, suggested? Or would it reinvigorate national democratic debate and spur a fresh approach to global opportunities? The Prime Minister is clearly struggling to convince his own MPs of the merits of EU membership. Sometimes he seems to struggle to convince himself. He wants the eurozone to save itself by forging ever closer union but has legislated to put the hurdle of a referendum firmly in front of any deepening of UK involvement. Behind his robust words, a moment's consideration of contenders for the 'winning nations for the twenty-first century' in terms of growth and trade would not include many of Britain's EU allies. Perhaps only Germany.

The government's timetable was gate-crashed by José Manuel Barroso when he announced his own plans in September 2012 to present a proposal for a new EU treaty before the next European Parliament elections in June 2014. In response to raised national animosities in the eurozone between struggling debtor nations and the solvent creditor countries, Barroso called for a true federation of nation states, because 'sharing sovereignty in Europe means being more sovereign in a global world'.[92] He was careful to say that he was not proposing a 'superstate' but 'a democratic federation of nation states that can tackle our common problems, through the sharing of sovereignty in a way that each country and each citizen are better equipped to control their own destiny'. It was the same fundamental argument about sovereignty used by Heath and Blair and practised by Thatcher but it found no resonance with the UK government of the day.

Britain and Brussels were now actively heading in diametrically opposite directions – and the prospect of a new treaty set the scene for the endgame of Britain's uncertain relationship with the EU. Perhaps beyond the three choices set out by Blair in 1997 – leaving, in but impotent or leading – Cameron could forge a fourth way, a new relationship based on the single market and the return of some powers while staying in a formal outer tier where the British position still counts in non-euro matters. This would avoid Blair's fear of 'perpetual isolation' and could see Britain 'leading' at least a secondary group of countries, albeit a dwindling band of non-euro members as one by one they join the single currency as originally planned.

Barroso's blueprint for new Brussels powers, intended to create the economic and political union of Europe, should become clear at around the same time that the government's two-year Review of the Balance of EU Competences is finalised. The government's report was intended to be the prelude to deciding which powers it wants to take back. Suddenly, with the likelihood of a formal conference of all the member states being called to hammer out a new treaty, Cameron will be gifted the chance to fight for the vision of Europe that he wants. The European Commission President's timing was deliberate. Barroso could have decided to announce his proposed new treaty in 2013 but chose 2014 partly because it would coincide with the outcome of the British review. He believed that this was the best way to keep the British on board and avoid the possibility of another veto from Cameron. Barroso intends that the treaty will make the UK an offer – a revised relationship with the EU. And the British people will then have their say at last.

THREE

The Balance Sheet

We are not asking for a penny piece of Community money for Britain. What we are asking is for a very large amount of our own money back.
— Margaret Thatcher at the EEC summit in Dublin, 30 November 1979

A strange womblike structure in a giant glass box is rising from the dirt of the European quarter in Brussels. The distinctive edifice in Rue de la Loi ('Law Street') will be the new office for Herman Van Rompuy, the Belgian who beat Tony Blair to the job of President of the European Council. Dismissed as a 'gilded cage' by David Cameron, Europa House is the latest addition to an EU property portfolio already worth €4 billion. Van Rompuy had a fourteen-page glossy brochure printed for the EU's national leaders to inform them all about his new base when they met for dinner at a Brussels summit held next door to the building site in June 2011. The architects described Europa House as a 'jewel box' and a 'humane gathering place'. His presentation was followed over coffee by debate on a second bailout for Greece and the €28 billion in austerity measures that would mean dramatic and painful cuts to jobs, pay and pensions for thousands of people. Budgeted at €300 million, Europa House seemed like small beer in comparison.[93]

This chapter is about the money that Britain sends to the European Union and what happens to it. An insight into the EU's approach to spending and redistribution, as well as the cost and benefits for the UK, is essential to any consideration of Britain's future relationship to the European club. Spread over the first and twentieth working days of every month, a ten-figure sum is deducted from the account of Her Majesty's Exchequer held at the Bank of England. The average monthly amount in 2012 was approximately £1,251,750,000. The money does not, initially, leave the building but is moved electronically to another sterling account also held at the Bank. This amounts to the biggest regular transfer of national funds ever committed in the history of the United Kingdom, averaging more than £41 million a day. It is subject to a special cashback deal – the British rebate – reducing it to £32 million a day. The recipient of the £15 billion annual payment was EC Account No 1 – the European Commission. What on earth do they spend it all on? And do we get value for money?

From the £2 million annual cost of the 39-person European Union office in Barbados that administers the £230 million budget for Caribbean countries, to the £2.5 million spent subsidising EU orchestras in 2011, hardly a week goes by without another example of extravagant Brussels spending splashed across the British media.[94][95] Who knew that there was both a European Chamber Orchestra and a Chamber Orchestra of Europe subsidised by the British taxpayer? The seemingly endless stories of largesse have spawned some powerful stereotypes that are now firmly fixed in the popular imagination – the fat-cat commissioner, the greedy MEP, the eurocrat gravy train. It is not difficult to find unusual individual items of expenditure in a budget that makes almost two million separate payments a year. But the EU accounts are notoriously so prone to error and fraud that they have not been signed off by auditors since 1994. Troubling at the best of times, the sight of the ever-rising EU budget at a time of painful national austerity measures has caused deep misgivings across Europe, particularly in those member states, like the UK, that are net contributors.

Any review of the vast EU spending operation can only give a flavour of the way the money is handled. This attempt to peer into the funding machine is necessarily selective but also revealing of some of the attitudes that shape its priorities, bearing in mind that all member states sign off the budget both in seven-year frameworks and on an annual expenditure basis. The EU is proposing to spend around €1 trillion in the seven-year period that starts in 2014 (€972.2 million, up from €925.6 billion in the 2007–13 period).[96] Britain is in a group of seven member states (with Austria, the Czech Republic, Finland, Germany, the Netherlands and Sweden) trying to ensure a freeze at 2013 levels. Fifteen nations led by Poland have teamed up to campaign for an increase in regional funds. The sums involved are mind-boggling and the detailed terms of the debate bamboozling for anyone outside the arcane world of EU funding. As a journalist who reported on the EU for five years, I am acutely aware how difficult and frustrating it can be to find reliable figures for spending, costs and benefits. Yet an insight into where the money goes and whether Britain gets value for money is essential at a time when the country is considering its future in the European Union. As the various attempts at a cost–benefit analysis of membership over the years have shown, it is difficult but not impossible to make an assessment of the £15 billion question – is it worth it?

The size of the membership fee that Britain pays to the EU has been controversial from the start. It was a sticking point of the accession negotiations, it was subject to attempted renegotiation by Harold Wilson in the 1970s and it was eventually moderated by a rebate set in stone by Margaret Thatcher after she famously (and apocryphally) declared: 'I want my money back.' The formula for raising and distributing the money was designed by the original six member nations without any input from the absent British. It relied heavily upon customs duties and agricultural import taxes, of which Britain generated a disproportionate amount, while much of the income was then spent on subsidising the type of small farms more prevalent in France than in the UK. Thatcher made her cashback case right from the start of her premiership in 1979, but it took five years of wrangling before the deal was eventually settled.

Ever since the rebate was won, the European Commission – the bureaucracy which proposes and oversees the EU's rules – has campaigned to end it, supported by the European Parliament and most member states. Tony Blair in 2005 negotiated a cut of around one-fifth, saying at the time that 'the cost of this is up to a maximum of €10.5 billion or about £7 billion over the next seven years of the financing period'.[97] (By 2012, the cut had cost the UK €8.65 billion at current prices, according to the European Commission.) It was part of a deal which promised a fundamental shake-up of the Common Agricultural Policy in return, or as Blair put it 'the prospect of a radically reformed budget midway through the next budget period'.[98] The CAP 'Health Check' that followed in 2008, however, fell far short of British expectations for reform. The proportion of the EU budget spent on the CAP at the start of the budget period in 2007 was 43 per cent and in 2013 it was due to be 39 per cent – hardly a seismic change.

Blair also explained that a reduced rebate was Britain's contribution to the extra costs of admitting ten former Communist countries to EU membership. 'The fact is that if we support and, indeed, drive through a policy of ending the post-war division of Europe, we have to be ready to accept our fair share of the costs of that policy,' he told the Commons.

I want to dispel one misunderstanding that has arisen – the impression that only the UK is contributing to the costs of enlargement. All wealthier countries are contributing. In terms of net contributions, our contribution will increase by 63 per cent over the next financing period in comparison with 2000–2006. France's contribution will increase by 124 per cent. Italy's contribution will increase by 126 per cent.[99]

The rebate reduction was 'backloaded' at the request of the Treasury, meaning that its value has fallen dramatically from a peak of £5.39 billion in 2009 to £3.14 billion in 2011 and an estimated £3.17 billion in 2012.[100] That has meant a corresponding rise in direct contributions, although the forecast £11.85 billion in 2012 (after the rebate has been deducted) was actually lower than the £12.21 billion after the rebate in 2011. (See the table on pages 319–20 for an annual breakdown of the UK's contributions, receipts and rebate.)

The rising cost of the UK's subscription fits a familiar pattern. In 1973, the year of accession, Britain made the fifth biggest contribution of the nine member states, a gross amount of £181 million (9.3 per cent of EEC funding) and received back £79 million in grants.[101] The bill for Britain overtook that paid by the Netherlands in 1976. It exceeded Italy for the first time in 1977. And in 1978 the UK contribution, now £1.35 billion (19.3 per cent of the total), was greater than that of France. By 1984, Britain was paying 21.3 per cent of the total budget while its per capita income was just 90.6 per cent of the EEC average. The case for the rebate had become clear. A review of the figures up to and including 2012 shows the incredible savings for Britain made by Thatcher's deal. Since 1985 the rebate – British money claimed back from the Brussels budget – has been worth £73.3 billion. That's £7.17 million a day.

All the twenty-seven member nations of the EU make a cash payment to its coffers, broadly based on the size of their economies. But only ten are net contributors once the money has passed through the European Commission's hands for redistribution and spending. The UK's gross subscription in 2011 was €13.8 billion, after the rebate, behind Germany (€23.1 billion), France (€19.6 billion) and Italy (€16.1 billion) and ahead of Spain (€11.1 billion).[102] But after the EU had redistributed funds back to the member states for farming, regional and infrastructure projects and assorted smaller items, the top five net contributors in 2011 were: Germany (€11 billion), UK

(€7.3 billion), Italy (€6.5 billion), France (€6.5 billion) and the Netherlands (€3.8 billion). Even allowing for the rebate, Britain is consistently the second largest net contributor to the EU.

EU budget net contributors 2011

1. Germany (€10,994 million)
2. UK (7,255 million)
3. Italy (6,492 million)
4. France (6,455 million)
5. Netherlands (3,805 million)
6. Sweden (1,577 million)
7. Denmark (975 million)
8. Austria (813 million)
9. Finland (662 million)
10. Cyprus (1.2 million)

EU budget net recipients 2011

1. Poland (€10,860 million)
2. Greece (4,634 million)
3. Hungary (4,394 million)
4. Portugal (2,981 million)
5. Spain (2,553 million)
6. Belgium (1,870 million)
7. Romania (1,434 million)
8. Lithuania (1,351 million)
9. Czech Republic (1,347 million)
10. Luxembourg (1,255 million)
11. Slovakia (1,091 million)
12. Latvia (729 million)
13. Bulgaria (712 million)
14. Slovenia (446 million)
15. Estonia (346 million)
16. Ireland (301 million)
17. Malta (69 million)

Source: http://ec.europa.eu/budget/library/biblio/publications/2011/fin_report/fin_report_11_en.pdf

---

Up to and including 2012, the total amount that Britain paid
to the EU in membership fees since it joined in 1973 was
£207.2 billion. Without the rebate and pre-rebate refunds, the
grand total would have been £283.7 billion. Of course the UK
also receives money back from Brussels, notably in the form
of farm subsidies and other rural payments, as well as grants
under what the EU calls structural funds which aim to promote
regional development. Over its forty-year history in the EU
to 2012, Britain received funding from Brussels worth £111
billion, leaving a net overall contribution of £96.3 billion.
While some argue that this is the true direct cost of the EU,
the Institute of Directors has argued persuasively that the net
figure can be misleading. 'When estimating the domestic tax
burden we do not deduct public expenditure from the total
tax burden. We don't say income tax is zero because of spending
on health and education. Consistency demands that we adopt
the same policy towards payments – which are essentially a
tax – to the EU.'[103] Moreover, the money returned under EU
schemes would undoubtedly have been spent differently by the
national government.

It is often said that at 1 per cent or so of the EU's gross
national income (GNI), the EU budget is very small in comparison with the amount national governments spend. While this
is true, it is not only misleading to compare EU and national
spending, it also misses the point. It is misleading because EU
GNI increased greatly in monetary value as the number of
member states expanded after Britain joined in 1973, putting
unexpected extra cost burdens on net contributors like the UK.
It is disingenuous because the EU does not pay nurses, teachers, social workers or an army. The UK government planned to
spend £682 billion in 2012, 45 per cent of GDP and six times
the entire EU budget of €129 billion. But the national government must foot the bill for defence, education, healthcare and
welfare. None of these areas are funded by the EU, even if its
regulations increasingly affect the way these systems are run.

One kind of quantitative comparison between the national and European budget might be instructive, however. In 1973, total UK government spending was £30.55 billion (roughly £340 billion in 2012 prices). In 1973, total EEC spending was around £2 billion (£22 billion today adjusted for UK inflation). The British contribution in 1973 was £181 million (equivalent to £2 billion today). These are the levels of commitment that the UK signed up to. But while spending by the UK government has roughly doubled in real terms since 1973, spending by the EU has – by the same measure – gone up more than five times. The UK contribution to the EU budget, even allowing for the rebate, is six times greater in real terms than when Britain joined.

There are two, related, reasons for the soaring cost of the EU since 1973. One is the enlargement of the club from six to twenty-seven nations, with most of the twelve new members that joined in 2004 and 2007, as well as Belgium, Greece, Ireland, Portugal and Spain, still net beneficiaries of the budget and likely to be so for a while. Contrary to popular belief, the other big ticket item of EU spending, the Common Agricultural Policy, is not a factor in the rising budget. Farm payments of various kinds made up 80 per cent of the EEC budget in 1973 when Britain joined, having peaked at 94 per cent in 1970, while in 2013 they were due to account for 39 per cent. There has been a steady shift away from direct production subsidies and market intervention, which made up the entire total in 1973 but three-quarters of the CAP budget in 2013.

The really big rise in EU expenditure has actually been in structural and cohesion funds, the cash handed to mainly poorer regions for infrastructure and other projects to help them catch up with the European average. These payments leapt as poorer countries continued to be admitted to the EU, starting with Greece in 1981 and culminating in Bulgaria and Romania in 2007, and Croatia in 2013. Structural and cohesion funds were worth €347 billion in the 2007–13 seven-year EU budget, or 35.7 per cent of the total, a rise of 47.3 per cent on the €235.6 billion allocated in the previous seven years. Almost half of the money was spent on infrastructure and around two-thirds of that was transport related. Around 15 per cent of spending went on environmental projects. This all marked an important change in philosophy in deploying the EU budget. As the European Commission website puts it: 'Hamburg is Europe's richest region with a per capita income four times that of Alentejo. These regional disparities are prejudicial to the Union's cohesion.'[104]

During the debate about how to save the single currency, one hot topic has been the call for richer eurozone countries to make huge fiscal transfers to poorer states to prevent the kind of debt crisis seen in Greece from snowballing into economic meltdown and triggering hostility and resentment between nations. This is the idea of a so-called transfer union, which exists in every well-functioning currency zone covering rich and poor areas, for example the way that wealth generated in the south-east of England is used to fund national rail and road infrastructure as well as specific projects like the regeneration of Manchester. But a system of transfers has been running in the European Union for many years already, seemingly unnoticed by financial markets. The EU's structural and cohesion funds are supposed to bring sustainable jobs to a region as well as enhance its competitiveness. Since it joined the EU in 1981, Greece has received €61.7 billion for regional and social projects designed to create jobs, improve infrastructure and raise standards of living.[105] That's €5.6 million a day for over thirty years of membership. Recently agreed projects range from €44.9 million to create a national land registry to €6 million for an astronomy park at Mount Orliakas. (See page 321 for the full table of money received by EU countries under structural fund transfers.)

Italy, a founder state of the EU, has received €80.3 billion for regional projects during its membership and yet, despite the government in Rome also transferring a further €50 billion in the same period from the prosperous north to the struggling south, per capita income in the southern region of Calabria remains less than half that in the northern region of Lombardy.[106] This in itself suggests that EU transfers have had little truly transformational effect. While the Greek and Italian sums are huge, they pale in comparison with those enjoyed by Spain, the main beneficiary of the EU's system of internal fiscal transfers. It has been handed a staggering €131.4 billion in structural funds from the EU budget since it joined in 1986. That's €13.3 million every day. As a rule of thumb, as the UK contribution to EU coffers was 11.6 per cent of its total budget in 2012, after the rebate (it was 12.5 per cent in 2011), around one-eighth of all payments from Brussels can be said to have been provided by Britain. At 11.6 per cent, that translates as €15.2 billion from the British taxpayer for Spain and €7.2 billion for Greece in structural funds alone.

Incredibly, the third biggest recipient of EU structural funds is Germany, the richest country in the union. It has received €73 billion back from Brussels over the years, around €8.5 billion of which came from Britain's contribution.

Most EU spending falls under two headings: sustainable growth (mainly the so-called structural funds for regional development but also research grants) of €55.3 billion in 2012, and preservation and management of natural resources (farming and rural funding) of €57 billion. The EU budget's three other headings are: administration (all those eurocrats, MEPs and their facilities), which takes care of €8.3 billion; 'the EU as a global player' (aid, development and overseas representation) at €7 billion; and 'citizenship, freedom, security and justice' (including border patrols and cultural spending), allocated €1.5 billion. The UK was expected to receive £5 billion in public sector receipts from the EU budget in 2012, most of which will be channelled to the private sector. Not included in the official UK figures are direct payments from the EU budget to the private sector, estimated at £890 million. By far the biggest category of money distributed to the UK by the EU is the Common Agricultural Policy (estimated at £4.7 billion in 2012–13), followed by £312 million for the European Social Fund (which gives grants to projects to improve employment opportunities) and £51 million for the European Regional Development Fund (money to regenerate areas by developing business).

Britain's slice of the main EU scheme for handing out money to needy areas, the ERDF, is barely one one-thousandth of the total pot of €52.8 billion in 2012. The UK has received more in the past, including £1 billion in 2007–8, but the money is increasingly being focused on the poorest areas of Europe. It also comes with strings attached. Money will only be released once there is a match-funding in place from the national and regional authorities, a method designed to ensure that EU plans fit in with and have the full support of the local area. So, for example, the new wing of the Museum of Science and Industry in Manchester, which opened in January 2011, was built with £2 million from the fund matched by £2 million from central government funds and a number of private investors. This came out of the total allocation from Brussels to the North West of England of €755 million in the seven-year budget for 2007–13.[107] Other sums allocated include £73.7 million for the Combined Universities in Cornwall, £1.7 million towards St Helens railway station, £12.8 million for the Eden Project in Cornwall and £48 million for the King's Dock redevelopment in Liverpool.

As regional funds have become increasingly harder to access for cash-strapped regions, the European Commission decided to relax the rules. But not for the UK. In the very poorest regions, European funds could already be triggered by a national contribution of just 15 per cent, compared to 50 per cent in the more prosperous UK. In December 2011, the European Parliament agreed to a Commission proposal to reduce the regional match-funding requirement to just 5 per cent for projects in Romania,

Greece, Ireland, Portugal, Latvia and Hungary. Portuguese media reported that this could release an extra €600 million for its regions.

For fraudsters and the mafia, the enormous rise in EU funding for regional development has proved irresistible. In Italy, the European Commission suspended ERDF payments worth €600 million to Sicily over 'serious deficiencies' in control and management of funds in 2012, while OLAF, the EU's anti-fraud office, discovered a racketeering scheme in 2011 that had embezzled €388 million from the Salerno to Reggio-Calabria autostrada project, a 430km highway from the historic capital of Campania to the very toe of Italy.[108] Among the many 'irregularities' in construction, repairs and upgrades discovered by investigators, Italian officials were accused of awarding lucrative contracts to companies that they worked for. It was the single biggest fraud bust by OLAF in 2011, part of the €691 million in misused EU funds recovered by the agency, €520 million of it from structural funds. OLAF expressed its concern that national authorities were becoming less likely to report suspected fraud to them, probably because of concerns that their country or region would then be labelled corrupt. Of the 1,046 reported tip-offs from public and private sources in 2011, only fifty-four came from national authorities. 'The decrease of information from public authorities is something which is worrying us,' said Giovanni Kessler, OLAF's director-general.[109]

Levels of agricultural funding have fallen but the EU continues to subsidise production and environmental farm management, as well as using high tariffs on imports to protect farmers from overseas competition. The initial rationale was to guarantee producers a certain level of income to ensure food security. To some, the CAP continues to offer vital support to preserve traditional farming activity, food supply and rural lifestyles, while others see it as a subsidy biased towards smaller-scale French farmers. At a cost of €338.5 billion over 2007–13, the CAP remains way out of kilter with its EU average gross value-added contribution to the economy of 1.7 per cent. The UK's agricultural sector is even less important to national wealth, at 0.7 per cent, and yet the 2007–13 EU budget calls for a CAP contribution from Britain of €41.1 billion, of which €32.5 billion will return to British farmers and landowners under the two main headings of direct farm payments and rural development. That means that the UK's net contribution – or subsidy to our competitors, if you prefer – was €8.7 billion over the budget period, equating to €3.4 million a day.

Independent research for the European Commission has put the cost of administering the complicated CAP direct payments, which make up four-fifths of subsidies, at €4 billion a year.[110] In 2007–8, the government put the average cost of processing each claim in the UK at £742.[111] With 106,341 claims in the UK in 2007, the administrative cost worked out at £78 million.

Unless there is a breakthrough in world trade talks, it seems likely that the EU import tariffs that distort global markets will also remain broadly in place, safeguarding expensive European production from cheaper producers in the developing world and keeping costs higher for consumers. Taking into account the costs of subsidies and tariffs, as well as national programmes, European taxpayers paid €105 billion in 2008 to farmers, according to analysis by the OECD, just over half of which came directly from the EU budget.[112] The UK's share of this has been put at €8.27 billion, meaning that British taxpayers contributed €4.6 billion in farm subsidies through EU and national spending, while British consumers paid an annual premium for their food of €3.67 billion.[113] With 25.5 million households in the UK, that works out at €324 each extra per year for agricultural support.

While the main two areas of the EU budget, structural funds and CAP, make up around three-quarters of spending, the range of EU activities has become ever wider, encompassing international trade negotiations and competition enforcement, as well as regulations to control business, environmental and trading activities, and the vast overseas representation of the

European External Action Service. Together with the European Commission, the EEAS helps to administer both humanitarian aid (with a budget in 2012 of €842.1 million) and international development (annual budget €1.31 billion). That's on top of the UK's own international development budget, forecast to be £8.16 billion in 2012–13.[114]

The EU is run by an institutional superstructure based mainly in Brussels, Luxembourg and Strasbourg but with a presence in most countries of the world. The European Parliament's budget in 2012 was €1.7 billion, the European Commission cost €1 billion, the European Council €533.9 million, the European Court of Justice €348.3 million, the European Court of Auditors €142.4 million and the European External Action Service €488.7 million.[115] The budget for paying MEPs' wages in 2012 was €69.9 million, with €80.8 million for their travel expenses and €39.3 million for their general expenditure. With David Cameron's salary frozen at £142,500 in 2010, worth €178,125 at an exchange rate of €1.25 to the pound, it meant that at least 236 eurocrats at the European Commission, fifty-nine at the European Parliament and forty-three at the European Council earned more than the Prime Minister in 2012.

Besides the institutions of the European Union, there is an ever growing list of agencies and quangos. The Committee of the Regions, created by Jacques Delors in 1994 to give district and city councillors a say in EU legislation, has 344 members seconded from the member states who meet in Brussels and write non-binding advisory reports. Its budget was €86.5 million in 2012. The European Economic and Social Committee is another 'consultative assembly', this time of employer organisations and trade unions, which shares its HQ with the Committee of the Regions in the unsurprisingly named Delors Building in Brussels. It cost €128.8 million in 2012. In 1989 there were three quangos and agencies; there are now fifty-two at an annual cost of €2.48 billion.[116] They include two separate human rights bodies, the Fundamental Rights Agency, set up in

Vienna in 2007 with a seven-year budget of €140 million, and the European Institute for Gender Equality, based in Vilnius with a seven-year budget of €52.5 million. While many member states host at least one agency, larger member states have two or three. The UK is home to the European Banking Authority, the European Medicines Agency and the European Police College. An independent assessment for the European Commission of the twenty-six decentralised agencies by Danish management consultants concluded: 'The process of establishing the agencies' budgets tends to be disconnected from performance information (which in itself is scarce)... the current process creates an indirect but powerful incentive for spending.'[117]

Accommodating the European Union is an increasingly costly business, with expensive new building projects continuously under way despite the austere times faced in the nation states. The most notorious extra accommodation expense is the monthly jaunt by the European Parliament from its main home in Brussels to Strasbourg, the French city on the border with Germany. It was originally chosen as a home base for MEPs to symbolise post-war reconciliation between the two old foes. As enshrined in EU law in the Treaty of Amsterdam, the European Parliament must meet twelve times a year in Strasbourg. The travelling circus which sees the 754 MEPs journey there along with more than 1,000 staff and a dozen lorries loaded with their paperwork costs €180 million a year. Holding the assembly full time in Brussels would cut 317 posts and save 19,000 tonnes of CO_2.[118] But since it is against EU law to drop even one session, and the MEPs do not sit in August, they go twice in September or October. To save a bit of cash, MEPs voted in 2011 to merge two of the sessions, a move immediately challenged at the European Court of Justice by the governments of France and Luxembourg, adding a bit more expense to the whole caper. The court case showed that MEPs were not able to vote for a change; it can only be made in a treaty by member states – a move that would unhesitatingly be vetoed by France.

The European Parliament's pet project at the moment is building the European House of History, defined as 'a place where a memory of European history and the work of European unification is jointly cultivated, and which at the same time is available as a locus for the European identity to go on being shaped by present and future citizens of the European Union'.[119] Originally budgeted at €18 million, the latest estimate to convert an Art Deco building in a park next to the European Parliament in Brussels came in at €31 million with a further €21.4 million to fit out the structure to open in summer 2014. It follows hard on the heels of another European Parliament scheme, a 65,000 sq ft visitor centre called the Parlamentarium, where 'a stunning 360-degree digital surround screen takes visitors into the heart of European Parliament action'.[120] This one cost €21 million to build. Admission is free.

As previously mentioned, the grandest current construction project is Europa House, the new headquarters for the President of the European Council being built in Rue de la Loi next door to the European Council. But just across the road the EU has recently welcomed yet another addition to its collection of buildings after the European External Action Service found a new home for an annual rent of €12 million. The EEAS, created in 2009 and first headed by Baroness Ashton of Upholland, the High Representative for Foreign Affairs and Security Policy, has more than 1,300 headquarters staff.

Law Street was also improved in 2006 with the addition of the Lex Building for the European Council at a cost of €262 million to house 1,200 staff including 800 translators for the twenty-three official languages. It has a Japanese-style garden on the ninth floor and the view from the two external elevators of the fifteen-storey building is spectacular. The Lex Building has a fifteen-storey sibling across the road, the Charlemagne Building, which cost €117 million in 1997 to house the trade and enlargement directorates of the European Commission. These are overflow departments from the Commission's main HQ, the Berlaymont, which underwent a thirteen-year refurbishment to strip out asbestos that cost a reported €824 million. Besides the EU's property portfolio around the world worth €4.05 billion, extra space is rented or leased at a cost of €506 million in 2012.[121]

Baroness Ashton promised when she was appointed in 2009 to make her EEAS 'cost neutral'. The service was expected by some to produce economies of scale by merging the overseas activities of the European Commission and European Council, but in 2012 she requested an extra €25 million. The annual budget was settled at €488,676,425.[122] Lady Ashton explained that her service was expanding its work in previously unforeseen ways, for example by opening a new office in Libya. The EEAS is the most obvious example of spending designed to project the EU as a global player. Many of the EU's measures have the direct or indirect advantage of helping to build its brand, from an ever growing array of contests and awards to the billions being ploughed into a satellite technology system which has quite literally taken spending on EU promotion into the stratosphere. Some of these examples show just how ill disciplined spending can become in Brussels with a lack of really rigorous controls and how Britain should continue to push for reform if it decides to halt its slide towards the EU's departure gate and retain its membership.

Prizes awarded by European Commission

European Capitals of Culture (First awarded from 1985, annual)
Prize money: €1.5 million each for two cities a year

European Union Prize for Cultural Heritage (from 2005, annual)
Prize money: €10,000 for up to six Grand Prix winners

European Union Prize for Contemporary Architecture (from 2001, biennial)
Prize money: €60,000 (plus €20,000 for Best Emerging Architect)

European Union Prize for Literature (from 2009, annual)
Prize money: €5,000 for eleven or twelve authors a year

European Union Award for Contemporary Music aka European
Border Breakers Award (from 2004, annual)
No prize money

Budget: Annual European Commission budget for Cultural
Heritage, Contemporary Architecture, Literature and
Contemporary Music prizes €1 million approx.

European Green Capitals Award (from 2010, annual)
Prize: Award ceremony but no financial prize
Budget: €580,000

European Business Awards for the Environment (from 1987,
biennial)
Prize: Award ceremony but no financial prize
Budget: €220,000

European Mobility Week Award (from 2002, annual)
Prize: Award ceremony but no financial prize
Budget: €260,000

European Enterprise Promotion Awards (from 2006, annual)
Prizes: Award ceremony and trophy in five categories, no financial prize

Lorenzo Natali Grand Prize for journalism (from 1992, annual)
Prizes: €60,000 total awarded to seventeen journalists

Prizes awarded by European Parliament

The LUX Prize for film (from 2007, annual)
Prize money: €90,000 approx., the cost of subtitling the winning
film into twenty-three EU languages and printing a copy for
each member state
Budget: €573,722 (2011)

Sakharov Prize for Freedom of Thought (from 1988, annual)
Prize money: €50,000
Budget: €652,348 (2011)

European Parliament Journalism Award (from 2008, annual)
Prize money: €5,000 each for four winners
Budget: €154,205 (2011)

European Charlemagne Youth Prize (from 2008, annual)
Prizes: €5,000 for 1st, €3,000 for 2nd and €2,000 for 3rd.
Representatives from one project from each member state travel
to Aachen for four days
Budget: €35,000 (2011)

Total budget for European Commission and European
Parliament prizes: €6.54 million a year.

Brussels journalists regularly receive emails from one or other
EU institution promoting its latest competition or awards ceremony. Whether the prize is for architecture, business, culture,
design, literature, music or journalism, the subtext seems
clear – these taxpayer-funded contests are intended to foster
that elusive feeling of Europeanness. Presenting the LUX Prize
for film in November 2011, Jerzy Buzek, then President of the
European Parliament, made its aims clear:

> [The Lux Prize] looks at the critical question of *what it means to
> be European today*. No other film prize has such a marked – and
> successful – pan-European dimension! Cinema is a mirror of soci-
> ety and identity. It helps us reach a clearer and deeper understand-
> ing of who we are, where we are going and what we want, and
> most importantly, what the citizens want... Europe is not only an
> economic superpower; it is also a cultural superpower. When we
> disregard our strength and unity, we undermine our actions.[123]

That was an extract (punctuation and style included) from a

European Parliament press release, which may give a flavour of what the hundreds of EU-accredited journalists regularly receive in their inboxes.

Even some MEPs are beginning to get nervous at the amount of cash being used to fund the burgeoning number of EU prizes. A report by the European Parliament's committee on budgetary control in April 2012 called for a reversal of the 89 per cent rise in spending on the parliament's four prizes from 2009 to 2011, saying that it 'could have been better deployed elsewhere'.[124] The cost of the journalism prize rose from €105,000 to €154,205; the Sakharov Prize for Freedom of Thought budget increased from €300,000 to €652,348; the Charlemagne Youth Prize rose from €24,000 to €35,000; and the LUX film award budget was up from €320,000 to €573,722. Grand total cost of European Parliament prizes in 2011: €1,415,275. European Commission competitions and awards cost at least a further €5 million a year. The budgetary control committee 'does not consider the prizes to be a core activity of Parliament and requests that a cost–benefit analysis be carried out before any new prize initiatives are developed, so as to take the continuing deteriorating financial and economic situation in all member states into account', it stated. The European Parliament swung into action. The journalism prize was scrapped.

In a rare public appearance, one of the most powerful euro-crats in Brussels gave an insight in 2012 into the campaign to create a European identity. The figure in question was Klaus Welle, the long-serving Secretary-General of the European Parliament. 'National systems have very much invested in constructing their own identity,' Welle, a German, told the Centre for European Policy Studies think tank.[125] Welle observed that people spoke of his native country as if it had existed forever. But the modern German state was created only in 1871. Not that long ago there were around 300 German-speaking statelets loosely connected under the Holy Roman Empire. 'It [1871] is very recent. We have reconstructed our own history as if we have always had a nation state which is completely false and untrue,' he said. 'In order to stabilise identity, we have created national museums, we have created national curricula, we have reconstructed national history.' The European Parliament was now seeking to do a similar thing with the Parlamentarium and the European House of History. 'If we want to build a lasting union of solidarity we also need to invest in European identity,' Welle said. 'We need to understand history as European history and not just as compilation of national histories.'

The greatest prize of all, judging by the amount of money invested by the EU, is conquering space. The Galileo satellite project was conceived in 1999 and was due to be in operation by 2008 as a rival to the American GPS system that provides the world with satnav technology. Allocated €1 billion for development, the original plan was for taxpayers to finance the first four satellites in the network, and for industry to pay two-thirds of the costs of the remaining twenty-six. The private sector pulled out in 2006, however, citing lack of commercial viability, but the EU decided to plough on using public money.

Completion costs for Galileo have climbed steadily and the project has been hit with a series of delays, meaning that the first two satellites were only launched in October 2011. The satellites were named Thijs and Natalia after children in Belgium and Bulgaria who won – what else? – an EU drawing prize. Having thirty satellites meant that, happily, a naming competition could be run in every member state so now, thanks to a talented ten-year-old from Watford, one of the spacecraft will be called Patrick.[126]

The delays to Galileo have led to concerns that it will miss out to rival Chinese, Russian or Indian satellite systems in the race for global commercial contracts and so the quest for fresh ideas for what to do with Galileo is on. The solution? Another prize of course! The annual European Satellite Navigation Competition has a budget of €1 million. The final satellites are not due to leave the launch pad until 2019, eleven years behind schedule, with the total bill expected to top €20 billion. EU officials continue to insist that Galileo 'will generate €90 billion worth of social and economic benefits over the next 20 years' while creating 100,000 jobs.[127]

There were always vague suspicions that Galileo was driven by a deep-seated continental anti-Americanism and a revealing insight was inadvertently given by Berry Smutny, chief executive of OHB-System AG, a German space company, in January 2011. According to a leaked cable published by WikiLeaks, he said that Galileo was 'doomed to failure' and 'a waste of EU taxpayers' money championed by French interests' just weeks before his company won a €566 million contract to develop the satellites.[128] American diplomats in Berlin recorded him alleging that the French were pushing Galileo because they did not want to rely on the US system. Smutny claimed that the desire to develop a 'redundant' alternative to GPS 'was spearheaded by the French after an incident during the Kosovo conflict when the US military "manipulated" GPS to support military operations', the cable said. Smutny added that 'France has aggressively corralled EU support to invest in Galileo development... France wants to ensure their missile guidance systems are free of any GPS reliance.' Berry Smutny was promptly sacked.

Warnings on Galileo were sounded by MPs on the Transport Select Committee in 2007. 'What taxpayers in the United Kingdom and other European countries really need and want is better railways and roads, not giant signature projects in the sky,' said the late Gwyneth Dunwoody, its Labour chair.[129] According to Open Europe, the British share of Galileo funding up to and including the first twenty years of operation was initially projected at €438 million but has risen to €3.35 billion.[130] Meanwhile GPS continues to provide satnav data for the whole of Europe.

Westminster and Whitehall are just as capable as Brussels of waste, extravagance and indulgence of course – the failed project to create a computer programme for NHS records was scrapped in 2011 after £11.4 billion had been committed, for example.[131] MPs claiming expenses for moat-cleaning and duck houses showed that it was not only MEPs who believed they were above scrutiny with their generous allowances. The question is whether the EU brings a serious net benefit despite its faults.

While no UK government cost–benefit analysis of EU membership has been attempted since accession in 1973, there have been various independent British and European studies that attempt to show the added value of the single market. Although they fall short of trying to assess the full direct and indirect economic impact of all EU actions, even an evaluation of the single market requires layers of complicated economic modelling and many 'heroic assumptions' according to a counterfactual study by the Centre for Economic Policy Research (CEPR) in 2008, written by academics from Oxford and Berkeley, California.[132] Its ultimate conclusion was that 'European incomes would have been roughly 5 per cent lower today in the absence of the EU.'

German coal and steel production would probably have restarted in the 1950s and put Europe back on the path to growth without the European Coal and Steel Community (the forerunner of the EEC), the CEPR paper concluded, because of other factors like support from the United States. But the creation of the Common Market and its customs union did bring about a step change in growth in the 1960s because politicians in the founding six member states could appeal to the spirit of European integration to overcome strong domestic resistance to labour market reforms and the liberalisation of protected sectors. The UK 'almost certainly' suffered substantial losses as a result of the Common Agricultural Policy but, if it had never existed, countries 'would probably have gone on protecting their farmers' anyway, the CEPR argued.

The single market achieved fewer gains than the original Common Market, the study argued, because the 1980s was a period that saw a good deal of domestic liberalisation and deregulation in Europe, spurred by the examples of Reagan in the United States and Thatcher in the United Kingdom. To take just one example, the interventionist French government had relaxed some of its tight hold over the financial sector well before the single market programme was launched.

Nevertheless the European Community

helped to coordinate these decisions and secure governments' irrevocable commitment to them. Often 'Europe' was used as a shield against domestic opposition to deregulation. Thus, the German telecommunications reform commission shifted the onus for difficult measures onto EC officials, helping to overcome opposition to deregulation from the Bundespost and the unions.

Two aspects of the single market which might not otherwise have happened, it added, were the opening up of domestic markets in public procurement and the mutual recognition of standards.

A revealing analysis for the Polish government in 2011 of the costs and benefits of the enormous spending by the fifteen 'old' EU member states on structural development funds identified a clear winner among them – Germany. The research aimed to show the impact for contributor nations of the €140 billion destined for the Visegrad Group (Czech Republic, Slovakia, Hungary and Poland) in 2004–15.[133] It concluded that, on average, every euro invested by the EU15 would generate 61 cents in extra exports from them to the four countries. But the estimated benefit ranged from €1.25 for each German euro spent to 20 cents for a French euro. UK exports to the four countries were forecast to grow by €4.8 billion, or 41 cents for every euro transferred. Germany, already the biggest trading partner of the four ex-Communist countries, won 43 per cent of the extra exports generated by structural spending while the UK gained just 6 per cent of them, the study concluded.

Perhaps the real lesson for Britain from the Polish study should be the difficulty of drumming up trade through aid to nations that have little tradition of doing business with the UK. Nevertheless, the report added:

> In addition to the quantitative analysis of additional exports, we also analysed external effects... in research and development, innovation, environmental protection and transport. Although the benefits in these areas are difficult to quantify in monetary terms, they are relevant for all EU countries. These effects are potentially very large and in the long term may prove even more important than extra exports.

It should be borne in mind that the main benefits of structural spending in central and eastern Europe were projected to occur in 2014 and 2015, a forecast presumably included in the study as part of the Polish government's campaign to maintain high levels of funding in the 2014–20 seven-year budget framework, which was still being negotiated at the time the report was published.

The trouble with cost–benefit studies is that just one of the many necessary 'heroic assumptions' can skew the results dramatically in one direction. An analysis for the Institute of Economic Affairs undertaken in 1996 and updated in 2001 concluded:

> Many costs and benefits of EU membership are intangible... An assessment of those costs and benefits which can be quantified suggests the net effect of withdrawal on the British economy would be small – probably less than 1 per cent of GDP. If a special relationship with the rest of the EU were arranged, there might be a small benefit.[134]

Leaving the Common Agricultural Policy would represent 'a

clear gain to Britain' and, while there might be a loss in foreign
direct investment, 'fear of adverse economic consequences
should not deter a British government from seeking to change
the relationship of the UK with the EU, or, in the last resort,
from leaving the Union'.

According to an Institute of Directors paper in 2000,

> the costs of EU membership outweigh the benefits significantly.
> Moreover, because of the significance of the CAP, there is a huge
> discrepancy between those who receive (farmers) and those
> who give (taxpayers). This means that at an individual level the
> costs of EU membership outweigh the benefits by an even wider
> margin.[135]

The IoD estimated the cost impact of the Common Agricultural
Policy as 1 per cent of GDP and the annual cost to the UK
economy of the 'EU social welfare model' at another 1 per
cent of GDP. It put the benefit of being inside the EU's customs
union at 0.5 per cent of GDP. Overall, it decided that the net
annual cost of EU membership was 1.75 per cent of GDP (then
£15 billion).

However, a report by the National Institute of Economic and
Social Research (NIESR) in 2000 concluded that 'the level of
real gross national income would be approximately 1.5 to 1.75
per cent lower outside the EU than inside' with GDP permanently 2.25 percentage points lower. A main reason for its
different conclusion to the IoD was a review of investment by
US-owned companies in Europe since the mid-1960s leading it
to conclude 'that membership of the EU... and hence participation in the single market programme [has] a significant positive
impact on the location and scale of investment. Thus the size of
national economies has to be viewed as partially determined by
the degree of integration with Europe.'[136]

In 2004 the think tank Civitas came up with another
opposing view, claiming that the annual direct net cost of EU

membership was probably 4 per cent of GDP, equivalent to £40 billion a year. This was made up of £20 billion from regulation, £15 billion from the CAP and £5 billion from the net membership fee. The study claimed that there was 'an absence of any convincing evidence in the UK or elsewhere that the single market has actually delivered net benefits for the economies of member states'. This conclusion was drawn despite successive European Commission studies that claimed a permanent GDP boost of 1 per cent (in 1996) and 1.8 per cent (in 2002).[137] A 2007 European Commission analysis of the single market effect from 1992 to 2006 claimed a 2.15 per cent rise in GDP, equating to a gain of €518 a year per person, with 2.75 million jobs created across Europe.[138] Competition in government procurement had enabled savings of 10 to 30 per cent, it said. An internal paper for the Department for Business, Innovation and Skills (BIS) from 2012 claimed that the European Commission's 2007 study, while giving no direct estimate for the benefits to individual member states, 'implies that the gain to UK GDP was in the region of £25 billion in 2006'.[139]

None of the European Commission studies take into account the lost or unrealised trade with the rest of the world as a result of EU membership. It is very hard to model the trade displacement effect of the single market (the likely pattern of trade with the United States, Commonwealth and other countries that was diverted by EU membership with its customs union and common external tariff to keep out products from non-member countries, especially in touchy areas such as agriculture). There is no question that joining the European club boosted British trading activity with our neighbours. It would be odd if it hadn't. Just 27.3 per cent of UK imports were from the six original members in 1968 and this had grown to 43.2 per cent by 1978.[140] The pattern has been well documented across the member states, with the share of exports from the original six members to each other's markets rising from 35 per cent in 1960 to 49 per cent in 1970.

It is fiendishly difficult to put a price on other variables due to EU membership such as the economic impact of all those EU laws. A thorough attempt to assess the cumulative effect of regulations and directives was made by the Open Europe think tank, which concluded that, between 1998 and 2009, 71 per cent of red tape had its origins in Brussels at a cost to the economy of £124 billion, or a total of £4,912 per household over that twelve-year period.[141] The cost had doubled since 2005, paradoxically the year that the government introduced its Regulatory Reform Agenda. According to an analysis of 320 official impact assessments issued in 2009 alone, the annual price of all regulation that year was put at £32.8 billion, with 59 per cent of the total coming from EU-derived rules.

However, the huge cost of red tape was apparently offset by benefits claimed in the official government calculations. Basing its calculations on 2,300 impact assessments, Open Europe put the benefit of all regulation at £1.58 for every £1 of cost, but within that, the benefit per pound spent on EU regulation was put at £1.02 compared to £2.35 for the domestic rules. 'Expressed differently, it is 2.5 times more cost effective to regulate nationally than to regulate via the EU,' they concluded. Nevertheless, it was intriguing to find that government assessments claimed an overall benefit for red tape, including a marginal benefit for EU rules and regulations.

A closer look revealed how the government was able to claim economic advantages from regulations. The official assessments strive to find benefits, including from effects such as a better work–life balance, reduction of accidents and higher productivity. Some of the assumptions made are ambitious, to say the least. The impact assessment on the EU's climate and energy package, which includes its emissions trading system, stated that the cost would be £20.6 billion and the benefits between £9.2 billion and £242.1 billion. The unfeasibly high potential net benefit of £221.5 billion was explained thus: 'Benefits will depend on other's actions and the emissions concentration trajectory the world is on. High end of range reflects world where EU action is pivotal in achieving a global deal.'[142] This effectively meaningless cost–benefit analysis was signed off by the then responsible minister, former Secretary of State for Energy and Climate Change Ed Miliband. No global deal has yet been achieved.

Isolating the UK's simple cash contributions and receipts for the sake of crude nationalistic comparisons is frowned upon in Brussels. Running a slide rule over EU membership simply misses the point of the intangible and incalculable benefit of nearly seventy years of peace, progress and international influence. Here is one reminder from the website of the UK's European Commission office that the EU is about more than a simple balance sheet:

> It is far too simplistic and perverse to confine the European Union to a price tag. There are an array of benefits – recognised and supported by a majority of the British public, according to a recent poll – that are difficult to quantify in cash: such as being part of a market of almost 500 million people, a cleaner and safer environment, and better security. It's like saying that it costs money to buy a house without saying that you need a house in the first place and that you would be in much worse situation without it![143]

It is difficult to know which poll was being referred to, since the closest EU-funded Eurobarometer survey, for spring 2009, found that just 28 per cent of British respondents thought EU membership was a good thing compared to the average across all member states of 53 per cent. The proportion of Brits who agreed that EU membership had benefited the UK was 34 per cent.[144]

Another reminder to take a more Community-minded view came from a European Commission official in an email response to a request for information on national cash contributions and receipts from the EU budget: 'Of course, one should refrain from drawing any conclusion from those crude figures ("How much did I pay in?" "How much did I get back? Therefore, How much am I worse/better off?") since that would be telling only half the story,' the official wrote.

> The other half is made up of two elements: Financial benefits of the Internal Market (£3,000 a year per British Household according to the British authorities); Non financially measurable benefits of the EU (legislation on consumers' protection, on environment, safe transport and all). With those two elements, one sees that comparing contributions to amounts of EU funds received is not only crude but also misleading.

Where was the evidence for the claim that the single market benefited every British household by £3,000 a year? The European Commission official said that his source was Vince Cable, the Secretary of State for Business, Innovation and Skills and President of the Board of Trade.

In a national newspaper article on his battle against bothersome EU regulation in May 2012, Dr Cable wrote: 'It is difficult to see how Britain could on the one hand continue to enjoy the benefits of the single market, worth £3,500 a year per UK household, while on the other refusing to engage on difficult issues.'[145] When asked for the background calculations, the BIS sent a link to a document on the Downing Street website called 'Let's Choose Growth' published in 2011. This included the claim that 'the single market already adds €600 billion a year to our economy. Further liberalisation of services and the creation of a digital single market could add €800 billion more. This is the equivalent of making the average European household almost €4,200 better off each year.' ('Our economy' in this context seems to refer to the EU rather than the UK.) But the household benefit figure was looking flimsier. The €4,200 gain was described here as something that 'could' only happen following two very significant further leaps forward in EU integration.

The Downing Street document sourced the €4,200 per household figure back to... a report on the BIS website, together with 'Eurostat data on EU GDP 2010 and number of households in the EU'. It sounded a bit back-of-the-envelope. The BIS report, Economics Paper No. 11 of February 2011, concentrated on assessing the potential gains for the UK of full completion of the single market, containing no new cost–benefit analysis on the benefits so far. But there was yet another potential source for Dr Cable's claim, one that would seem to contradict his confident assertion of a £3,500 benefit per UK household. This came in the answer to a parliamentary question in September 2011 by his Liberal Democrat colleague in the BIS, Ed Davey.

Asked for the department's estimate of the effect on national and household income of trade with other EU member states for every year since 1981, Davey was unable to give a comprehensive answer. Instead, he replied:

> There is no doubt that the single market is important to the UK's prosperity: it gives UK business access to the world's largest market with 500 million people generating about £10 trillion economic activity. EU countries account for half of the UK's overall trade and foreign investments. As a result, around 3.5 million jobs in the UK are linked to the export of goods and services to the EU. Available estimates show that the greater level of trade liberalisation achieved through the single market leads EU countries to trading currently twice as much with each other as they would do otherwise. As a result, the single market may be responsible for income gains in the UK between 2 per cent and 6 per cent, that is, between £1,100 and £3,300 a year per British household.[146]

This showed that the Cable figure was actually above the top end of his own departmental colleague's estimate of the benefits per household. It was more than three times the lower end of the estimate given by Davey eight months earlier. Moreover, Davey's answer was unsourced. Then another email arrived.

This contained the BIS department's explanation of Cable's assertion that the benefits of the single market are worth £3,500 a year per UK household:

> Looking just at the impact of the single market programme of 1992, income benefits e.g. from productivity gains and price-cost mark-ups are estimated at 2.2 per cent. However, if we take into account the broader period of time from the accession of the UK to the then EEC until today, estimates then take into account well documented positive effects of trade integration on investment, innovation, specialisation and product diversification. Since the late 1970s, domestic bias in economic consumption in the EU has decreased by a third in Europe. As a result, EU countries trade nowadays twice as much with each other as they would do in the absence of a single market [referenced to a 2004 study by Fontagne]. Given that, according to the OECD [referenced to a 2003 report], a 10 per cent increase in trade exposure is associated with a 4 per cent rise in income per capita, increased trade with Europe since the early 1980s (around +15 per cent) may be responsible for benefits of between 2 per cent and 6 per cent of UK national income. The figure of £3,500 is derived from this percentage and is an upper estimate. These estimates are in line with the recent research literature on the benefits of the single market. [Two references: the Centre for Economic Policy Research study from 2008 and a Netherlands Bureau for Economic Policy Analysis from 2009].

All of this just illustrates how hard it is to nail down any kind of reliable figure on the true economic benefits of the single market, let alone the effect of the EU in its entirety. Of the 'recent research literature' cited by the BIS, the CEPR study claimed a general 5 per cent GDP gain across Europe with no UK-specific figure and the Dutch research found a gain of 2 to 3 per cent of GDP across the EU from extra trade in goods and services.[147] Confidently stated, in a carefully prepared article for a newspaper, Vince Cable's figure of a benefit of £3,500 for each household in the UK turned out to be both an estimate and the upper end of the range, two provisos that he neglected to mention.

Neither minister took into account the impact on family budgets of distorted food prices or the effect on businesses of extra regulation. A quarter of a century after the Single European Act and forty years after Britain joined the Brussels club, a clear official figure for the value added to the British taxpayer from the European Union remains elusive. The latest European Commission assessment of the impact of the single market, in a glossy brochure celebrating twenty years since its full implementation, stated that 'EU27 GDP in 2008 was 2.13 per cent or €233 billion higher than it would have been if the single market had not been launched in 1992'.[148] Despite being the main claim in a leaflet published in October 2012, this calculation was based on figures from 2008, the final year of the boom before the dramatic bust of the financial crisis plunged the EU into economic meltdown and triggered talk of a lost decade.

Britain has undeniably benefited from the greater ease of commerce within the EU, by more than the member state average given its openness to trade and attractiveness to investors, most likely to the tune of somewhere between 2 and 5 per cent of GDP. It has probably forgone trading opportunities elsewhere but the overall impact is unknown. The UK's membership fee, after the rebate, amounts to under 1 per cent of GDP (0.8 per cent in 2011) and less once receipts are taken into consideration. The OECD's analysis of the net cost of the Common Agricultural Policy to consumers (i.e. beyond what is paid through the EU budget) was around £3 billion a year in

2008, or 0.2 per cent of GDP. The annual cost of regulations is disputed because it is arguable which would have been necessary if Britain never joined the EU, although two of the biggest and most expensive, the working-time directive and agency workers directive, would not have been created by British lawmakers. Through an exhaustive review of government impact assessments, Open Europe calculated the annual cost of EU regulation as £19.4 billion in 2009, or 1.3 per cent of GDP. On the back of this envelope, at best there is a permanent net benefit to the UK from EU membership of 2 to 3 per cent of GDP, and at worst the purely economic effect is negligible. But then, of course, no cash balance sheet can capture the full impact of forty years of EU membership on British life, and no simple amount of money can be entered into columns marked peace and freedom.

FOUR

Direction of Travel

There are twenty-seven commissioners, which means twenty-seven directorate-generals. And twenty-seven directorate-generals means that everyone needs to prove that they are needed by constantly producing new directives, strategies or projects. In any case, the rule is: More and more, more and more, all the time.
– Guenther Verheugen, German member of the European Commission 1999–2009[149]

Being photographed holding hands with your chief of staff shortly after promoting her and while wearing nothing but a baseball cap on a naturist beach in Lithuania could have finished the career of a lesser man. But Guenther Verheugen is made of sterner stuff. The German Social Democrat and two-term European Commissioner rode out the political storm, parted from his wife and after retiring formed a consultancy with his ex-chief of staff to sell advice about the EU. The entire episode played straight into the corrosive stereotype of the unsackable eurocrat, untouchable in office and inhabiting an elite and rewarding echelon of the European project, even in retirement. Verheugen was also remarkably candid about the way the system worked. He knew better than most the forces driving the European integration process, having been in charge of preparations for the accession of the ten nations that joined the EU in 2004 as enlargement commissioner, and then holding the enterprise and industry portfolio where he battled to cut red tape on behalf of business.

The ever growing European Commission is the engine room of the EU perpetual motion machine. This is the body that has sole responsibility for originating laws and where every country must have a commissioner with all the paraphernalia that goes along with them (chief of staff, seven-person cabinet, team of secretaries, chauffeur-driven car, legislation to work up). But the other big institutions cannot be left out of the picture. All are keen to push their own agendas in the constant jockeying for influence that goes on in Brussels: the European Council, where member states bang the table and attempt to change the Commission's legislative proposals to suit national interests; the European Parliament, which piles ever greater numbers of amendments into legal acts; and the European Court of Justice, which increasingly forges fresh obligations as it seeks to apply EU law in scenarios undreamt of by the original legislators. Increasingly, the European Central Bank in Frankfurt will take on more powers of supervision and oversight to haul the single currency out of crisis.

With the UK poised in the not-too-distant future to take a momentous decision on whether to keep faith with the EU or find another way to organise its relations with its nearest neighbours, it is crucial to know what reforms and future developments are in the minds of key European policy-makers. It seemed absurd when Britain joined the nine-member EEC that seventeen European nations would one day be sharing a single currency, yet it came to pass within three decades. The appointed European Assembly turned into a directly elected European Parliament less than ten years after British accession. No one can possibly look as far as thirty years ahead, but another UK referendum would settle the membership question for at least that time frame. Senior European politicians have made proposals for the EU that they would like to see for all its member nations, beyond those measures that the eurozone must take to preserve the single currency and which will directly affect only the countries concerned. There are plans being discussed from Luxembourg to Warsaw which will reshape the EU in the years to come, a dynamic given extra impetus by European Commission President José Manuel Barroso's determination to set out plans for a more federated EU before the end of his mandate in 2014. What, then, lies in store for a Britain that decides to change course and recommit to a role at the heart of Europe, or at least stick with the EU as best it can?

'At the moment, the idea of a single European state is simply irrelevant to the political reality. In fact, it is really just parts of the British media that constantly claim that there are people who want such a thing. But I do not know anyone who does.'[150] So said Verheugen in the same valedictory interview quoted at the start of this chapter. He was right to say that the post-war dream of a single European state failed to become reality. The absence of a superstate has been painfully apparent in the drawn-out battle to save the single currency from meltdown, with national governments in wealthier northern eurozone countries – notably Verheugen's own – refusing to allow the pooling of debt or the wholesale fiscal transfers necessary for a properly functioning currency union. But the absence of a fully fledged superstate has not meant much let-up in central-ising measures taken in the spirit of ever closer union. While asserting that the single European state is a mythical monster kept alive only by the British media, Verheugen went on to set out several of the key ambitions for the next few decades of European integration which are still very much alive and well in Brussels. For example, asked if the EU really saw itself as a global player, he answered:

> It is not one yet. But in ten or twenty years, Europe will be forced to compete with new economic superpowers which will also have their own political agendas. And at that point, we will not be able to play an equal role if we do not have a single EU repre-sentation in international organisations such as the International

Monetary Fund or the UN Security Council and are hence unable to speak with one voice.

While Britain retains a veto over any such consolidation of international seating arrangements, bolstering Europe's 'soft power' presence on the international stage is never enough for an ambitious federalist like Verheugen, whose most fervent hope is to revive a plan rejected by France in the 1960s but one which will not go away. These hopes were only fed by Europe's divisions over the Iraq war, which led to the drive for a more coherent EU foreign policy under its European External Action Service. 'It is in precisely those areas where we need more Europe that you can find the largest emotional resistance from the member states,' said Verheugen.

I believe that having a global role will not be possible as long as Europe continues to see itself exclusively as a 'soft power'. It is an illusion to think that you can conduct global politics just with humanitarian assistance and diplomacy. One also needs to have the means to enforce your decisions... I believe it is necessary to have a common EU military force, for reasons of efficiency apart from anything else. Today, Europeans have two million soldiers under arms, but they are not even able to deploy 60,000 of them somewhere.

So there you have it: a single seat on the UN Security Council and a European army. But not a superstate, that is a figment of the British imagination, and Verheugen knows nobody who wants such a thing.

His successor as Germany's member of the European Commission, Guenther Oettinger, belongs to a rival political party, Angela Merkel's Christian Democratic Union, but also has strong views on the direction of the European project. Talking in February 2012 about the likelihood of Germany eventually accepting common eurobonds and of his support for proposals put forward for greater fiscal coordination by the European Commission and others, he said:

> I feel that the proposals are an outstanding basis for engaging in the structural debate about tomorrow's Europe at all levels in the coming weeks. We are talking about a banking union, common economic policy, more democracy and democratic control and, ultimately, the founding of the United States of Europe.[151]

Oettinger is not some oddball outlier in German politics but represents the authentic voice of mainstream opinion among senior representatives of Europe's most powerful nation. Both Wolfgang Schaeuble, the long-serving Finance Minister, and Chancellor Merkel talked increasingly during 2012 of the need to build 'political union' in Europe. 'Without doubt, we need more and not less Europe,' Merkel told an audience of students in February 2012.[152] 'That is why it is necessary to create a political union, something that was not done when the euro was launched.' The European Commission would act as a government reporting to a strong European Parliament, she said. 'We believe that we will stand better together if we are ready to transfer competences step by step to Europe.' This is a cross-party view in Europe's strongest nation – it is shared by the German Socialist and President of the European Parliament, Martin Schulz, who would love nothing more than to become European Commission President so he could put it into action. 'I could do that job,' a German magazine quoted him as saying.[153]

For obvious historical reasons, post-war Germany has been the most consistent supporter of European federation, an approach which holds less fear for a country that, on the one hand, is often reluctant to assert its own national self-interest, and on the other hand is already organised in a strong internal federal system which entrusts much power to its sixteen states. The German upper house, the Bundesrat, is entirely composed of representatives from the states and Oettinger, a former Minister-President of Baden-Wuerttemberg, clearly finds the model inspiring. Pressed on how the EU would ensure democratic control if sovereignty over further fiscal powers was transferred to the supranational level, Oettinger added:

> We will need a two-chamber system in the future. The representatives of the countries could sit in the second chamber, based on the model of the United States Senate. And, incidentally, the European Parliament has to play a decisive role in all other deliberations on the amendment of our EU treaties.[154]

These ideas, it will be remembered, were precisely the ambitions of Jacques Delors to which Margaret Thatcher issued her famous 'No, No, No!' in the House of Commons in 1990.

Wolfgang Schaeuble is sometimes seen as the last of a generation of prominent politicians born during the Second World War who sees a European superstructure as the best way of controlling nationalist forces in order to cement peace on the continent. The German Finance Minister spelt out in 2012 that he could foresee reforms to the way the EU was run in the near future that would necessitate a historic change to the German constitution. This, in turn, would require the assent of the German people in the country's first referendum since the war. 'The European Commission should become a genuine government and for that it needs to be elected by the parliament or by the direct election of its President. I am for the second option,' he said.[155] 'One can give more power to Brussels but the German people will have to have their say.' A popular vote was conceivable within the next five years, he added.

The task of corralling support around Europe for a further push at EU reform was taken on by another member of Merkel's government, Guido Westerwelle, the Foreign Minister, from the junior party in the ruling coalition, the liberal Free Democrats. A generation younger than Schaeuble, he too is pushing for much greater concentration of powers in Brussels that would require the consent of the German people: 'I hope that we have a real European constitution and that there will also be a referendum on it,' he said in August 2012.[156] Westerwelle's role in German politics is coming to an end with the dramatic loss of support for his party, but he could yet be a candidate for the country's next European Commissioner. There is, however, very little appetite among member states for another push for a constitution after French and Dutch voters rejected the first attempt in 2005 and showed how distant federalist politicians had become from the general public's expectations for Europe.

Nevertheless, the idea of a directly elected 'EU President', who could also serve as unified head of both the European Commission and the European Council, seems to be gaining a head of steam. It is seen as a way of strengthening the global brand of Europe while giving the EU greater democratic legitimacy and some much-needed personality. Both Presidents are currently chosen by the group of twenty-seven national leaders, usually from among their own number, a method that has been criticised for tending to produce low-key figures who present no threat to Europe's main national leaders. An injection of democratic uncertainty could throw up new EU leaders more likely to challenge or even outshine the national heads of government, not least because they would owe a certain allegiance to voters rather than simply to the heads of, say, France and Germany for anointing them.

José Manuel Barroso used to argue indignantly that his mandate was 'doubly democratic' because he was elected first as Prime Minister of Portugal and then 'elected' again by the national EU leaders.[157] But there would be a different order of democratic legitimacy if the post was put to a vote of the people of Europe. Those who campaigned for greater democracy in Brussels would then find themselves with, potentially, an extremely powerful figure on their hands.

The push for institutional change in the coming decade

is not just coming from the big countries. Viviane Reding, Luxembourg's long-serving member of the European Commission, is also calling for a strong President uniting both Commission and Council. Reding, who is believed to harbour her own ambitions for such a post, added:

> European leaders should agree that the new Council President will convene a convention to draft a treaty on European political union. Such an agreement should ensure that the European Parliament becomes a true European legislature, with the right to initiate legislation and the exclusive right to elect the Commission. A treaty on political union should also ensure that the Commission President receives the right to dissolve the European Parliament if needed. From 2016–19, the treaty on political union would be subject to ratification in all member states by way of referendums. It would enter into force once two-thirds of member states have ratified it. Citizens should be given two alternatives: either to accept the new treaty, or to reject it and remain in a close form of association, notably by continuing to participate in the single market.[158]

Here was the logical lesson to be drawn from the Lisbon Treaty and the Fiscal Compact – to get round the awkward squad (i.e. Britain and the Czech Republic), the EU should forge ahead through a new type of qualified majority, that of the committed integrationists. A simple two-thirds majority just happens to equate to the combined number of the eurozone states plus one (and with Latvia keen to join the single currency as soon as possible).

A public election for the most senior EU job would not only strengthen the post but could surely not be less edifying than the bizarre behind-closed-doors spin-the-bottle stitch-up that currently characterises senior appointments. An unwritten law prevails which stipulates that the top jobs must be shared out equally between big and small member states, east and west, left and right and, preferably, male and female too. The result is a parlour game of who can be found to fill the gaps in this complicated jigsaw, rather than who is personally best qualified to carry out the duties of the role. So, in the last round, with a right-of-centre male from a medium-sized country in the west (Barroso) on track for a second term at the Commission, and a centre-right man from a large eastern country in place as President of the European Parliament (Buzek) in a deal which would more or less guarantee that a centre-left male from the largest country would take over from him for the second half of the parliament (Schulz), not forgetting that an apolitical French male civil servant was already in charge of the European Central Bank (Trichet), and that an apolitical German male civil servant was chosen to be Secretary-General of the European Council (Corsepius), the two remaining big vacancies, for President of the European Council and High Representative for Foreign Affairs, clearly had to balance the whole thing out by ticking the boxes marked 'small country' and 'centre left' and 'female'. Since Tony Blair had attempted a high-profile tilt at the presidency but had been thwarted, Britain was in the frame for a consolation prize. Thus Herman Van Rompuy of Belgium and Baroness Ashton of Upholland fitted the bill for the two posts very nicely. Helmut Schmidt, the former Chancellor of Germany, summed up the choice of the EU's top trio: 'At the head of the Commission, Barroso is weak. The President of the Council is Mr Nobody. The chief of European diplomacy, Ms Nobody.'[159]

One proposed variant of the directly elected President scheme would involve a two-stage election with the final pair campaigning from Limerick to Limassol, igniting new passions about the EU along the way. It was not surprising, then, that the idea of the super-President was taken up by Westerwelle's Future of Europe Group, which reported in September 2012 and comprised the foreign ministers of Austria, Belgium, Denmark, France, Italy, Germany, Luxembourg, the Netherlands, Poland,

Portugal and Spain. All of the EU's big players, in fact, with one rather obvious exception. Westerwelle denied that he had snubbed William Hague because he feared British wrecking tactics. 'It was just a choice I had to make,' he said. 'Every selection is in a way unfair. We wanted a creative group, big enough so that all groups were represented and yet not too big.'[160] The irony of Britain being excluded from a gathering called the Future of Europe Group spoke volumes for others' perception of its place in the EU. It seemed that the idea of Britain playing no part in the continent's destiny was catching on.

The proposal for a unified President did not meet with unanimous approval from the eleven-nation Westerwelle group. 'Some ministers suggested the creation of a double-hatted post of President of the Commission and President of the European Council,' the final report stated, revealing divisions over the idea. Austria and the increasingly eurosceptic Netherlands were understood to be the most vocal opponents of the combined post, leaving the idea dangling for now. Nor was the group united on the idea of holding a direct election for the President of the European Commission.

> At the end of a longer process, we need a streamlined and efficient system for the separation of powers in Europe which has full democratic legitimacy. For some members of the group, this could include the following elements: a directly elected Commission President who appoints the members of his 'European Government' himself, a European Parliament with the powers to initiate legislation and a second chamber for the member states.[161]

The report showed both that federalism retains its long-term appeal for some member states but also that others are feeling a certain reform fatigue. What this means for Britain is that some European politicians will never let go of the EU's founding principle of ever closer union, although they will find it difficult to take the whole club with them and may forge ahead in an inner core of federalists. But a positive decision by the UK to stay in the EU and fight for a distinctly British vision of greater market liberalisation and competition would probably also come up against resistance to change, unless the British were prepared to concede ground in other fields like some of those raised by the eleven foreign ministers. That is how the EU has always developed – a liberalising advance has often been achieved only at the expense of deepening the institutional or federalist agenda.

The model of the US Senate for the role of European member states inside the EU is another perennial federalist dream that would certainly be vetoed by Britain and almost as assuredly by France, which has traditionally acted to preserve its national sovereignty within the European framework. And while the reach of the European Parliament has steadily increased to include a say over the annual EU budget as well as a potential veto on the next European Commission President, Britain is also likely to block any further extension of MEPs' powers that included proposing new laws. As for the European Council, the Future of Europe Group said that 'in the medium term, to improve the European Union's capacity to act, we should extend the scope of decisions taken by qualified majority'. This could refer to areas such as taxation and foreign policy which currently remain under the preserve of national vetoes. Again Britain would be expected to block any such proposals.

In fact, given that almost all of the proposals debated by the eleven countries would seem completely unacceptable to the current British government, the path forward for most of the rest of the EU seems clear. They will go ahead anyway, just as the Fiscal Compact went ahead after David Cameron's veto in December 2011. As the group concluded:

Most members of the group believe that both the adoption and entry into force of treaty revisions (with the exception of enlargement) should be implemented by a super-qualified majority of the member states and their population. A large majority of member states should not be restrained of further advancing in integration due to either lack of political will or to significant delays in the ratification process... They would be binding for those member states that have ratified them.

It would hardly be worth Britain attempting to block some of the recurrent ideas such as a European border police or a European visa to replace national visas, both of which could be limited to countries within the Schengen travel zone, which covers most of the continent apart from the UK and Ireland. With 'some members' of the Future of Europe Group also 'eventually' wanting a European army, there is little prospect of Britain being able to veto it in future. As with most of these proposed measures, if they come to pass, Britain will find itself simply left on the outside whether it stays in the EU or not.

What would the EU do with its own 'hard' power if a group of member states did agree to a European army? Here's Rachida Dati, an MEP for the French conservative UMP party, speaking in 2012 about Syria: 'The weakness of Europe will not be forgotten or forgiven... 19,000 people have died, that is the weight to bear for the weakness of the EU.'[162] This desire to use 'hard power' in Europe's neighbourhood is not limited to MEPs. Barroso, the Commission President, speaking in his state of the union speech in September 2012, said:

> The appalling situation in Syria reminds us that we cannot afford to be bystanders... The world needs a Europe that is capable of deploying military missions to help stabilise the situation in crisis areas. We need to launch a comprehensive review of European capabilities and begin truly collective defence planning. Yes, we need to reinforce our Common Foreign and Security Policy and a common approach to defence matters because together we have the power, and the scale to shape the world into a fairer, rules based and human rights abiding place.[163]

This was not Barroso's only cunning plan. In the same breath with which he set out a timetable for considering a new treaty to complete economic and monetary union, he promised 'elements for reinforced democracy and accountability' as well as 'a Single Market Act II' and measures 'to create a European labour market, and make it as easy for people to work in another country as it is at home'. In line with the Lisbon Treaty, he added: 'Our commitment to upholding the rule of law is also behind our intention to establish a European Public Prosecutor's Office.' This old chestnut, long resisted by Britain, can now be brought forward under so-called enhanced cooperation so long as at least nine countries agree. The prosecutor would then serve the countries that want it. The Lisbon Treaty stated that the European Public Prosecutor 'shall be responsible for investigating, prosecuting and bringing to judgment, where appropriate in liaison with Europol, the perpetrators of, and accomplices in, offences against the Union's financial interests'.[164] Cases would be brought in national courts. Its work could be extended 'to include serious crime having a cross-border dimension'. The UK coalition government made its position clear in its programme for government: 'Britain will not participate in the establishment of any European Public Prosecutor.'[165]

While the debate over the future shape of the European Union continues largely without the UK, there is one area where Britain has tried hard to ensure that its influence is strongly felt – the establishment of the European External Action Service, the prototype EU Foreign Office, created in the Lisbon Treaty from the merged overseas operations of the Commission and Council. Here, Britain's engagement has been in another great tradition of the country's involvement with the European project – it is designed to restrain the true potential of the policy, as evidenced by the move to water down the proposed name of EU Foreign Minister to High Representative. Nevertheless, ambitions remain high across many member states for the future of the EEAS, with a new High Representative due to take over in November 2014. A number of medium and small-sized EU nations would dearly like a change of style from Baroness Ashton's 'quiet diplomacy'[166] to get more visibility on the global stage and the Future of Europe Group called for the role of the service to be expanded. Rather ominously for Britain, they said that this could include 'joint representation in international organisations'.

While the UK government will certainly fight hard to preserve its permanent place on the UN Security Council – where it sits alongside France, the United States, Russia and China – the EEAS will equally certainly continue to expand its role. From 1974, the EU had observer status at the United Nations but that changed in May 2011 when the EEAS won the right for Baroness Ashton to address the General Assembly no differently from the British Prime Minister or US President.[167] Following a vote pushed by the EEAS, the UN changed from an assembly of nation states into a body with representation rights for regional blocs. This also gave the EU 'the right to speak in a timely manner, the right of reply, the right to circulate documents, the right to make proposals and submit amendments, the right to raise points of order and more seats' in the chamber for the High Representative and her officials. This recognition led the EEAS to go on and secure representation rights at numerous other UN bodies. The direction of travel for the EEAS seems clear – it will seek to represent the EU wherever and whenever it can. That's its job.

The mission creep of the EEAS was evident from the start. Quite literally. All talk of the EU's representatives being called 'Head of Mission' was soon forgotten in favour of the full-blown 'Ambassador' title that the UK feared made the EEAS sound like a Foreign Office for Europe rather than a service of the member states. And while Baroness Ashton adopted a low-key approach, the office megaphone was taken up by João Vale de Almeida, the former chief of staff of fellow Portuguese eurocrat José Manuel Barroso, who was appointed to represent the EU in Washington DC in 2010. In his first public statement upon arrival, he said: 'In this area code, you call me. I am the first new type of ambassador for the European Union anywhere in the world.'[168] This led William Hague to warn British diplomats to resist any attempts by the EU foreign service to usurp their position. 'We see some evidence of EU delegations in particular parts of the world where they try to push for an enhanced leadership role,' David Lidington, the Europe Minister, said.[169]

> William has sent out instructions to all our posts around the world to be vigilant about any risk of competence creep. It is things like an EU delegation assuming and asserting that it has the right to speak on behalf of member states. There is a pressure from some parts of the EU machine to push competence and we are very keen to make sure it is pushed back and clear lines are drawn.

There seems little doubt that the EEAS will look more and more like an EU Foreign Office as the years go by. Whether Britain remains in the EU or not, it has helped to create a new overseas power much loved by smaller European countries, for which the EU representation offices provide their only foothold in far-flung places. This will increasingly be the case as the example of the Irish and Swedish governments is followed by others seeking to save money during tough economic times by closing their own embassies and relying on the EEAS. Ireland's Special Group on Public Service Numbers and Expenditure Programmes concluded its review on consolidating spending with a report that 'recommends that the Department for Foreign Affairs... embrace the opportunity that this supranational service will present to further rationalise Ireland's network of overseas missions and to achieve significant savings'.[170]

Calls for the EEAS to be given consular powers have been made by the foreign ministers of Austria, the Netherlands and Estonia, the last of these a country with just one embassy of its own in the whole of Africa and the Middle East. These consular powers could range from the most basic, such as assisting with the medical evacuation or emergency financial aid of an EU national, to helping those who find themselves under arrest or who lose their passports. The EEAS could of course be embraced by the Foreign Office, to provide representation in hard-to-reach places or countries where Britain lacks expertise. From July 2012, for example, the UK relied on the Swedish embassy in Tehran to represent its interests after closing the British embassy when it was attacked by protestors. David O'Sullivan, the Irishman who acts as Chief Operating Officer of the EEAS, said: 'Scale will matter in the twenty-first century. Individual western countries will struggle. If Europe is to be relevant in the twenty-first century, it will be so only as the EU.'[171]

Another development that is likely to gain momentum in coming years is the growth of the EU as a 'rights body' as it encroaches upon territory traditionally seen as the preserve of the Council of Europe, the separate 47-nation organisation set up in 1949 that runs the European Court of Human Rights in Strasbourg. The EEAS is playing its part in expanding this EU role. In 2012 it created the new post of EU Special Representative (EUSR) for Human Rights, an envoy who will be expected to roam the globe to press the case for better treatment of downtrodden minorities and ill-treated democracy campaigners. Stavros Lambrinidis, a former MEP, Vice President of the European Parliament and Foreign Minister of Greece, was chosen in July 2012 as the first EU human rights ambassador. 'As a lawyer he will bring discipline and rigour to the new human rights and democracy strategy and action plan adopted by EU foreign ministers,' said Edward McMillan-Scott, a Liberal Democrat MEP and the European Parliament Vice President responsible for human rights and democracy. 'Furthermore, as a former MEP, he will understand that the public expects the European Union to do more in this field. The latest Eurobarometer survey of 25,000 citizens shows that the highest appetite for EU action lies in the field of human rights and democracy.'[172]

A further step change in EU activity in the realm of human rights is being prepared by the EEAS with its project to develop a European Institute of Peace. Baroness Ashton's service allocated €200,000 in the 2012 budget for a cost–benefit analysis to 'consider questions such as institutional set-up, including cost structures, managements systems and funding requirements'.[173] While the size, scope and location of the European Institute of Peace have yet to be determined, work to create the body has been under way since 2010 despite the squeeze on resources across European governments which has seen so many of their own services cut, including a 24 per cent reduction in the budget of the UK's Foreign Office under the 2010 Comprehensive Spending Review. The Peace Institute was the brainchild of the foreign ministers of Finland and Sweden, Alexander Stubb and Carl Bildt, who called for 'an independent body focusing on conflict resolution and peace mediation' which 'could engage in conflict resolution activities worldwide, not least those of the UN. It could train Europeans for service in situations where classic diplomacy is not always optimal'.[174]

The European Institute of Peace was made legally possible by the Lisbon Treaty. A study for the European Parliament stated:

The background is the fact that as the Lisbon Treaty has now come into force the Union should be capable to carry out the role of a global actor in the pursuit of peace as set up by the treaty. The world as it looks today with the challenges and threats described in the European Security Strategy has given the Union a vast and complex task in its ambitions to create security and work for peace also on a global level. The challenge for the Union at this stage is to acquire the capabilities needed in analysis, knowledge and training based on a common strategic vision to pursue this... The question to be answered by this report is whether an EU Institute for Peace would give an added value to the Union. This question can be answered by yes.

According to a research project for the EEAS into setting up the institute, the European Institute of Peace could develop a far-reaching role around the world. Its tasks could include 'advice, research, training, mediation and informal diplomacy aiming at conflict prevention and peaceful resolution of conflicts'.[175] Having secured peace in Europe in the last century, not to mention a Nobel Peace Prize, the EU has added global peace to its manifesto for the new century. This is yet another example of the unforeseen developments stemming from the creation of the EU's foreign service in 2009. If Britain's destiny lies inside the European Union, it may be able to clip the wings of the EEAS, although as this example shows, now that it is up and running it will seek to grow into the fully fledged Foreign Office envisaged by its supporters with or without the support of the UK.

There is also no guarantee, of course, that the next High Representative will be as benign towards British interests as Baroness Ashton, who has not sought consular powers for the EEAS nor tried to compete openly with national foreign ministers. As jockeying for position continues among potential candidates to succeed the Labour peer, the two foreign ministers behind the European Institute of Peace seem likely to be in the frame, as well as Germany's active representative Guido Westerwelle. Another likely contender is Radosław Sikorski, the Polish Foreign Minister, and not least because Poland expects to claim one of the top European jobs on offer at the next major rotation. Sikorski, an outspoken Oxford-educated former Bullingdon Club member, has been developing a vision of his own for Europe as Poland, which joined in 2004, seeks to play a fuller role in EU decision-making. The Germans do not have the monopoly on plans for the EU's future, far from it. But it was at the German Council on Foreign Relations in

Berlin in November 2011 that Sikorski – speaking in English – gave a Polish vision of what could lie ahead. He called for a new treaty that would create a European federal state to solve the euro crisis. He reminded his audience that the United States and Switzerland only became real federations when rules were created for the transfer of wealth between their richer and poorer regions. Such a move would allow the European Commission to become a real government with an elected President, he said.

> Eurosceptics are right when they say that Europe will only work if it becomes a polity, a community in which people place at least a part of their identity and loyalty. 'Italy is made, we still have to make Italians,' Massimo D'Azeglio said in the first meeting of the parliament of the newly united Italian kingdom in the nineteenth century. For us in the EU, it is easier: we have a united Europe. We have Europeans. The eurozone's failings are not the exception but are typical of the way we have constructed the European Union. We have a Europe with a dominant currency but not a single Treasury to enforce it. We have joint borders without a common migration policy. We are supposed to have a common foreign policy but it is divorced from real instruments of power and often weakened by member states cutting their own deals. [176]

This thinly veiled hint of the need for a European army, as well as a common European visa, sounded very much like the German agenda, and, combined with a massive centralisation of economic policy-making, they add up to a substantial federalist programme. Sikorski also threw in a smaller and more powerful European Commission for good measure. 'We have to decide whether we want to be a proper federation or not. If renationalisation or collapse are not acceptable then only one way remains, making Europe as Europe governable at last and hence in due course more credible.' The ultimate goal for Sikorski 'if we get our act together' is to 'become a proper superpower in an equal partnership with the United States'.

Another advocate of closer European political union, also from the centre right and also thought to have his own ambitions to lead the European Commission (he is taking English lessons), is Sikorski's boss, the Polish Prime Minister Donald Tusk.

'We are standing at a crossroads, in front of us is a very serious choice, whether in this time of crisis we choose the community path or national and state egoism; selfishly seeking rescue and seeing the community as ballast is not the best way out of the crisis for Europeans,' he told the European Parliament during an appeal for talks on a more efficient Europe.[177] He argued that European integration could not be blamed for the financial and political crisis. 'The last six months have shown that it is exactly the opposite... Europe, not only for the duration of this crisis, but also for the future requires strong political leadership.' It sounded like a tilt at the top Commission job, although with the intense focus on saving the euro the big founding member states are likely to want a Commission leader deeply rooted in the single currency.

A key area where the EU claims to lead the world and which is certain to develop in the coming years is the battle against climate change. Measures intended to help meet energy efficiency targets include the binding instruction for member states to renovate 3 per cent of the floor area of central government buildings every year from 2014 to cut energy use – an expensive outlay at a time of budget cutbacks. Work is already under way on the successor targets to the EU's 20–20–20 package for mandatory 20 per cent emission cuts and 20 per cent of fuel to come from renewable sources by 2020, as well as the non-binding goal of 20 per cent energy efficiency (reduction of fossil fuel use against projected levels). The European Commission launched a debate in July 2012 on the next set of targets for 2030. It identified three options: new targets for greenhouse gas emissions cuts but no new goal for renewable energy; targets at national level for renewable energy, cutting emissions and improving energy efficiency; and new EU level targets in the three areas mentioned. The EU's Emissions Trading System (ETS) would continue to issue carbon credits to industry and airlines, and extend this to the maritime and forestry sectors.

The European Commission has also prepared an 'Energy Roadmap 2050' which envisages a reduction of 80 to 95 per cent in greenhouse gas emissions from 1990 levels. Although supported by twenty-six member states, Poland used its veto in June 2012 because of its continued reliance on coal-fired power stations. But the EU's direction of travel on climate change seems clear – more targets, less carbon emissions and more use of renewables, which means more subsidies for wind and wave power. The European Renewable Energy Council, made up of twelve associations from the sector, has asked the EU to increase the share of renewable energy to 45 per cent of the energy mix by 2030.[178] This is opposed by the British government, which has privately urged the scrapping of the renewables target when it expires in 2020. In a leaked submission to the European Commission, it said: 'The UK envisages multiple low-carbon technologies: renewables, nuclear and carbon capture and storage, all competing freely against each other in the years to come... For this reason, we cannot support a 2030 renewables target.'[179] Oxfam is also opposed to any renewal of the target in renewables for transport fuel after 2020, saying that the 10 per cent target agreed in 2008 led to crops in the developing world being given over to biomass production, causing evictions, land grabs and rising food prices. Nevertheless climate change is one area where Britain has had and can continue to have a leading role in the EU if it chooses to stay and commit to developing the policy.

How much bigger will the European Union get? The enlargement of the EU from fifteen to twenty-seven states since 2004 has been seen as a triumph of British foreign policy. Against

resistance from France, which feared the dilution of its influence, London was the chief cheerleader for a speedy entry for the
new members because of its belief that the EU would entrench
core European values like the rule of law in vulnerable young
democracies. A welcome side effect was that all these vibrant
newly independent countries would kill off any lingering plans
for a European superstate by sheer weight of numbers. Wider,
not deeper, was the mantra. Surely, the British thinking went,
no country recently emancipated from the Communist yoke
would want to surrender its new-found freedom to another
remote overlord, this time based in Brussels. This reckoned
without Poland's ambition to rival France and Germany as a
leading EU power.

There are five countries recognised as candidates to join the
European Union and three potential candidates. Their entry
would bring the total membership to thirty-six. But not all of
them will join. The two most advanced applicants are so small
as to barely impact upon British influence inside the EU or the
running of the club – apart from to add to the twenty-three
official languages, provide an extra commissioner each and add
a handful more MEPs. These two – Iceland and Montenegro
– have a combined population of just over one million people
and would become the smallest and fourth smallest members
respectively. While Montenegro could expect to join in around
2017, the people of Iceland seem to have gone off the idea. The
fervour to apply in 2008 at the height of the island's financial
meltdown has been replaced by a steady stream of polls showing opinion against joining, not least because of the impact on
Iceland's fiercely protected fishing rights.

The next two official candidates in line also have their problems. Macedonia, known internationally as FYROM (in full,
'The Former Yugoslav Republic of Macedonia', which means
it sits in between Thailand and Timor-Leste at the United
Nations), is still held back by its name dispute with Greece,
which claims to fear FYROM's territorial ambitions over the

Greek province of Macedonia to the south. The Greek Foreign Ministry refuses to recognise its neighbour's preferred name, the Republic of Macedonia, accusing it of 'a falsification of history and the usurpation of Greece's historical and national heritage'.[180] The fourth candidate, Serbia, shows signs of turning back towards nationalism and is repairing traditional ties with Moscow. With a population of 7.1 million, Serbia would receive around seventeen MEPs and cause a realignment of voting weights in the European Council that, all other things being equal, would just tip the balance so that the eurozone members would no longer be able to command an automatic qualified majority by themselves. The recognised potential candidates are Albania, Bosnia and Kosovo, while further afield, pro-EU forces in Ukraine are on the back foot and Georgia has long-term ambitions to join.

But none of the other would-be EU members will have anything like the impact of the longest-waiting candidate country, Turkey, if it finally joins. With its population of more than seventy-four million people, and the second-largest army in NATO behind the USA, Turkey would easily become the second-largest EU nation. Its population is forecast to overtake that of Germany, currently the largest member, by 2020, which would give it the most MEPs and the biggest voting weight in the European Council.[181] The population of Turkey is forecast to reach 97.8 million by 2050, compared to 79.1 million for Germany and 66.2 million for the UK. [182]

Turkey would extend the EU's borders to Syria, Iraq and Iran. It would also be the member state with the youngest age profile, given that more than a quarter of its population is under fifteen. The centre of EU activity would move dramatically eastwards. Turkey's formal application to join was made in 1987 but since then at least eighteen countries have leap-frogged it in the queue, fifteen of them becoming members. Little wonder that the Turkish are losing faith in the EU, with popular support for membership falling from 73 per cent in 2004 to 38 per cent in 2010.[183] 'The European Union, with its population of half a billion people, should not be scared of a country of 60 or 70 million citizens,' said Abdullah Gül, the Turkish President, in 2010.[184]

There is good reason for Turkish scepticism. While Britain has a long history of promoting its case, Nicolas Sarkozy legislated so that France would have to hold a referendum on Turkish accession, unless a large majority of deputies decided otherwise. Austria followed by declaring that it, too, would hold a referendum and public opinion remains against Turkish entry. Angela Merkel, the German Chancellor, has long favoured a 'privileged partnership' for Turkey rather than full membership. 'We have already got a privileged partnership. There is a customs union. We want to become a full member,' said Gül in 2011.[185] Turkish membership of the EU has more support from the USA than from some European states. President Obama, speaking on a trip to Ankara in 2009, made no secret of the American belief in keeping the world's most modern secular Muslim state bound closely to the west. 'I think it is the right approach to have Turkey join the European Union,' said the US President.

> I think if Turkey can be a member of NATO and send its troops to help protect and support its allies, and its young men are put in harm's way, well, I don't know why you should also not be able to sell apricots to Europe, or have more freedom in terms of travel... I also think it would send a strong signal that Europe is not monolithic but is diverse and that that is a source of strength instead of weakness.[186]

François Hollande softened French policy after Sarkozy but nevertheless appeared to rule out Turkish membership for five years during his election campaign. Official UK policy notwithstanding, it is hard to see a British government allowing the free movement of people, one of the EU's four freedoms, to apply to Turkish citizens following the debacle of the ten-country accession in 2004, when between 5,000 and 13,000 eastern Europeans were forecast to come and stay in the UK but by 2008 at least 704,000 had done so.[187] However, as diplomats in Brussels are quick to point out, Britain has the luxury of being able to maintain its benign attitude towards Turkey because France and Germany have become so openly hostile. In the light of this overt opposition, negotiations have slowed to a snail's pace. José Manuel Barroso said in 2006 that the accession process would take at least until 2021.[188] The latest unofficial target date mentioned by Turkish analysts is 2023, the centenary of the founding of the modern Turkish state. It could even be the case that the trajectories of Turkey and the UK, the one inching forward, the other backing away, eventually meet in some kind of associate membership status as bookends to a more closely integrated eurozone.

The single market is usually cited as the single most important reason for Britain's continued membership of the European Union, given that the UK is likely to remain opted out of the single currency and the single travel zone. Yet the single market is far from the static or completed construct that some may imagine. Much remains to be done. Barriers to internal trade in the form of tariffs on goods and physical barriers like border posts have successfully been removed. But non-tariff barriers such as national licensing, technical and administrative rules remain, to say nothing of the impediments to the cross-border trade in services like banking, healthcare, insurance, maintenance and training. Services account for 70 per cent of GDP and are the most important source of foreign direct investment and net job creation in the EU. Yet only 20 per cent of the services provided in the EU have any cross-border dimension and it has been estimated that the potential economic gains from the implementation of the EU's services directive of 2006 range between €60 billion and €140 billion, representing a growth potential of between 0.6 and 1.5 per cent of EU GDP. Moreover, there are emerging sectors, such as digital and energy, where the British government and others are pushing EU policy-makers to hurry up and complete a truly single market approach.

Whether Britain stays in the EU or leaves, work will go on to adapt the single market and this could well follow a far-reaching blueprint drawn up by a former commissioner who oversaw the system from 1995 to 1999. Mario Monti, before he became Italy's technocratic Prime Minister in 2011, was asked to draw up a plan for the future of the EU which some believe he may yet get to implement himself as the next European Commission President. Whether or not the politically non-aligned professor remains active when the next Commission is chosen, his report gave Britain and others a clear idea of the kind of challenges and compromises that lie ahead in the battle to liberalise the EU.

A New Strategy for the Single Market, delivered in May 2010, opened with a quote from Paul-Henri Spaak, the Belgian states-man seen as a founding father of the Common Market, who in 1961 declared: 'All those who, in trying to meet the economic challenges set out by the treaty of Rome, neglected the politi-cal dimension have failed. As long as [those] challenges will be addressed exclusively in an economic perspective, disregarding their political angle, we will run – I am afraid – into repeated failures.'[189] Monti was here signalling right from the start what so many British politicians either will not, cannot or do not want to grasp – that the single market is not viewed anywhere on the continent of Europe as a simple economic trading system but rather as a complicated political construct involving many social checks and balances in order to function acceptably.

Monti consulted widely among the twenty-seven member states and concluded that there were three main types of atti-tude towards extending the single market: the *radical critics*, who 'see the single market as a source of tensions, dislocations and fears... They would rather see less economic integra-tion and perhaps a lesser role for markets in general in our societies'; the *conditional supporters*, the 'vast majority of member states' who regard the single market as important but believe that it is 'insufficiently mindful of other objectives (for example, social or environmental)' and 'that a relaunch of the single market is likely to meet serious opposition unless it addresses such concerns'; and finally the *unwavering supporters*, 'who fully support the idea of a relaunch' but 'do not seem to be fully aware of the concerns that, in many other countries or contexts, have reduced the acceptance of the single market'.[190] Clearly the UK falls into the third category, while one could easily imagine Germany in the middle group and France, historically resistant to unrestrained competition, in the first. Monti's identification of the three factions is important because it shows just what the UK would be up against, and would have to accept, if it wanted to stick with the EU and force the pace of greater liberalisation. In Monti's view, this would involve significant political commitment.

Monti proposed reforms to complete the single market in energy by introducing new regulatory frameworks for the large-scale deployment of renewable resources, smart metering, smart cross-border grids and transparent wholesale energy markets, as well as a single market for green products with EU-wide standards for measuring and auditing carbon footprints and energy-efficient products, and targeted EU funding for energy infrastructure. He suggested reforms to facilitate a single digital market, with new legislation to harmonise rules for delivery, warranty and dispute resolution; proposals to simplify cross-border retail transactions; an EU framework for copyright clearance and a legal framework for EU-wide online broadcasting. There were also many transport-related suggestions such as a single market for maritime transport and rail reforms to harmonise track gauges, energy supply and signalling systems across member states. He also called for moves to increase the mobility of European workers, such as portable pension rights and the automatic recognition of professional qualifications, which at that time only applied to seven out of 800 professions.

The quid pro quo for further market opening should be 'actions in the area of free movement of workers, social services, public procurement, industrial policy, coordination of taxation policies and regional policy', Monti said. 'These are building blocks for a reconciliation between the single market and the social and citizens' dimension in the treaty logic of a highly competitive social market economy.' He urged greater clarity on the right to strike following two European Court of Justice rulings that limited collective action aimed at protecting the conditions of workers in 'old' member states from being undermined by cheaper labour from 'new' member states.

Most controversially, Monti set out to allay the fears of the 'radical market critics' by taking aim at tax competition between member states, one of the key British (and Irish) red lines. 'Europe has a highly fragmented tax landscape. In many areas, the operation of twenty-seven different sets of rules implies significant compliance costs and administrative burden for citizens and business operating cross-border,' he said. Monti argued that when countries compete for international business by cutting their corporate tax rates, this tends to reduce the money available for government social programmes: 'The functioning of the single market – coupled with the wider globalisation process – places a growing challenge for the operation of domestic tax systems and may erode in the long term their revenue raising capacity, as well as their ability to pursue social and redistribution policies at the national level,' he said.

> It is important to devise solutions that minimise harmful tax competition... This does not mean depriving national systems of a tool to exploit the full potential of the single market. Business surveys show that corporate tax levels are only one of the factors taken into account by business when weighing the attractiveness of alternative locations for direct investments. Other factors, such as stability of political and regulatory environment,

infrastructure, productivity and labour costs are considered more important than corporate taxation.

This was the argument he hoped would convince Britain and others to stop aggressively competing with fellow EU nations to be the destination of choice for international business head-quarters on the basis of corporation tax cuts.

His answer came from the UK government in the Budget of March 2011, when George Osborne cut the rate of corporation tax from 28 to 26 per cent, falling to 25 per cent in 2012. In the following year's Budget he set out a further reduction to 22 per cent by 2014. That compared to a company tax level of more than 30 per cent in France, Germany, Italy and Belgium. Britain is not alone in opposing the harmonisation of corporation tax by Brussels. Sweden, which has also refused to join the euro, announced in 2012 that it would cut its corporation tax from 26.3 per cent to 22 per cent. 'This is the most harmful tax of all,' Prime Minister Fredrik Reinfeldt said.[191] The cut would 'strengthen the investment climate and growth in Sweden'. A large group of national capitals see things Monti's way, however. The UK has a veto over changes to any tax rates at EU level but corporate tax harmonisation has not gone away.

Monti was in effect proposing a repeat of the kind of grand bargain that Thatcher rather unwittingly signed up to in the Single European Act of 1985, which introduced the single market at the cost of the loss of the national veto in many areas. His report showed just how strongly tax coordination is linked to single market reform in mainstream EU thinking and signalled to market reformers, like Britain and Ireland, that significant further liberalisation will come at a price. It should act as a wake-up call to all those who believe that 'completing the single market' can be achieved in isolation from social, employment and fiscal concessions, without hard-fought political debate and compromises. Following the EU Act of 2011, which requires a referendum on any further transfer of power to Brussels, deepening the single market, Monti style, would certainly trigger a vote on Britain's future relationship with the EU.

At the same time as Monti was toiling away with his crystal ball for the European Commission, a Reflection Group chaired by Felipe González, the Socialist former Prime Minister of Spain, was hard at work on a similar mission for the European Council across the road. The group's report, published in 2010, *Project Europe 2030 Challenges and Opportunities*, warned:

> If our mission is to be shared, politicians and citizens must take ownership of the European venture. If governments continue as and when it suits them to treat the EU and its institutions as alien or hostile, there is little hope of creating the kind of popular identification with the EU which is needed for its success.[192]

It could well have been aimed at British politicians in the tradition of Gordon Brown and David Cameron, who believe that they can harangue the EU into action without having to work long and hard at alliance-building and compromise.

This was another report prepared for an EU institution which repeated the familiar call for 'more Europe' and better centralised coordination as an answer to the economic crisis. It reached some familiar conclusions, including:

> The EU must strengthen the single market against temptations of economic nationalism and complete it to include services, the digital society and other sectors, which are likely to become the main drivers of growth and job creation in a market of 500 million users and consumers. The strengthening and completion of the single market should be accompanied by improved tax coordination.

This was further proof that fiscal sovereignty is in the EU's long-term sights as a trade-off for greater market liberalisation. Without giving any specifics, this report, prepared by a small group of experts led by a Spaniard with vice chairs from Finland and Latvia, emphasised the role of tax coordination in deepening the single market:

> The development of the single market has long been hampered by two simultaneous processes: a resistance in some Member States to applying internal market, competition and state aid rules; and a tendency in other Member States to oppose even moderate initiatives of tax coordination that could improve the functioning of the single market and remove the concern that the single market may hinder the pursuit of social objectives. Left unattended, these trends would aggravate the bias of tax systems against job-creation and the difficulties of Member States in addressing inequalities. They would also lead to a race to the bottom in social protection and would exacerbate the opposition to integration.[193]

Both reports, then, are instructive on the quid pro quo to be expected of Britain for developing the single market, the core achievement of the EU that is most celebrated in Westminster but also most misunderstood. Further liberalisation will not be won without tough compromises which may never be acceptable to British politicians or business.

Monti claimed that his blueprint was written from the perspective of a proactive reformer. Some of his proposals were taken up by the Barroso Commission but it was too distracted by the existential battle to end the euro crisis to pick a new fight with member states on far-reaching reform of the single market. But what if the next European Commission President was not a Monti but from one of those countries in his 'radical critic' or 'conditional supporter' category? France, as it happens, may well have a contender for the presidency in one of its former commissioners who has since gone on to lead the key global body for liberalising commerce – Pascal Lamy, Director-General of the World Trade Organization. But Lamy in this context is not your typical Frenchman. He comes from the same political family as President Hollande, the Parti Socialiste, but has devoted his recent career to attempting an un-Gallic opening up of trade – which many believe is exactly what the EU needs.

Lamy backs a scheme to spice up the European Parliament's next elections in May 2014. The idea would be for the major political groups to put forward a candidate for European Commission President together with a manifesto for the next five years that would be promoted during the election campaign. The choice of President would thus be tied to the outcome of voting by the electorate and effectively taken out of the hands of the leaders of member states. Not only would this add an extra touch of democratic legitimacy to the Commission President, who is usually hand picked by the national leaders sitting in the European Council, but it would advance the federalist dream of the European Commission forming the true government of the EU, deriving its legitimacy from the citizens who express their democratic will through votes for the European Parliament and relegating the Council (where the member states' ministers sit) to the senate-like second chamber, as already described by prominent German and Polish politicians, as well as the eleven-nation Future of Europe Group.

'I refuse to countenance this French and British idea that the Commission is merely the secretariat of an executive Council,' Lamy added, distancing himself from his country's tendency to choose intergovernmental solutions over the 'Community method' led by the European Commission.

> The Council should be the member states' senate... The Council is the venue for compromise among the member states, but none of those member states speaks for Europe's broader interests. The President of the European Council is the President of the European senate and he should act in that capacity, representing the chamber of the regions. The executive is the Commission.

Lamy, it must be borne in mind, is a disciple of Delors, having served as his chief of staff throughout his tenure as Commission President. Could the pupil become the master? If so, or if a fellow federalist does seize the European Commission crown at the next opportunity, Britain will find a strong centralising tide replaces the current era of member states holding the whip hand during the euro crisis.

Another old Brussels chestnut of self-funding for the European Union was also raised by Lamy despite the repeated efforts of many governments to kill off the idea. 'The EU needs independent resources, such as a common tax on financial transactions, a climate tax and project bonds, to finance its growth plan,' he said.[194] One of the key missing ingredients in the creation of a federation of Europe is the question of its tax-raising powers. Almost all of the funding currently received by the EU comes from its member states in direct transfers from national treasuries, based primarily on a gross national income calculation supplemented by VAT, agriculture and sugar duty receipts. Holding the purse strings gives member states the ultimate power in the EU system, much to the annoyance of the European Commission, which regularly proposes direct revenue-raising schemes to bypass national capitals. These are always vetoed by member states.

Brussels will never escape the thrall of the national capitals without tax-raising powers, because otherwise it will always be vulnerable to a rent strike. None of the possible schemes could go ahead as a revenue-raising exercise for the EU without the unanimous support of all its members, however, as tax remains one of the last sacrosanct areas subject to the national veto. Britain and others, including eurozone member Ireland, are especially opposed to a common financial transaction tax (FTT), for example. The European Commission has accepted that its goal of a wide-ranging FTT is dead but vowed that 'now it is clear that agreement on this can only happen through enhanced cooperation [i.e. a group of at least nine countries agreeing to work together], the Commission will do all it can to move this forward rapidly and effectively with those member states that are willing'. By blocking its introduction across the EU, Britain denied the Commission the chance to claim the considerable revenue from the intergovernmental FTT planned between a group of eleven countries led by France and Germany in October 2012. As for the reforms needed to repair the single currency, Barroso backed moves towards banking and fiscal union, as well as forms of risk-sharing, such as 'steps for genuine mutualisation of debt redemption and debt issuance'. In other words, the rich eurozone countries should help to lower their poorer neighbours' debt costs through issuing common 'eurobonds'.

These last suggestions were a rebuke to Chancellor Merkel and her ruling coalition, which resisted pooling debts, seeing it as a 'moral hazard' and a reward for failure. But slowly the political tide began to turn in Germany despite opinion polls showing a big majority of taxpayers against throwing more money at struggling southern eurozone members in the name of European solidarity. During 2012 the main opposition, the Social Democratic Party, swung behind common debt issuance and closer fiscal integration. Peer Steinbrück, the candidate to fight Merkel for the Chancellorship in autumn 2013, said that the eurozone crisis left the EU with a choice: either the member states gave up more of their sovereignty to Brussels or moved towards a 'renationalisation'. For an export nation like Germany 'that would be a fatal way to go', Steinbrück said.[195] The SPD's conversion to pooling eurozone debt will liven up the German election and, if the party plays a role in the next government, will undoubtedly hasten much deeper economic integration by the euro nations. This, in turn, will mean that the UK only finds itself even more marginalised outside a single currency club that is on a path towards the closer federation envisaged by José Manuel Barroso and the European Commission.

Of all the many ideas covered in this chapter, it has to be said that most if not all European governments are heartily fed up with grand European schemes. Most of them in 2012 were also waist deep in difficult economic reforms and austerity measures designed to combat the worst downturn for years. National politicians generally do not have the time or inclination to push through yet more European changes, especially as popular sentiment has piled at least some of the blame for the record levels of unemployment and debt on the EU. But it is also true that in most capitals there is an acceptance, albeit often reluctant, that the solution to the continent's dire straits involves more, not less, coordination at a European level. There is also a realisation that any increase of EU powers must be accompanied with action to restore legitimacy to a system tarnished by years of unaddressed accusations that it lacks proper accountability. This criticism has deepened with the imposition of austerity measures in struggling countries. So, along with inevitable reforms such as banking union to consolidate the eurozone, there is bound to be a push soon for democratic measures such as an elected European Commission President. Any new treaty to make these changes will inevitably seek to enhance the powers of the EU in other ways, or perhaps reformulate its structure to allow the eurozone to convene separate structures – and the non-euro members like the UK to formalise their different status. One thing is clear, the status quo is not an option for Britain.

FIVE

Repatriation

The dogma of 'ever closer union' has taken the EU to the brink and Britain should now be articulating an alternative vision for the future and mapping out a fresh start in its own relationship with the EU... We believe that a new relationship should protect and develop Britain's membership of the single market but lead to the return of powers in many other areas where policy would be better set by our own Parliament.
– The Fresh Start Project[196]

There can be no higher praise for a Conservative euroscep- tic than to be hailed as the new Iron Lady and doubly so when the honour is bestowed by Fleet Street's most eurosceptic newspaper. Yet that was the sobriquet chosen by the *Daily Express* for Andrea Leadsom, a former investment banker and MP for South Northamptonshire, one of three founders of the Fresh Start Project in 2011. The project's aim was to identify overbearing areas of EU control that the British government should either reform or claim back. Nine months before José Manuel Barroso, the European Commission President, fired the starting gun on a new EU treaty, Leadsom forecast that 'the eurozone crisis is going to be a catalyst for change and a chance to ensure a better relationship for Britain within the EU'.[197] Her reported top priority was a 'an EU rule allowing member states to opt out of Brussels directives whenever they have a change of government'. This would have allowed the coalition to end the maximum 48-hour week under the working time directive, the paper said (even though the UK has already negotiated the right to opt out of the 48-hour week). It quoted Leadsom as saying:

> The EU still holds to directives and measures signed forty years ago. It is ludicrous to say you can change national governments every five years but that you can never change anything that comes out of Europe. You can go from a right-wing government to a left-wing government but you cannot change anything from the EU, even though it accounts for about half of the laws of the land.

It was an odd demand, given the extreme difficulty that would face any British negotiator tasked with delivering a mechanism for unravelling the entire European Union. But Fresh Start – a group entirely drawn from the ranks of the Conservative Party – would go on to produce a detailed and well-researched report setting out a range of ideas for repatriating powers from the EU.

The idea that Britain can negotiate a better, looser and less intrusive relationship with Brussels has obsessed the Conservative Party for more than a decade. With a new treaty looming, the Cameron government will finally have the opportunity to push for a repatriation of powers, a negotiating feat unprecedented in the history of the EU, which has so far consisted only of steps going deeper into the European cave (with the one exception of Greenland's decision to withdraw in 1985 after home rule from Denmark). This chapter looks at some of the main areas of EU control that are considered ripe for retrieval, and assesses the obstacles faced by British negotiators. It is an approach considered by Britain's allies in Europe to be negative and potentially damaging to the single market concept, which relies on a network of checks and balances to guarantee rights for all sections of society and is not supposed to be unpicked by one member state going back on what it previously agreed. But the pressure on the Conservative leadership to slim down Europe is unrelenting and comes from the heart of the parliamentary party. Given the difficulty of a satisfactory outcome, renegotiation is set to be the next staging post on Britain's seemingly unstoppable journey out of the European Union.

Leadsom and her Fresh Start colleagues insisted that they did not want Britain to leave the EU, but wished to forge a better and less involved relationship. No similar programme has been proposed by the other two main parties, Labour and the Liberal Democrats, while UKIP campaigns for the ultimate repatriation of powers – complete British withdrawal. In a Westminster Hall debate, Leadsom showed the depth of suspicion with which Brussels is regarded among mainstream backbenchers, like herself, from the country's main ruling party. Praising the government for the 'fast track' training programme for young British civil servants to go and work in the EU institutions, she added:

> When we visit MEPs and Commissioners in Brussels, we find that they have all gone native; they even speak with a sort of weird part French, part German, part English accent – if there is such a thing. They lose track of whom they represent. What we need is British people in the Commission representing British interests.[198]

Quite apart from her utter rejection of the principle of allegiance to the European cause sworn by all new Commissioners ('neither to seek nor to take instructions from any government or from any other institution, body, office or entity'), this sounded unerringly like the original Iron Lady, who declared her own mistrust of the eurocrats in Brussels: 'They are paid much too much – from our taxpayers' money. It looks like a real gravy train.'[199]

Britain already has more opt-outs from EU policy than any other member nation. Besides the single currency and the Schengen travel zone, the UK has avoided the full force of the Charter of Fundamental Rights and can opt-in on a case-by-case basis to justice and home affairs legislation. It refused to take part in the Eurocorps, a prototype EU army garrisoned at Strasbourg with troops from Belgium, France, Germany, Luxembourg and Spain. David Cameron decided not to take part in the formal eurozone bailout funds and, of course, stayed out of the Fiscal Compact. But Britain's semi-detached status, memorably characterised as its hokey-cokey approach by Lord Mandelson, still does not satisfy many euro-sceptics, notably on the Conservative backbenches, who want less intrusion from Brussels. It also does not satisfy ardent euro-philes, like Lord Mandelson, who believe that only full-hearted involvement in the EU is in Britain's long-term strategic interests in a world of rising new superpowers. Nor, apparently, does it satisfy David Cameron, who said during the party leaders' debate in the 2010 election campaign: 'We are part of Europe, we want to cooperate and work with our allies in Europe to get things done. But... we have let too many powers go from Westminster to Brussels, we have passed too much power over and we should take some of those powers back.'[200]

The Fresh Start Project sought to distil some of the concerns into concrete suggestions for a renegotiation and return of powers from Brussels to Westminster. The group's first meeting in September 2011 was attended by more than 100 Conservative parliamentarians. William Hague, the Foreign Secretary, gave them a green light to push for ambitious reform when he said it was 'certainly not career suicide' to attend the meeting.[201] The project was also no doubt further encouraged by the Prime Minister in October 2011 when he tried to limit the size of the non-binding Commons vote for an EU referendum. 'Fundamental questions are being asked about the future of the eurozone and, therefore, the shape of the EU itself,' Cameron said.

Opportunities to advance our national interest are clearly becoming apparent. We should focus on how to make the most of this... Changes to the EU treaties need the agreement of all twenty-seven member states. Every country can wield a veto until its needs are met. I share the yearning for fundamental reform and am determined to deliver it... Like you, I want to refashion our membership of the EU so that it better serves our nation's interests. The time for reform is coming. That is the prize. Let us not be distracted from seizing it.[202]

The question remains whether British diplomats can muster the required unanimous support from their EU allies for a reverse power grab – and whether Cameron's own party will give him time to formulate and conduct a satisfactory renegotiation before pressure to hold a public vote on membership becomes overwhelming.

Cameron's goal won support from the previous Conservative Prime Minister, Sir John Major, who had tried to limit EU competence during his time in office by refusing to agree to the Social Chapter and securing an opt-out for sterling from the euro. Major forecast that EU states were heading towards a 'federal state within the eurozone' as they tried to solve the currency crisis.

At some stage there will be another treaty because if there is fiscal union in Europe it changes our relationship to Europe... it gives us an opportunity to negotiate for the looser form of Europe that I would have liked to have seen in the 1990s. I think there are some areas that are worth looking. Fishing is one. I think there are some elements of employment law... things like the working-time directive, which I think is a very foolish piece of legislation – we could look at repatriating part of it.[203]

The reality of attempting to use the British power of veto to win repatriation was dramatically shown just a couple of months

later, when Cameron's demands for greater powers over financial services in return for agreeing to the Fiscal Compact were
rejected by fellow leaders in the European Council. Nevertheless,
various policy areas were identified for renegotiation by Fresh
Start in their *Options for Change* Green Paper in July 2012,
informed by research from the eurosceptic think tank Open
Europe and others. The report set out green, amber and red
objectives, covering measures deemed to be easily achievable,
those that would probably require negotiated treaty change
and those which might only be won by unilaterally breaking Britain's treaty obligations. Some areas were suitable for
repatriation only by actually leaving the EU, such as regaining the right to conclude international free trade agreements.
But a number of reforms were identified that at least would
give British diplomats a negotiating challenge. There was also
an encouraging foreword to the document by William Hague,
who wrote: 'Public disillusionment with our membership of the
European Union has never been so deep. Now, then, is the right
time for serious thought to be given to how Britain's place in
the EU can be improved.' It sounded like the stamp of official
approval, notwithstanding the government's own review of EU
powers due to report in 2014.

All the while it must be borne in mind that successive
generations of British politicians, diplomats and civil servants
– including some of those who will now be primed for the repatriation battle – have helped to fashion the self-same laws that
will be targeted for retrieval. Some of the aggravations of EU
life were conceded to win gains in other policy areas that were
felt to be more important to the UK's national interest, some
were agreed by governments of a different stripe with different
priorities, some were unforeseen developments that resulted
from cases at the European Court of Justice. It is the same deal
that all EU member nations have so far signed up to – such
complex arrangements between a group of twenty-seven allies
with deeply felt national prerogatives simply could not function

without a number of compromises. The single market, which is the prize that Fresh Start believes makes the EU worthwhile, would never have been so liberalised and open for business without Britain conceding ground on areas like employment regulation to nations wary of brutal capitalist competition. Every country would like to tweak its EU deal unilaterally to national advantage. There is therefore a real danger that Fresh Start may be raising hopes that are doomed from the start – and if public expectations are too unrealistic the frustration of failure will drive Britain more assuredly towards the exit door.

True, some of the annoyances of the EU pre-date British accession, such as the Common Agricultural Policy, which has been reformed substantially in application from the days of wine lakes and butter mountains when surplus produce was bought up at guaranteed prices, but remains incredibly expensive for the value it delivers the taxpayer. In some other areas, particularly those with arduous business or social impacts, Britain felt suckered into accepting them through majority voting, most notably the working time directive, which is estimated to cost the economy £3.5 billion a year. In yet other areas, costs have risen exponentially in the past few years, such as the giant regional funding budget, following the British-led policy of rapidly enlarging the EU to take in a dozen poorer countries.

While some areas of EU activity provoke deep divisions along political lines, there has been long-standing cross-party pressure for reform of the way money is spent in Europe's regions. The money is targeted by the European Commission at the regional level rather than the central national government, meaning that poor areas of relatively wealthy countries qualify for aid. In 2003, a year before the admission of the ten mainly ex-Communist new member states, Gordon Brown proposed that all the richer countries, including the UK, should be given back full control over their own regional spending without the requirement to filter any money through Brussels.

He pledged that the government would preserve UK regional funding at the same level, which he could confidently promise because Britain would make a net gain of at least €4.6 billion over the seven-year budget period by not having to help fund regional schemes in prosperous countries like Italy and France any more. Countries with a GDP below 90 per cent of the EU average, which include most of the twelve new entrants since 2004 as well as Portugal, would still benefit from EU money. This would also help cut administration costs, which were put by the European Commission at between 3 and 4 per cent of the entire budget for structural funds, or between €10.4 billion and €13.9 billion in 2007–13.[204] So far, calls for reform have fallen on deaf ears and are resisted by a powerful lobby of fifteen states in the Friends of Cohesion group led by Poland, which includes all the former Communist countries of central and eastern Europe as well as Greece, Spain and Portugal.

Britain's net contribution to structural funds in 2007–13 was €25.3 billion.[205] Of the €10.6 billion that was allocated to projects in the UK, five-sixths was taken from and then given back to the same UK region, according to Open Europe calculations. The UK is divided into thirty-seven regions by the EU and only two, Cornwall & Scilly Isles and West Wales, were net gainers from the scheme.

> We estimate that the West Midlands, which has the lowest disposable income per capita in the UK, pays £3.55 to the structural funds for every £1 it gets back. Merseyside, which has a disposable income of 88 per cent of the UK average, pays in £2.88 for every £1 it gets back.[206]

If structural funds were limited to countries with a GDP of 90 per cent of the EU average or lower, the entire EU budget for 2007–13 would have been cut by 15 per cent and the UK would have made a net saving of around €5 billion. All the 'new' member states that joined since 2004 would also have made net savings, apart from Cyprus and Slovenia, but there would have been three big losers – Spain, Greece and Italy, which all had GDP per capita above the 90 per cent level. Given the drama of the euro crisis, which was felt particularly harshly in these same three countries, a reorganisation of structural funds has therefore become politically even less likely than when Gordon Brown tried unsuccessfully to push it onto the agenda for the 2007–13 budget framework.

The EU's method of allocating funds was also based on regions that were too large to catch pockets of real deprivation, Fresh Start pointed out. 'For example, Tower Hamlets in east London has high relative poverty, but it sits within the EU region of "Inner London" which also includes Kensington & Chelsea and the City of London. Hence "Inner London" does not qualify for any special structural fund status,' they said.[207] The European Commission admitted in 2011 that structural funds lacked performance criteria to link them to clear results. 'Implementation has focused more on successfully spending and managing funds and complying with control rules than on how effective interventions are,' the Commission reported.[208] The current system seems to contradict the EU's own principle of subsidiarity, as defined in the Maastricht Treaty, that the EU 'shall act only if and so far as the objectives of the proposed action cannot be sufficiently achieved by the member states, either at central level or at regional and local level'.[209] This could leave it open to a challenge at the European Court of Justice, one possible avenue for Britain to explore if, as seems likely, reform attempts are again thwarted.

Repatriating a big chunk of regional payments would have one big advantage over similarly dramatic reform in almost every other policy area in that it would not require a change to the EU treaties. It could be done as part of the negotiations for the next seven-year budget due to begin in 2014. But it seems as if the government has given up on radical reform for this period. Baroness Hanham, the minister with responsibility for European regional development funds (ERDF), said in July 2012 that 'that is not a possibility within the next round. It might be from 2020 onwards.'[210] She added: 'In order to do that, you have got to get every European country to sign up to it, because it is a completely different way of doing it.' Asked if the government could push for it in the future, she said:

> We have got to wait and see, I think. It depends how things develop over the 2014–20 programme. We are already looking for less money to come back to the wealthier countries and more to go to the poorer countries, so there are changes which will come about within the next programme.

For the EU, the philosophical justification for the money-go-round of structural funding is the logic of the single market. 'We are ensuring that money is well spent all over Europe, in the interests of all Europe, so there is an internal market factor, and two-thirds of all exports in the EU for all countries, including Britain, are done within the EU,' said Ton Van Lierop, spokesman for regional policy.[211] 'The exports of Britain to Ireland are bigger than the exports of Britain to China, Brazil and the United States combined. So you still have very much a regional economy in Europe, and investing in that regional economy is in the interests of all member states.'

The idea of reclaiming power from Brussels has been an issue at the last three general elections. In 2001, William Hague as leader proposed 'a treaty flexibility provision' which meant that 'outside the areas of the single market and core elements of an open, free-trading and competitive EU, countries need only participate in new legislative actions at a European level if they see this as in their national interest'; Michael Howard in 2005 vowed to 'restore our opt-out from the European Social Chapter and liberate small businesses from job-destroying employment legislation'. He also planned to 'restore national and local control over British fishing grounds'.

Besides pledging that the British people must have their say on any future transfer of powers to the EU in a referendum, David Cameron's manifesto in 2010 vowed that

> a Conservative government will negotiate for three specific guarantees – on the Charter of Fundamental Rights, on criminal justice, and on social and employment legislation – with our European partners to return powers that we believe should reside with the UK, not the EU. We seek a mandate to negotiate the return of these powers from the EU to the UK.

In the end these ambitions were tempered in the coalition's programme for government, which committed the government to 'examine the balance of the EU's existing competences and, in particular, work to limit the application of the working-time directive in the United Kingdom'.

The issue of greatest economic importance to the future of the country, however, was the debate on whether the UK could regain better control over the regulation of the financial services industry, a sector that provided £63 billion in taxes to the Treasury in 2011 and accounts for 8.9 per cent of GDP. This assumed central importance for the coalition government in the face of a raft of proposed new EU rules to regulate bankers and financial markets following the excesses that contributed to the global economic crisis. David Cameron showed that financial services was top of his priority list when he tried to secure several safeguards in return for agreeing to make the Fiscal Compact part of EU law in December 2011. In a nutshell, he wanted a guarantee that greater fiscal coordination in the seventeen-nation eurozone would not distort the single market that covers all twenty-seven EU members; a legal protocol to protect the City of London from excessive regulation including the ability to enforce higher bank capital requirements than the suggested EU maximum; agreement that the European Banking Authority would stay in London; and protection from EU regulation for US financial institutions based in London that do not trade with Europe. It was a first attempt at repatriating some powers over financial services.

Cameron's attempt failed both on tactics and substance, providing two lessons for future renegotiations. Not enough time was spent building up allies around the table before the meeting and the details were not seen as directly relevant to the subject in hand, namely the coordination of national budgets. Naturally, British eurosceptic commentators put the blame on the French, sensing that President Sarkozy all along preferred an ad hoc agreement (rather than a full EU treaty) that would leave eurozone governments (i.e. France) with the whip hand. 'The events of the past twelve hours have exposed a truth that many chose to ignore, namely that in its relentless pursuit of its national interest, France's strategic objective has been to drive the UK to the margins – if not out of the EU – and to destroy the City,' wrote Ben Brogan in the *Telegraph*.[212] Suspicions about French motives had been roused by Sarkozy's reported outburst in 2009 upon succeeding in placing his candidate, Michel Barnier, as the European Commissioner for the Internal Market and Financial Services. This was a victory for France against the 'excesses of Anglo-Saxon financial capitalism', the President exclaimed, and the British were 'the big losers'. It showed that he set as much store by the European Commission's oath of allegiance as Andrea Leadsom.[213]

Essentially David Cameron's failed renegotiation in December 2011 was about restoring the British veto to financial services regulation. In common with many aspects of the single market, the veto was replaced with QMV to speed up decision-making and break through vested national interests under rule changes agreed to by Margaret Thatcher. Critics of Cameron's stance felt that he was trying to turn back the clock to 1985 and unpick liberalising measures agreed by his predecessor. But Open Europe explained eurosceptic thinking on why Britain deserved special treatment on financial services, a sector of the economy as important for the UK as agriculture in France and fishing for Spain: 'Unlike agriculture where the French have a veto over the Common Agricultural Policy... or fishing where Spain wields a veto over the Common Fisheries Policy, the UK has no comparable protection from EU financial regulation.'[214]

Moreover, Cameron had solid support from the industry for his tough stance. Seventy per cent of managers at UK finance firms told a poll in December 2011 that they agreed with the statement 'The UK Government needs to renegotiate existing EU treaties to safeguard the City of London, limiting agreements to trade and association only'. And 68 per cent agreed that 'the UK government should take back more control from the EU over financial regulation and governance even if it risks compromising the possibility of easier access to other European countries'.[215]

In the face of Barnier's intense activity in updating or devising regulation for the financial sector, Open Europe came up with a 'double lock' wheeze to guarantee greater British control over financial services proposals from the European Commission. The first 'lock' would require the Commission to reconsider proposals that impact disproportionately on Britain due to the special influence of financial services on the economy. The second lock would give the UK a right of appeal to the European Council for any proposal at any stage during the decision-making process before the proposal had been finally agreed, effectively giving Britain a veto.

The idea was supported as an 'amber option' in the Fresh Start Green Paper, which said that it could only be possible by a change to the EU treaties. But the group added:

> The financial services are a critically important industry for the UK, and the European Union is by no means their only market. The EU must not be allowed to strangle them with red tape, nor impose crippling costs on them, nor dissuade financial companies and workers from locating or staying in the UK... They may

not always be popular and they are widely misunderstood, but financial services matter to the whole of the United Kingdom, and indeed to the European Union. The EU should be their champion, not their executioner.[216]

A new protective mechanism would take enormous diplomatic energy to bring in, however, and might not have a significant effect, given that the UK has very rarely actually been outvoted under the qualified-majority system. Most proposals undergo a long negotiation, which helps Britain tailor them towards its goals, such as the proposed ban on short selling which ended up trimmed back by the European Parliament to a ban on 'naked' short selling of sovereign debt (i.e. selling an asset without even borrowing the security to back up the sale). Moreover any British attempt to claim greater control over financial services legislation will also, ironically, be viewed in Brussels as an assault against the principles of the single market – the EU achievement that even eurosceptic MPs claim to support.

The main bone of contention between Britain and the EU under Labour and Conservative-led administrations has long been the extent of social and employment legislation, all decided by QMV. Suspicions began when John Major's opt-out from the Social Chapter was circumvented by the use of employment law to bring in the working time directive. Its provisions were then advanced by successive rulings from the European Court of Justice. These included: the Simap judgment in 2000, which added on-call time to working hours calculations; the Jaeger judgment of 2003, which ruled that time spent asleep at hospital counted as working time for doctors; the Stringer judgment of 2009, which meant paid annual leave continues to accrue when workers are off sick, even if they are off sick all year; and the Pereda judgment of 2009, which ruled that if an employee falls sick just before taking annual leave, he can take the holiday that overlapped with his sickness at a later date. These added extra cost to employers from the original, much-amended directive, which brought in a 48-hour week subject to various provisos, as well as mandatory daily and weekly rest periods (at least eleven hours uninterrupted time off per day and one 24-hour block per week) and a minimum four weeks of paid annual leave.

Britain has negotiated an opt-out for individuals who choose to work longer than the 48-hour week, a concession which is currently used by at least fourteen other countries but under constant attack in Brussels and still subject to difficult negotiations. The European Parliament wants to phase out this derogation within three years of a revised directive coming into force. In late 2012, talks were bogged down as Britain could still muster a blocking group of fellow member states against the demands of MEPs and the European Commission.

An estimated three million workers in Britain make use of the opt-out to work longer than forty-eight hours a week some or all of the time. From the hospitality industry to night porters, construction workers and contract labourers, all manner of British employees find themselves occasionally needing or wanting to work longer than the EU maximum. The directive reaches deep into different areas of British life. David Dalziel, the secretary of the Chief Fire Officers Association in Scotland, said:

> The potential loss of the individual opt-out in the UK would have catastrophic effects. Ninety-one per cent of the UK landmass is protected by firefighters on the retained duty system. These men and women crew two out of every three fire stations in the country. They hold other jobs in their local communities and also provide around 120 hours availability every week of the year to deliver a local fire and rescue service. Any adverse impact on that would expose this country to an unacceptable level of risk.[217]

The biggest single impact of the working time directive has been on the NHS. It seems mind-boggling that this one directive could account for the bulk of the annual £1 billion bill for agency workers to fill the gaps in health service cover.[218] With the tradition of British junior doctors working ridiculously long hours becoming unsustainable, the government brought in a 'new deal' that saw their hours limited to fifty-six hours a week from 2000, superseded by the working time directive's forty-eight hour week from 2009. But it is the directive's requirement for mandatory rest days and periods which has had the most disruptive effect on hospital doctors, who complain that patients lose continuity of care and trainees no longer feel they belong in a team as shift patterns have become more erratic. 'The new shift patterns have broken up teams of trainee doctors and their seniors. Morale is certainly lower and junior doctor sickness rates much higher,' said a hospital doctor who was in training between 2009 and 2011.[219]

Some countries have tried to find a way around the impact of the working time directive on their health services by exempting training from the legal definition of work so trainee doctors fall outside its scope (Ireland) or classifying trainee doctors as 'autonomous workers' so most of the directive cannot be applied to them (the Netherlands). But the European Commission, in its role as 'guardian of the treaties', is ever vigilant in its policing of EU laws. Ireland and Greece have been sent a 'reasoned opinion' (basically a final warning) over trainee doctors' excessive hours with the threat that they will be referred to the European Court of Justice where they could face heavy fines.[220] According to the government's impact assessment, two-thirds of the cost to the British economy from the working time directive comes from the requirement for mandatory daily and weekly rest periods, while one-fifth comes from the four-week leave entitlement, 8.5 per cent from restrictions on night working and only 2 per cent from the 48-hour requirement, because of workers' ability to opt out.[221] Open Europe has estimated that the annual extra cost of losing the opt-out will be between £9.2 and £11.9 billion a year.[222]

The opposite case was put by the Trades Union Congress, when the UK blocked an attempt in 2009 to end the 48-hour opt-out: 'We are disappointed that another opportunity has been missed to end the UK's dangerous long hours culture,' said Brendan Barber, the TUC General Secretary.

> Long hours cause stress, illness and lowers productivity. And when many employers are moving to short-time working, the need for an opt-out of the 48-hour week is even more out of date. The UK government still needs to tighten the law on working time, otherwise the EU could take it to court in order to protect UK workers from abuse of the 48-hour week.

Speaking at a TUC debate which voted overwhelmingly to end the British opt-out, Tony Woodley, then joint leader of Britain's biggest union, Unite, said: 'People don't want long hours. They work long hours because it is the only way to make ends meet. People should work to live – not live to work.'[223]

Yet anger at the distorting and costly effects of the working time directive is shared across the political spectrum. Vince Cable, the Liberal Democrat Business Secretary, said that the

> heavy-handed, one-size-fits-all approach... incorporates the idea that is most clearly expressed in the French 35-hour week: that work should be compulsorily restricted and shared out, whether or not it suits the needs of individual workers or firms. Not only is this dreadful economics, it is also deeply illiberal. It suppresses the right of workers to choose how long they work to earn overtime, to help their company safeguard employment by working flexibly, or simply because they enjoy and take pride in what they do.[224]

Cable's department has forecast that the 2009 ECJ judgments on sick pay and annual leave could add more than £100 million to employers' costs.[225] In government, Labour staunchly defended Britain's opt-out from the 48-hour working week. Pat McFadden, Labour's employment relations minister in 2009, said that the government 'refused to be pushed into a bad deal for Britain'. He added: 'The current economic climate makes it more important than ever that people continue to have the right to put more money in their pockets by working longer hours if they choose to do so.'[226]

While the working time directive has become the most notorious example of ever increasing rules and costs on employers and employees alike, the 2008 temporary agency workers directive has also hit the British economy hard, imposing extra annual costs estimated at £1.87 billion.[227] The main aim of the directive is to insist that general working conditions for agency workers should be the same as if they were recruited directly to the same job by the same organisation. The government negotiated with the Confederation of British Industry (CBI) and the Trades Union Congress (TUC) for this requirement to come into effect once an agency worker has completed twelve continuous calendar weeks in the same role, at the same organisation. This was implemented by the Agency Workers Regulations 2010, which entered into force in October 2011. The government's impact assessment estimated that around 40 per cent of agency workers, around 520,000, would be covered by the principle of equal treatment. It also said that about 65,000 agency workers could have their postings cut short to prevent them meeting the twelve-week qualifying period for equal treatment. In a survey of 200 medium-sized and large UK organisations in 2011, one-third of respondents said that they would consider ending an agency worker's job before they had served twelve weeks, in order to avoid the increased costs of equal treatment.[228]

There are dozens of other EU social and employment laws, many concerned with technical aspects of health and safety, which the UK would wish to preserve in national legislation even if it withdrew from Brussels. Ordinary workers have undoubtedly benefited from some, notably on maternity and paternity provisions. For example, after Tony Blair agreed to reverse John Major's opt-out of the Social Chapter, the UK soon adopted two pieces of European legislation which had already flowed from the chapter for all the other member states: the works council directive of 1994 and the parental leave directive of 1996. The first required large companies, usually with offices in more than one EU country, to form a joint consultative committee where workers are informed and consulted on company decisions. The second ushered in a new right, later included in the Employment Relations Act 1999, for every parent to take thirteen weeks' unpaid leave to care for each child (in addition to maternity leave) before the child turns five years old. It was the kind of social provision emanating from Brussels that Conservative governments had blocked – in this case since it was first proposed by the European Commission in 1983.

Then there is the pregnant workers directive, which established the basic right of a working mother to time off with 90 per cent pay for six weeks, and which MEPs are proposing to extend to fully paid leave for twenty weeks. Vince Cable warned that 'European Parliament amendments to the pregnant workers directive could cost the Exchequer up to £2 billion extra in full pay during maternity leave, an excessively prescriptive and grossly disproportionate measure we are fighting with the support of Germany.'[229]

Cable has helped to form the 'Like Minded Group' of fifteen EU countries, which is 'committed to rolling back excessive regulation emanating from Brussels and to expanding the single market'.[230] Following a meeting in Vilnius, the Lithuanian capital, Cable vowed to press on with negotiations to reduce the red tape burden. Clearly rejecting the route of repatriation, he claimed some success and insisted that more would only come through hard talking despite his own misgivings about the working time directive and pregnant workers directive:

These examples may be taken by some as evidence that the UK

could somehow detach itself from the EU altogether. Or that we could carve out a comprehensive opt-out of all EU employment legislation. But in practice it is difficult to see how Britain could on the one hand continue to enjoy the benefits of the single market, worth £3,500 a year per UK household, while on the other refusing to engage on difficult issues. But the tide is turning. Beyond the Like Minded Group, Spain and Italy want the EU to focus more single-mindedly on a growth agenda, including deregulation. Last November the European Commission agreed to attack the regulatory burden with exemptions for micro businesses. And earlier this year, following sustained UK lobbying, we achieved agreement in Brussels to exempt around 1.4 million UK small businesses from burdensome EU accounting rules. When foolish and costly initiatives come out of Brussels, it is tempting to wave the Union flag and plead British exceptionalism. I discovered in Vilnius that we are not on our own. We are part of a new progressive European majority replacing the dinosaurs of the past.

Nevertheless the Fresh Start group believes this to be a priority area for treaty change to take back powers. They would seem to be in tune with David Cameron's thinking, given a telling passage in the Prime Minister's speech at Davos in January 2012 which seemed to list his top three priority targets:

In spite of the economic challenge, we are still doing things to make life even harder. In the name of social protection, the EU has promoted unnecessary measures that impose burdens on businesses and governments, and can destroy jobs. The agency workers directive, the pregnant workers directive, the working time directive. The list goes on and on.[231]

But wholesale repatriation is complicated by the way that different legal grounds are used by the European Commission to propose employment and social laws, as seen by the way that the working time directive was brought in through 'health and safety' law, bypassing the British opt-out of social legislation.

Open Europe have proposed a 'double lock' that would involve an opt-out from all social policy along with a right to refer any proposed law to the European Council for decision by unanimity if the UK believed it would have an unacceptable impact on domestic social or employment policy.[232] Fresh Start proposed a third 'lock' to prevent the European Court of Justice forcing a proposal on the UK through a judgment once it had been subject to a double-lock opt-out. 'This sort of treaty provision would be unprecedented in the EU and very radical,' the Fresh Start group conceded.[233] It was an admission of the extraordinary lengths that the UK would have to go to in order to blockade future social and employment legislation from the EU, while remaining a full member of the club and enjoying complete access to the single market. All the measures targeted are regarded by many member states as essential requirements underpinning Europe's social market system.

What would be the likely response of Britain's friends in Europe to such an attempt to wrest back national control over key areas of legal jurisdiction? From Fresh Start:

> One complaint other member states would be likely to raise is that this new arrangement would allow the UK to take part in the EU single market on the basis of 'unfair competition'. In other words, the UK would be allowed the same automatic access to EU markets without having to apply the minimum EU requirements in labour conditions, which is likely to give UK traders a competitive edge.

It argued that it would be 'a little naïve' of the UK's allies to think that there was currently a level playing field in Europe given that 'some EU countries have a patchy record of actually implementing EU laws'. Secondly, it argued that 'the ' is not going to regress to some Dickensian state' in w

they want to have the cake and eat the cake, this is how they have behaved since they became a member of the Union... But what is an internal market? Is it only that you have no barriers or that you also have rules for this internal market? This crisis has taught us that the best supporters of the free market are the socialists. Because they are the ones able to define regulation for the market – when the market is on its own it is only driving us to a foolish situation.

As a leading French socialist, her words can be taken as an insight into President Hollande's own thinking and the attitude that British negotiators will face when they enter the room to discuss reclaiming powers over areas of the single market to suit the British way. The clue to the European Parliament's approach lies in the formulation of the committee chaired by Ms Berès: the employment and social affairs committee. The two policy areas, seen as separate matters by successive British governments, are regarded as indivisible in Brussels.

It is not just politicians from the 'old' member states who will seek to defend 'social Europe' from raids by the British wishing to repatriate selected powers to suit their national advantage. László Andor, the Hungarian member of the European Commission responsible for Employment, Social Affairs and Inclusion, warned in February 2012 that it would be pointless for David Cameron to attempt to repatriate some of the EU's social laws because this would require treaty change and the assent of all twenty-seven member nations. 'I therefore think it is clear that repatriating social policy competence is a non-starter – legally, socially and politically,' he told a trade union audience in London. Andor also attacked Britain's 'seemingly unreasoning belief in the primacy of the market in the governance of the economy'. He added: 'I find it curious that the unbridled power of the market should be viewed so positively.'[235]

Fresh Start suggests that the Germans may be won over to deregulation for Britain if the government were to offer to reverse its veto on the Fiscal Compact from becoming a full EU treaty. Angela Merkel would indeed be happy for this to happen because then there would be no confusion over whether the European Court of Justice and other EU institutions could enforce the compact sanctions and help to prevent eurozone nations losing control of their budgets as Greece did. But the French were quite content to have the compact as an intergovernmental agreement, reluctant as they have been to hand more sovereignty to EU institutions, so there is no reason to suppose that they could be won round using this ploy. Nevertheless, there might just be enough leverage here, or in the negotiations over the coming EU treaty proposed by the European Commission, to score a repatriation victory of some kind. As Fresh Start says, the government just has to decide where its priorities lie in recovering power – in social and employment law, in financial services, fishing, regional funding?

As with all of these matters of the potential repatriation of powers from the EU, there is always a nuclear option. The ultimate tactic that Britain could deploy is unilateral action by Parliament to revoke any European law that a previous British government had agreed to. This would represent the last throw of the dice by any national government. 'It is open to Parliament in the UK's legal order to disapply EU social and employment law,' argued the Fresh Start group in their 'red option' for reversing these measures.

> This would, however, be a clear breach of the UK's EU treaty obligations in international law. While, ultimately, the EU cannot enforce its treaties against the UK, under general international law the other member states might be able to suspend obligations they owe to the UK internationally, including but not limited to EU treaty obligations. In short, such unilateral action would not provide a sustainable long-term solution. It could, though, create the conditions to force a meaningful negotiation if other member states had previously refused to take the UK

seriously. The suitability of this approach is likely to depend on the UK's priorities and its bottom line regarding its future relationship with the EU.[236]

In fact, the EU has a rather potent method of enforcing its treaties. The European Court of Justice can issue unlimited fines to member states in breach of EU law, pegged at a daily rate until the rules are followed. A failure to pay the fine could, effectively, result in money for British farmers or regional projects being withheld, forcing the government to meet the costs directly. The resulting clash would end in one of three ways – Britain refusing to pay any more money to the EU and effectively withdrawing, capitulation and business as usual, or some kind of hard-fought compromise to relax EU law from which neither side emerges unscathed.

There is one very significant area, however, where the government is set to secure a major repatriation of powers without any of the time-consuming business of building a vote-winning group of supportive allies or the risk of being hauled before the courts. The Lisbon Treaty dramatically increased EU control over policing and criminal law, ending the pillar structure of the Maastricht Treaty and moving the entire policy area into the realm of QMV. This means that these measures also now require oversight by the European Court of Justice. But because this was such a significant shift from a situation so carefully negotiated in the early 1990s by British diplomats as an inter-governmental area, the UK was given a one-off opportunity to decide whether to retain or reject all of the policing and criminal justice laws passed before the Lisbon Treaty entered into force. This comprises some 133 separate measures, including one of the most controversial EU justice agreements ever made, the European Arrest Warrant. The UK has until 31 May 2014 to state whether it would continue with the whole package of laws or opt out en masse. That will not be the end of the story, however, as the UK has the possibility of negotiating to re-enter individual provisions on a case-by-case basis, albeit under the ultimate jurisdiction of the European Court of Justice and at the risk of extra conditions being imposed by the EU. In October 2012, Theresa May, the Home Secretary, told Parliament that the government was minded to use the block opt-out but had not yet agreed which measures to try and opt back into:

> The government's current thinking is that we will opt out of all pre-Lisbon police and criminal justice measures and then negotiate with the Commission and other member states to opt back into those individual measures that it is in our national interest to rejoin. However, discussions are ongoing within the government and therefore no formal notification will be given to the Council until we have reached agreement on the measures that we wish to opt back into.[237]

Measures subject to the block opt-out include those which set up two EU bodies that the UK might want to stick with: Eurojust and Europol, both based in The Hague. Eurojust, set up in 1992, and joined by the UK under Michael Howard while Conservative Home Secretary, exists to foster cooperation between national prosecuting authorities in crimes that concern more than one member state. Member states are obliged to provide Eurojust with 'any information necessary for the performance of its tasks'. The European Commission in 2010 proposed legislation to enable Eurojust to initiate criminal investigations. Europol, the European Police Office, became operational in 1999, and collects, stores, analyses and exchanges information, while also having the power to ask member states to initiate, conduct or coordinate criminal investigations. The concept behind Europol was explicitly federal – Chancellor Helmut Kohl said that the EU should have its own FBI.[238] It is currently headed by a Welshman, Rob Wainwright, formerly of the Serious Organised Crime Agency. Europol and Eurojust coordination has been central to smashing two global paedophile rings in joint police investigations known as Operation Koala and Operation Rescue. Koala began when a child abuse video was discovered in Australia that had been made in Belgium by an Italian producer with 2,500 global customers. It led to coordinated arrests including several men in trusted positions such as teachers and swimming instructors, as well as the identification of twenty-three children aged under sixteen.[239] Operation Rescue led to the arrest of 184 suspected paedophiles when Dutch police seized the servers of a chatroom after British police traced two perpetrators to Spain and discovered their use of the website. The three-year operation across thirty countries led to the rescue of 230 children.[240] These are the kind of transnational inquiries that show the strength of EU coordination.

Transposed into British law by the Extradition Act 2003, the European Arrest Warrant (EAW) has become the most notorious of the EU justice measures. By one measure – the rate of use – it has been very successful. Britain arrested forty-six suspects on behalf of fellow EU nations in 2004 under EAWs, rising to 661 in 2008 and 1,355 in 2010.[241] Britain issued ninety-six warrants in 2004, leading to the transfer of nineteen suspects; this rose to 256 warrants in 2010 and 116 transfers. The EAW was originally pushed through the European Council in the wake of the 9/11 attacks in the US and talked of as a necessary measure to fast-track the extradition of suspects in serious criminal matters including terrorism. 'There will be nowhere in Europe for terrorists to hide,' wrote Peter Hain, the Europe Minister, in October 2001.[242] Hussain Osman, one of the would-be London bombers of 21 July 2005, was arrested under a European Arrest Warrant by Italian police in Rome and extradited in under two months. This was in stark contrast to the way that Rachid Ramda, convicted of financing bombings in France in 1995, was able to spin out his extradition from the UK for ten years before the EAW existed.

But it turned out that there would be no place for a number of innocent Britons to hide either, as extradition was increasingly demanded by EU countries under the European Arrest Warrant on spurious grounds. Under the rules, the UK authorities cannot refuse a warrant provided that the potential sentence faced by the suspect is at least twelve months. This was predicted eloquently by the late Hugo Young, who in 2002 warned:

> We don't need to throw every legal protection away. Least of all in Europe, which has been complaining piously about Guantanamo. Europe, blindly on the nod, is about to indulge in its own sinister overreach... The dream of integrationists, who insist that the EU should in all respects be a single legal space, begins rather dramatically to materialise. How can this friend of Europe possibly object? Very easily... the warrant will be a mighty weapon. It is by no means confined to the terrorist emergency that has given it life, but will apply to every crime carrying a sentence of twelve months or more.[243]

Young foresaw further dangers when the ex-Communist countries joined in 2004.

> They will include several states with no tradition of an independent judiciary. Whether the finer points of due process have yet fully penetrated the bones of the average judge in Prague might be a matter of sceptic speculation. But the EU arrest warrant will make that unamenable to the intervention of an English judge.

And so it proved.

Fair Trials International has campaigned to raise awareness of several deeply concerning British cases. Edmond Arapi was subject to an Italian EAW to serve sixteen years after being convicted in absentia of a murder in Genoa, a city he had never visited and which took place on a day he was at work in a café in Staffordshire. Italy only dropped the EAW after he had spent weeks in custody. Andrew Symeou was extradited to Greece in

July 2009 in connection with the death of a man at a nightclub, despite evidence that the charges were based on statements extracted by Greek police through intimidation of witnesses who later retracted their statements. Symeou was bailed after spending more than ten months in a Greek prison but was not finally cleared until June 2011. Deborah Dark was acquitted of drug offences in France in 1989 but, unknown to her, French prosecutors appealed and a two-year sentence was imposed in her absence. She was arrested in 2006 and after a three-year legal ordeal, the case was dropped. As Dominic Raab MP, another campaigner against the EAW, has said:

> These are not isolated cases. The number of British citizens surrendered to foreign authorities under an EAW has risen from two a month in 2004 to two a day. For every warrant the UK issues abroad, we receive twenty back. Not a very balanced deal, given the high price paid by blameless Britons.[244]

But as well as miscarriages of justice, there have also been some ridiculously trivial cases. Suspects have been demanded under these fast-track measures for the theft of two car tyres, possession of 0.45g of cannabis and piglet-rustling.[245] By far the highest number of warrants are issued by former Communist countries with very different justice systems to the UK: Poland tops the list with 1,659 warrants (until the end of March 2011) followed by Lithuania (355, including the alleged piglet-rustler) and the Czech Republic (162).[246]

David Cameron was urged to take the block opt-out from the EU's 133 pre-Lisbon Treaty police and justice measures, including the arrest warrant, by 102 Conservative MPs. 'We have deep concerns about the operation of the European Arrest Warrant for our citizens. We want the UK Supreme Court to have the last word on UK crime and policing, not the European Court of Justice,' they wrote.[247] 'As British co-operation with Norway after its recent terrorist attacks and our long-standing intelligence relationship with the US shows, we do not have to cede democratic control with close partners in order to co-operate effectively with them.' The Fresh Start group proposed that the UK could seek to conclude international agreements with other member states to establish any cooperation needed. The government has pledged to put the block opt-out and those measures it proposes to opt back into to a vote in Parliament before taking a final decision.

The law and order professions, which are especially keen on the simplified extradition process of the arrest warrant, have conducted an intense lobbying campaign to keep the UK in the European measures. This was exposed in a leak of a letter signed by a former director-general of the Serious Organised Crime Agency, two former Metropolitan Police Commissioners and an ex-head of MI5. 'The growth in cross-border criminal activity within Europe is both an inevitable by-product of the free movement of goods, services, capital and people under the single market, and a serious policing and security challenge,' they wrote.[248] 'British law enforcement bodies are now constantly communicating, co-operating and collaborating with EU agencies and other national policing partners in pursuing serious organised criminal and terrorist networks.' The decision on whether to opt back into the European Arrest Warrant is set to become a battleground between Britain's law and order agencies and human rights campaigners, who are compiling a growing catalogue of abuses.

One former member of the Commons Home Affairs Select Committee who will have a decisive effect on the fate of the European Arrest Warrant has already shown his strong dislike of one aspect of it. The outraged young MP spoke out against the way that it abolished the principle of 'dual criminality' by obliging EU states to extradite suspects for misdemeanours that are not considered criminal offences in the arresting country's law. 'We are in new territory here. Never before have we given up the dual criminality protection,' David Cameron told the

Commons in 2003, during the passage of the Extradition Bill, which enshrined the warrant into British law. 'I believe that we are making a great mistake... It is an important safeguard that people in this country have had for years.'[249]

The general push for the repatriation of powers has manifold political as well as practical purposes. Firstly, moderate euro-sceptics have welcomed it as a way of softening the sometimes unattractive image of hysterical anti-Europeans who seek to smash the EU and paint it as the most evil empire since Darth Vader got the keys to the Death Star. By ostensibly negotiating with the enemy, as Brussels is seen by some, then eurosceptics can claim to have tried to engage in a process rather than just shouting from the sidelines. Secondly, it plays for time during a phase when the future shape of the EU is not clear, given the chaos in the eurozone and the different views on what constitutes the political and economic union that key continental leaders claim to want. Thirdly, it begins in earnest the necessary debate on what type of Europe Britain wants, by forcing opponents and supporters alike to study the real impact of EU policies and determine which of them could better be handled domestically, or reformed in Brussels. Fourthly, it recasts euroscepticism as a positive force that can change Europe for the better.

All of the above applies whether or not you believe that the Fresh Start Project is being undertaken with the best of intentions or is really just a Trojan horse for withdrawal. Renegotiation is seen as a necessary process by many eurosceptics, some who hope it will work, others who believe that it can only fail in a bruising battle which will lead to a British exit. Do its main supporters really believe that sufficient powers can be reclaimed to justify all the effort that renegotiation will take? George Eustice, Conservative MP for Camborne and Redruth, one of the three founders of Fresh Start, claims to think so, despite his past occupation as a press officer for UKIP. 'Where there is a political will there is a way... if you decide something

politically, you bring the lawyers in, you give them their march-
ing orders and they will sort the treaties out,' he said.[250]

Hardline withdrawalists and committed europhiles alike are
extremely doubtful about the entire repatriation movement.
Nigel Farage, the UKIP leader, dismissed renegotiation as David
Cameron's 'next con trick' after the 'cast-iron guarantee' of a
referendum on the Lisbon Treaty which did not come to pass
because the treaty was already in force by the time Cameron
came to power. Farage, writing in *The Sun*, added:

> I am sceptical as to whether we would ever get the best deal
> for Britain [by renegotiating]. Any agreement needs to get the
> go-ahead from all the other countries in the EU. It would be like
> trying to have an amicable divorce with twenty-six ex-partners
> who all blame you for their problems – partners who cost you
> £50 million a day, by the way. They are not going to send us
> home with a box of Belgian chocolates and a bottle of French
> red. At the very best, Mr Cameron will arrive back from Brussels,
> cheeks flushed with victory, telling us we're just in the single
> market now and that means trade – nothing more, nothing less.

But even this level of repatriation, which would be an extraordinary feat given the negotiating complications to wrest back
control over fisheries, agriculture, regional spending and the
like, would not satisfy UKIP. Farage continued: 'The single
market is responsible for all those health and safety regulations
and environmental directives... More than that, if we remain a
part of it, we still won't be able to strike trade deals with the
rest of the world.'[251]

Seasoned political operators from the pro-EU camp have also
poured scorn on the renegotiation route. Powers, once ceded to
Brussels, 'frankly are un-negotiable', said Sir Stephen Wall, the
UK's ambassador to the EU from 1995 to 2000.[252] Philip Collins,
a chief speech-writer for Tony Blair in Downing Street, said that
he saw his own former employer curse the EU for making it

difficult to send prisoners back to their countries to serve their sentences. But the system was extremely difficult to change.

> Nobody will be receptive to the British Prime Minister scribbling 'return of powers' at the bottom of the agenda. Let's assume, with heroic generosity, that we manage to inveigle the others into this national obsession. Let's assume too that we are able to define those powers we are seeking to repatriate... Even assuming all that, we are then being asked to suppose that our list would pass a process of negotiation that had to be signed off by twenty-seven countries, each pursuing its own pork-barrel interests... Were we to demand that the social chapter be collapsed, what would France demand in return? Do we not think that Germany might find something it wanted in return for signing off the abolition of the directive on maternity rights? And so on, until twenty-seven nations had prizes. Every British government finds itself in this position and every British government comes to much the same conclusion. Every single instance, every single demand for a repatriated power will fall over on the sheer administrative difficulty of achieving it.[253]

Whatever the repatriation pessimists say, Britain will have several opportunities in the coming months to 'take a pick and mix approach', according to Mats Persson, the Swede who runs Open Europe.[254] He insists:

> As Europe goes through profound political changes in the wake of the crisis, Britain will have plenty of opportunities to advance this position, including in budget talks and future treaty negotiations, over which it will have vetoes. Once new terms have been agreed, they could confidently be put to the electorate in a referendum.

But he urged David Cameron to get to work, if he wanted to avoid UKIP scoring even greater success at the 2014 European

Parliament elections than its second place, thirteen MEPs and 2.49 million votes in 2009.

> Britain has leverage in Europe. If the choice is between the UK leaving or getting some powers back, liberal, northern EU countries in particular may – after a lot of posturing and negotiation – go for the latter. The alternative would be losing a key ally in upholding a rules-based system of liberal trade as Europe goes through a highly defensive phase. Germany fears a Mediterranean-dominated EU as much as anyone.

But treaty change, which would be necessary in most cases for the permanent repatriation of powers, requires the unanimous agreement of every member state, as Nigel Farage pointed out. The EU landscape has changed since November 2009 when Pierre Lellouche, the French Europe Minister under President Sarkozy, warned the Conservatives that it would be 'a waste of time for all of us' to attempt treaty change just for Britain. 'It is not going to happen for a minute. Nobody is going to indulge in rewriting [treaties for] many, many years. Nobody is going to play with the institutions again. It is going to be take it or leave it and they should be honest and say that,' he said. 'We need to be united, otherwise we will be wiped out and marginalised. None of us can do it alone. Whether you're big or small, the lesson is the same. And [Britain's] risk is one of marginalisation. Irrelevance.'[255]

That outburst came before the real prospect of a new treaty negotiation sprang from Barroso's 2012 state of the union address to the European Parliament.

But François Hollande, Sarkozy's replacement as the French President, wasted no time upon his election victory in May 2012 in making his own views clear on the hokey-cokey of *les rosbifs* towards Europe. 'Let's recognise that the British have been particularly timid about the question of financial regulation and only concerned by the interests of the City,' Hollande told *Slate*, a French news website, in an apparent reference to the way that Gordon Brown in particular resisted EU regulation on financial activity which the French feel could have cushioned the financial crisis.[256] 'And to that is added a relative indifference to the fate of the eurozone, because Great Britain is protected against speculation since its central bank can intervene directly to finance its debt. Europe is not a cash till and less still a self-service restaurant.' He did not sound like a man prepared to let Britain pick and mix.

There is no doubt about the seriousness of the movement on Conservative benches to reclaim power from Brussels over various aspects of EU control that are felt to be excessive or damaging to Britain. The goal is shared right through the party up to the Prime Minister and Foreign Secretary, who have launched a comprehensive review of EU influence in order to assess where to strike back in a renegotiation. But the programme will meet stiff opposition once it moves from the comfort zone of the House of Commons onto the hostile terrain of the European institutions. The EU has never relinquished powers in this way before. When Greenland, an autonomous area of Denmark, wanted to regain its full fishing rights, it found that the only way to do so was to withdraw from the Union. Britain is altogether larger and more important, not least because of its net financial contribution. There will be an opportunity to pursue repatriation in the next EU treaty negotiations but the defeat of earlier attempts to water down the huge regional spending programme under the Labour government, or to win reassurances on financial services under the coalition, does not bode well. The likely failure of an extensive reorganisation will trigger even greater disillusionment with the European project and confirm the grounds for divorce between London and Brussels. The country will then be faced with repatriation on an altogether different scale – a wholesale reordering of our relationship with the EU.

Six

Another Way?

I never felt in the 1960s or now that Europe was or would ever become my country. Europeans are friends and neighbours, but not my fellow citizens. The eurozone crisis now presents us with a clear choice: do we want to be part of a country called Europe? Or should the UK be a self-governing nation in a new, looser European Community?
– Lord Owen[257]

David Owen resigned from top political jobs twice over his belief that Britain belonged at the heart of Europe. Both times he fell out with his party because of its failure to commit to membership – firstly when Labour voted against joining the EEC in 1972, secondly when the party decided to campaign to withdraw in 1981. It was one of the issues that motivated him to leave Labour and form a new pro-European party. After forty years of reflection on Britain's relationship with its nearest allies, the former Foreign Secretary has proposed a new deal – ostensibly with the UK on the outside of the European Union. Britain should join with other nations that do not wish to share the single currency and its inevitable pull towards greater federalisation and 'a country called Europe'. There should be a less integrated European Community which would still guarantee access to the single market as well as common environmental measures. This arrangement would clearly define Britain's place outside the full European Union, with no part in economic, agricultural, fishing, industrial and social policies. It sounded like everything that the Conservative Fresh Start group or most other eurosceptics could ever want – retention of the single market, repatriation of sovereignty over many key areas and a reduction in payments, all rolled into one simple package. Surely there must be a catch? For the plan to emerge from a pro-European source, albeit one who campaigned against the euro and believed in a Europe of nations rather than federalism, showed just how far the argument had run away from Britain's europhiles.

Lord Owen's intervention in June 2012 came as federalist thinkers at the other end of the telescope in Brussels were plotting a similar fate for the UK. The key motivation here was not a concern for Britain's destiny but quite the opposite – it was a response to years of annoyance with London acting as a brake on attempts to achieve ever closer union. The 'British problem' finally had to be faced, with proposals either for associate membership for the UK or for an 'avant-garde' of Europe's true believers that would leave recalcitrant nations behind. These plans showed how far and how fast Britain's future in Europe was being debated, without any input from the UK government, by Europeans primarily focused on saving their core project – the single currency. Listen to major speeches in 2012 by Angela Merkel, or François Hollande, or Mario Monti, or Mariano Rajoy, and the centrality of the euro to their thinking is obvious. The concerns of non-euro states pale into insignificance in comparison.

Angela Merkel has demanded that eurozone countries subject themselves to stricter budget rules and tough enforcement regimes to keep their public spending and borrowing in line if there is to be any chance of Germany permanently underwriting the single currency. The contender for Merkel's job from the German opposition Social Democrats, Peer Steinbrück, thinks similarly – closer fiscal coordination is necessary to save the single currency. As the pre-eminent economy, Germany is determined to lead the eurozone to the next level to save the currency with measures such as the European Semester, which requires all participating countries to share details of their annual Budgets with Brussels at an early stage. This has already led to the extraordinary spectacle of the Irish Budget being discussed by the finance committee of the Bundestag before it reached the floor of the Dáil, much to the embarrassment of the Taoiseach.[258] Needless to say, the thought of German MPs poring over the British Budget before the Chancellor of the Exchequer had even pulled it from his red briefcase is as unthinkable to the government in Westminster as any of the extra integrationist moves under way for the eurozone, and the UK has refused to send its Budget plans until MPs have heard them. Yet the redesign of economic affairs in Europe is sure to have spillover effects on the non-eurozone countries, from the extra surveillance of the banking regulator being created at the European Central Bank in Frankfurt to the impact of the French-inspired financial transaction tax.

To a seasoned observer like Lord Owen, the coalescing of the eurozone out of self-preservation is sure to lead to the creation of something that looks a lot more like a European government. He foresees that Economic and Monetary Union, the Common Agricultural Policy, the Common Fisheries Policy and the Common Foreign, Security and Defence Policy will all end up becoming government departments for the countries which stick with them, especially if they are freed from naysayers like Britain who have always tried to put a spanner in the federalist works.

Although logically the inner eurozone should be called the United States of Europe... in all probability its members would wish it to be seen as the EU so as to present it as a continuous development and help ensure minimal changes in the treaties. In which case, the wider Europe should seek to stress its continuity by reverting to calling itself the European Community, which some have already been members of and in the case of Turkey initially applied to join.[259]

With pressure building on the government to commit to a referendum on Europe amid an era of rapid change, Owen believes that it must act fast to set out a clear position for Britain so that voters can be sure what they are voting for.

The EU is reaching a point where muddling through will cease to be an option any more. This calls for a line in the sand, and only a new and well-defined status will convince voters that Britain has achieved a stable relationship that will not be subject to the kind of competence creep seen in the four decades following the 1975 referendum. 'Any UK political party that from 2012 on ignores the rapidly emerging political, not just economic, challenge over eurozone reform is putting its head in the sand. Only the complete collapse of the eurozone will stop a redesign and that now looks unlikely,' Owen wrote. 'In the UK, but also in some other countries, there are growing public demands for a principled and consistent position... because the people in these countries want to remain self-governing, in that they are determined to retain their own currency and remain in control of foreign, defence and fiscal policies.' Owen calls for an early referendum to establish a negotiating mandate for Britain to create a level of membership that involves primarily the single market. The key is deciding where to draw the line on the level of commitment involved in this new European Community – and then successfully convincing everybody else to go along with it.

Upon closer inspection, Owen's plan has a number of potential drawbacks. There would be no need to retain Members of the European Parliament, he suggested, meaning that the deal would lose its democratic aspect, at a time when the European Parliament has never had such extensive powers of revision. As Britain would remain inside the common customs union, the EU would retain the power to conduct international trade negotiations and set import and export rules, which are freedoms sought by some eurosceptics. The Community would continue to respect the single market's 'four freedoms' for goods, services, capital and people, and Turkey would be invited to join, meaning potentially that Turkish passport-holders would be waved through Britain's borders. Owen was aware that this would lose some support for his scheme, so he added that

> a new mechanism, without involving the totally free movement of labour but within any restructuring, brings Turkey in, in an honourable way, allowing it to identify itself with and join in a single market, and would settle the long-standing problem of Turkey being an associate member but as yet without any hope of being admitted to full membership.

Owen suggests that the European Community would attract the Czech Republic, Denmark and Sweden from among current EU members which do not use the euro (although the Czechs may take a more europhile turn once their staunchly anti-EU President Václav Klaus retires in 2013), as well as non-members Norway and Switzerland. However, while the former trio are fairly eurosceptic, none is pushing for the kind of much-reduced semi-detached role foreseen. And neither of the latter two nations currently accepts the European Commission as its international trade representative nor belongs to the customs union, both of which would act as strong disincentives. Switzerland would be bound to put it to a referendum that would almost as certainly be lost. In fact, it is hard to see any other country rushing to take up the offer of the European Community, which really appears like special pleading for Britain. That is not to say it could not work, indeed it seems a very attractive option for many eurosceptics, only that it will make it much harder to convince all the other member nations to allow the UK to continue to have full access to the single market and European Council while opting out of almost everything else. Turkey, of course, still wants to become a fully fledged member of the European club, but could be persuaded by the reality of continued French and German opposition to join with Britain as the book-ends to the real EU. Owen's suggestion that British voters could be asked whether they want either full integration or semi-detached European Community status was perceived by UKIP as a 'trick' to deny the public the chance of an all-or-nothing in/out vote and the chance to leave altogether.

One alternative to reformulating the European Community for half-committed countries is the idea that a cadre of more deeply integrated eurozone nations forges ahead by signing a new treaty between themselves. This would be open for all member states one day to catch up and join in. The 'avant-garde' approach to European development was recently revived by the man who wrote the technical drafts of the last five EU treaties, Jean-Claude Piris, the Frenchman who served as legal counsel of the EU and head of its legal service from 1988 until 2010. Piris considered four options for the next stage of the EU in his book *The Future of Europe*, rejecting both the substantial rewriting of the EU treaties as unworkable and the status quo as insufficient. The final two options are based on an avant-garde of eurozone nations either using the existing treaties or writing a new one under the EU's little-used provision for enhanced cooperation (meaning that a minimum of nine states can agree to new measures between themselves).

Piris freely admits that his five treaties have not stopped the EU from being 'slow, heavy, not flexible enough, not able to decide rapidly' when faced with tough decisions in the economic crisis.[260] 'The implementation of the Lisbon Treaty, even after a normal period of adaptation, will not deliver what is needed,' he added. 'The status quo and the system of "one-decision-fits-all" are not satisfactory... The fact is that a number of the twenty-seven member states are not presently in a position to accept the measures that would be necessary in order to strengthen the EU and, in particular, to stabilise the euro area.' The next treaty should cover not just a convergence of budgetary and economic policies but also 'in relation to the internal market, a reduction in the differences in tax and social policies'.[261] All the financial consequences of an additional treaty would have to be borne 'by participating states only' and democratic legitimacy could be ensured by a new body of representatives from national parliaments, as well as meetings of ministers from the countries involved, paving the way for parallel structures for a eurozone assembly. This was timely given that Herman Van Rompuy, the President of the Council, was simultaneously preparing plans for just such a structure for the eurozone as a quid pro quo for extra economic coordination.

In a short section of his book on 'How to guarantee the rights and interests of the non-participating EU member states', i.e. Britain and several others including Denmark and Sweden unlikely to join economic union or a eurozone assembly, Piris concludes that to stop them gaining unfair advantages, the avant-garde must be overseen by bodies that are trusted by everyone, i.e. the European Commission and European Court of Justice. Piris, whose words count for much in Brussels even in retirement, has proposed a formal process for developments that should have been foreseen once Britain and Denmark obtained their opt-outs from the Maastricht Treaty. The alternative structures envisaged for the eurozone nations will soon become clear and the British government, having called repeatedly for them to take the necessary measures to shore up the single currency, is in no place to object.

An altogether more sinister plot to marginalise the UK was prepared over summer 2012 by the President of the Union of European Federalists. It should come as no surprise that federalist Members of the European Parliament want to 'park' Britain in a new category where it cannot block reforms designed to advance the centralisation and harmonisation of the European project. The only surprise might be that the federalist President who wants 'associate membership' status for Britain is himself a Brit, Andrew Duff, the Liberal Democrat MEP for the East of England. The long-serving and influential Duff foresees a formal convention of representatives from all member states taking place in 2015 based on the blueprint for the next treaty promised by José Manuel Barroso for 2014. But the 'British problem' hangs over a treaty-making process which requires unanimity from member states to succeed. Writes Duff:

> The immediate problem for Britain's EU partners is to present a package at the 2015 convention which will circumvent the British veto and allow the large majority of states which will by then wish to take the federal route to do so. In the shorter term, the UK needs the option of a parking place short of the federal destination. The inevitable British referendum, therefore, will proffer a two-tier federal package. Without the option of becoming more clearly detached from the federal core, the British voter, in my view, is certain to answer No.[262]

Duff sat on the convention that compiled the ill-fated EU constitution and represented the European Parliament in the formal conference which drew up the Lisbon Treaty, leaving him well placed to join the group which prepares the next treaty, so his views must be taken seriously.

He proposes a new clause in the next treaty to create associate status, which will mean access to the single market but the withdrawal of elected representatives.

> Participation in the EU institutions would be limited. In the case that the UK opts for associate membership based on trade and the single market, retention of a British judge at the Court would be eminently sensible, but the case for a British Commissioner would be less convincing. As for MEPs, those Brits who manage to get elected in 2014 would surely be the last: one might envisage instead twice yearly meetings of a joint parliamentary committee of the European and Westminster parliaments.

Duff added that associate status could make 'a satisfactory permanent accommodation' for Turkey, just as Lord Owen envisaged semi-detached membership for both Britain and Turkey in his European Community. Moreover, all future treaties should be able to enter into force after being ratified by four-fifths of members, to avoid all that messing about with referenda that can happen in countries like Ireland with quaint traditions of direct democracy.

> Such a modification would relieve the Union of the risk of being trapped by the refusal of one national parliament or one referendum vote to accept the constitutional evolution desired and needed by everyone else. The Treaties of Maastricht, Nice and Lisbon were all delayed unconscionably by just such recalcitrance.

Referred to by Duff at one point as 'second-class membership', the associate status he proposed seems almost punitive, with the loss of representation in the European Parliament and Commission, even as it solves the federalist dilemma of circumventing the British veto. His suggestions show that an important evolution in federalist thinking is under way. Now that the imperative is to save and progress the core project, there is open talk of how to sideline non-believers rather than try and cajole them along with the programme. This provides an opportunity for British eurosceptics to work hand-in-hand with their old federalist enemies to find a formal role for the UK which is more acceptable to both. Faced with this pincer movement, would Britain be simply better off out, or at least better placed in the kind of neighbourly arrangement practised by two self-assured countries that have forged close but not suffocating relationships with the EU?

Former Europe Minister David Davis certainly sees some advantages. 'If we do not like a new law, Parliament should be able to reject it. Norway and Switzerland – with their more flexible trading relationships – do not subordinate their democracies to the EU. Neither should we.'[263] Could Norway be our way? Should we shun Brussels to become Britzerland? Norway and Switzerland are Europe's richest nations, prosperity which could have been jeopardised by full EU membership and the loss of respected currencies, trading advantages and, in one case anyway, less than respectable banking practices. These two smallish yet self-assured countries offer the only road-tested models we have of modern European nations living comfortably – very comfortably – outside the ever closer union headquartered in Belgium. It is hard not to share Davis's desire for unsubordinated democracy. After all, isn't that what democracy is supposed to be about?

Appearances can be deceptive. Norway and Switzerland have distinctively different relationships with the EU but both suffer from a troubling democratic deficit which may not be acceptable to British voters – especially if they have just taken the seismic democratic decision to break with Brussels for reasons of sovereignty or economics or both. But nor does their approach necessarily leave them completely estranged from polite international society. Modern-day Norway could never be described as isolationist. Neutral in the two World Wars, it emerged from Nazi occupation to embrace the global community as a founder member of the United Nations, NATO, the Council of Europe, the Organisation for Economic Cooperation and Development, the European Free Trade Area and the General Agreement on Tariffs and Trade. For a country of just five million people, it punches way above its weight on the international stage – and not just because it is home to the Nobel Peace Prize. It hosted secret talks to kick-start the Middle East Peace Process which led to the Oslo Accords of 1993 and has taken a leading role in peace and reconciliation efforts in Colombia, Haiti, the Philippines, Somalia, Sri Lanka and Uganda. Its 2012 aid budget of 27.8 billion kroner, or 1 per cent of GNI, was its most generous ever at a time when the UK government was coming under heavy domestic pressure to scrap its commitment to reaching 0.7 per cent – and the average among EU nations fell to just 0.42 per cent.[264]

Twice the political leaders of Norway tried to take it into the EU and twice they were rebuffed by their voters in referenda. Norway linked its membership application to the UK's from as far back as 1961 when Macmillan first applied to join. Alongside Denmark and Ireland, it was thus forced to spend the next dozen years biding its time thanks to de Gaulle's resistance. But while the other three northern European nations eventually joined the EEC, Norwegians voted by 53.5 per cent to 46.5 per cent to stay out in 1972. After all, they still had the benefits of the then six-nation European Free Trade Association (EFTA), set up by Britain in 1960 as a rival structure to the Brussels-based club. But EFTA membership became less attractive as membership dwindled over the years when first Portugal and then Austria, Finland and Sweden prepared to join the EU, encouraging the Norwegian government to have another go for Brussels. In the 1994 referendum the result was closer, at 52.2 per cent to 47.8 per cent, but still the verdict was 'No'.

Sovereignty was a very prominent issue in both Norwegian referendum campaigns, Norway being extremely proud of the independence it gained from Sweden in 1905. The major oil discovery in 1969 led to a new era of confidence and wealth that made independence a whole lot more attractive than it was to debt-ridden, recessionary, Britain. But after the second unsuccessful EU bid, the country entered into a new arrangement so that it could participate in the single market. This was done through extending the market into the European Economic Area (EEA) to encompass all the EU member states plus Norway, Iceland and Liechtenstein. The deal promised formal sovereignty to Oslo so that it kept out of the EU's farming and fisheries programmes as well as the customs union (allowing Oslo to make bilateral trade deals with other nations, unlike the UK) but Norway would agree to make a contribution towards 'cohesion' and follow the EU's single market rules. Norway's good times continued. In the two decades from 1992 to 2011, GDP increased by 60 per cent and unemployment fell from 5.9

per cent to 3.3 per cent.[265] In the same period, UK unemployment went from 9.8 to 8 per cent, and French unemployment from 9.3 to 9.7 per cent. Norwegians' purchasing power also increased substantially and its welfare state provision was developed into some of the most generous on the planet.

All this has led some to think that a simple EEA agreement outside the EU would also be a better arrangement for the UK. After all, what's not to like? Norway gets to retain its sovereignty. It gets to stay in EFTA and yet its traders have access to the EU single market through the EEA in a similar way to those in a member state. It does not have to pay a formal EU membership fee. So why was David Cameron right to warn against Britain turning into Norway should it leave the EU during his foreign policy speech to the Lord Mayor of London's banquet in November 2011? The answer lies in *Outside and Inside*, an impressive and extensive assessment of Norway's relationship with the EU written by its EEA Review Committee, an independent group composed of twelve of the country's top academic researchers. It reported in January 2012 with the stark conclusion: 'There are few areas of Norwegian democracy today where so many know so little about so much as is the case with Norwegian European policy.' This would seem to go as much for the country's own inhabitants as for those British eurosceptics who have a hankering for Norwegian-style independence. The detailed 911-page analysis, on a scale never attempted by any EU member state, tells a salutary tale of subordination and self-denial.

The EEA deal entails the adoption of all of the legislation associated with the single market including every social and employment law, competition law, state aid rule and consumer and environmental protection measure. In addition, Norway has signed up to the Schengen travel zone and to a range of agencies and justice measures including the European Defence Agency, Europol, Eurojust and even the Eurodac common system of fingerprinting irregular migrants. As we have seen, Brussels draws the boundaries of single market legislation somewhat more widely than many British MPs find palatable. Norway's MPs cannot afford to be at all squeamish. In the days of paper-based communication, the Oslo method became known as fax machine diplomacy – the Storting, Norway's parliament, simply receives regular faxes from Brussels telling them which laws to enact. The *Outside and Inside* team said that they themselves were surprised at the extent of EU influence over their country. All seventeen Norwegian government ministries had to engage with Brussels as well as all 430 local authorities, 'who feel that EU/EEA-related issues make up a large part of their everyday life', the report concluded. Between 1992 and 2011, Norway adopted three-quarters of all EU laws despite not being in the Common Agricultural or Fisheries Policies and free of the European Commission's control of overseas trade policy. 'In general it appears that Norwegian society has been greatly Europeanised in this period,' the report noted.

Apart from anything else, the EEA deal does not sound very democratic. As a non-member, Norway has no European Commissioner, no MEPs and no place at the European Council for its ministers to cast votes among the member states there. Although it can make some limited suggestions through officials at Commission and Council committees, it has no formal input at all to the European Parliament. There are also some trade barriers because Norwegian products are subject to 'Rules of Origin', which means that they face EU tariffs if components or supply chains do not meet single market requirements. Norway's arrangement sounds like a more profound surrender of national sovereignty than that of any EU country which has the right to trade freely and send elected representatives and civil servants to Brussels to fight their corner.

The Norwegians manage to live with this by making a distinction between 'formal sovereignty' and 'actual sovereignty', according to Fredrik Sejersted, director of the Centre for European Law at Oslo University and chair of the EEA

Review Committee. 'A distinction that has been important in Norway is between formal sovereignty and real sovereignty. Formal meaning legal, constitutional sovereignty. Real or actual sovereignty would be not competence in the legal sense but power, who decides – can you decide for yourself or does someone else decide?' he said.[266]

A small country like Norway is used to sharing real sovereignty – of course we do not decide everything ourselves in the modern world. We are intertwined with other countries and bigger powers decide a lot. But for Norway a lot of the debate has been on the formal sovereignty and you could say that the EEA agreement is a way of preserving formal sovereignty. When it comes to real sovereignty there is not much distinction between the EEA and EU membership. Because we are taking the same legislation, we have the formal right to say no to new legal acts but we have already taken almost 7,000 legal acts and we have not exercised that right of formal veto once because it is very difficult to do so.

The *Outside and Inside* report concluded that

the most problematic aspect of Norway's form of association with the EU is the fact that Norway is in practice bound to adopt EU policies and rules on a broad range of issues without being a member and without voting rights. This raises democratic problems. Norway is not represented in decision-making processes that have direct consequences for Norway, and neither do we have any significant influence on them. Moreover, our form of association with the EU dampens political engagement and debate in Norway and makes it difficult to monitor the Government and hold it accountable in its European policy. This is not surprising; the democratic deficit is a well-known aspect of the EEA Agreement that has been there from the start. It is the price Norway pays for enjoying the benefits of European integration without being a member of the organisation that is driving these developments.

Norway has no formal, legal arrangement to pay the EU for the privilege of taking 75 per cent of its laws and participating in the single market and Schengen. Instead it negotiates an informal deal every five years, or rather, it tries to limit EU demands for funding, which have risen exponentially since the EEA came into force. The EU regards it as Norway's obligation to pay 'EEA grants' which are the equivalent of structural and regional funding provided by member states and are partly based on a GDP calculation. 'Norway, Iceland and Liechtenstein say it is not an obligation but we do it out of our good heart, voluntarily,' said Professor Sejersted. 'Of course in actual terms it is an obligation, so once again you have this distinction between formal obligation and actual obligation.' From 1994 to 1998 and 1999 to 2003, the EEA grants were only collected for projects in Greece, Ireland, Spain and Portugal. For Norway, they amounted to around €150 million for each five-year period. But when the ten new member states joined in 2004, the rates shot up, further augmented by Norway's rising GDP in relation to the rest of the EU. 'They demanded a twenty-fold increase, negotiated it for a year or two and settled on a ten-fold increase,' said Professor Sejersted.

> The Norwegians and people in Iceland were screaming a bit but we paid out in the end. Then there were negotiations for the next five-year period and in the meantime Bulgaria and Romania had joined and it was increased again, but this time only something like 25 per cent. The total amounts are the result of negotiation with the EU, in which the EU has the upper hand.

From paying €150 million over five years when it first joined the EEA, Norway paid €1,300 million in 2004–8 and €1,800 million in 2008–13. This put Norway seventh among the main net contributors in euros per capita to the EU budget – without even being a member. The Norwegian contribution was still less than if it had been a member, in which case it would probably have been the largest per capita contributor to the EU budget because of the strength of its GDP. In return for the extra cash, Norway would have had a vote for its ministers in European Council decisions (weighted to reflect its size as the twentieth largest member), one European commissioner and fourteen MEPs – just 1.8 per cent of the seats in the European Parliament. While some of its senior politicians still pine for membership, the vast majority of voters seem quite content with the current arrangement. Anti-EU feeling has risen steadily and reached its highest ever levels during the euro crisis, with an opinion poll in April 2012 showing that 74.7 per cent were in the 'No' camp.[267]

The *Outside and Inside* report did not provide a cost–benefit analysis of Norway's EEA relationship with the EU but asserted: 'The economic benefits of cross-border trade, investment and migration, modernisation of Norwegian industry, the increase in employment and benefits for Norwegian consumers far exceed the budgetary costs of the agreements.' Since Norway under the EEA accepts the 'four freedoms' of the EU single market – the free movement of goods, services, capital and workers – it has no control over immigration from EU countries. Around 200,000 eastern European workers arrived following the enlargement of the EU in 2004, but the *Outside and Inside* report noted that this was 'without negative consequences for wages and working conditions' for Norway. In fact, Norway regards the influx of migrants as a key benefit of its arrangement with the EU. Farmers, for example, used to be among the most eurosceptic groups but have benefited enormously from a flow of willing labour, as have the oil industry and the construction, hotel and transport sectors.

'We don't have this "British work for British workers" issue,' said Ulf Sverdrup, director of the Norwegian Institute of

International Affairs and head of the EEA Review Committee secretariat.[268]

> Since 2004, the Norwegian economy has been growing very strongly and this would not have been possible without migration. The workforce increased by 2 or 3 per cent, it removed bottlenecks in the labour market and kept inflation low without having a negative salary development. This has strengthened competitiveness of Norwegian industry and also reduced incentives for Norwegian businesses and firms to move their businesses to other countries. Migration has been the biggest gain [of the EEA] and it coincided with boom in Norway. In 2008 in the crisis, lots of Poles left and it showed an interesting dynamic element to this, that you can increase the capacity and downscale quite easily.

Probably because of its oil-funded national wealth, fears of 'benefit tourism' or other abuse of the welfare system have not yet emerged in Norway as they have in British eurosceptic circles. Sverdrup added:

> We have a welfare state that is quite generous in this country. On the one hand these welfare standards make people attracted to come to Norway, so we get labour, while at the same time some of these labourers earn social rights and could export these social benefits. At the present level the volume of these exports are small, so it is not a problem as such. But in the future there might be a problem.

For Norway, the key to accepting the quasi-EU membership deal of the EEA lies in knowing its place in the world and feeling entirely comfortable with its status. This points in turn to a main reason why the EEA is unlikely to be acceptable to British politicians or voters. 'There is a fundamental difference to being a great power like the UK and being a small state,' said Sverdrup.

Whereas you have always been concerned about how can we shape the world or shape Europe in the way we would like it, Norway has always been small and saying, how can we adapt to the things that are happening out there? This is why the small states are doing well in globalisation. It is because we are good at this, we know how to adapt. And the UK is becoming a small state as well in a world of China and India. But, like France, they still believe they are big states, great states, shaping the environment. They should think about themselves as small states, adapting to a new environment. For Norway, we believe that what twenty-seven countries that are fairly similar to us agree upon would not be too bad for us.

Even more disconcerting from the point of view of a future British relationship with the EU should it decide to leave, is the view in Norway that it has become a 'lobby nation' vis-à-vis Brussels, arguing its case from outside the room in much the same way as a non-governmental organisation like Amnesty or Greenpeace or a multinational corporation. 'We think [the EEA] is suitable for small states that like to adapt, that have small aspirations for themselves,' said Sverdrup.

It is for states that are willing to bite the bullet when it comes to democracy, and say, OK let's take on these rules and regulations and comply with them and be monitored and held accountable for them, but without participating in influencing or shaping them. Norway is a lobby nation. In terms of influencing the EU, it is like going into a nightclub and the door is getting more and more narrow and the club is getting more and more filled up by members themselves. So they in general have fewer seats available to others. And the queue of people standing outside is getting longer, so it is not only Norway but Yahoo or Apple or Samsung or China or Turkey. Because as the EU is enlarging and affecting global regulation more and more, other actors want to participate and influence it, it is a huge lobbying process.

Then, what you hate most at nightclubs, there is the queue and the waiting to get in but there is also the selection, there is the doorman picking people: 'You at the back can come in.' Norway used to have some kind of privileged partnership but now the issue is, if we bring in Norway to talk about defence, we should bring in Turkey as well, and what about the candidate countries? Sometimes, ideally, they would like to bring us in but cannot do it because it would not be equal treatment for the others.

Clearly the experience of Norway would not translate directly if Britain was to leave the EU and decide to base its new relationship on the EEA. Britain would benefit much more from the freedom to trade globally, given that only half of UK trade is with the EU compared to 81.2 per cent of Norwegian exports and 63.9 per cent of its imports.[269] The UK would not, unlike Norway, opt to join Schengen or, probably, the European Defence Agency, and it would not have to pay into the EU's External Action Service. It would be more likely to use its formal right of veto over new laws from Brussels, potentially setting up some almighty clashes with the EU and also with fellow EEA members. And with the UK no longer at the EU discussion and voting table, the qualified blocking majority led by Britain that has held back the working time directive from enforcing the 48-hour week could crumble. It would then be applicable in the UK through the EEA. Britain, as the EU's new largest external trading partner, would certainly expect to be at the front of the 'lobby nation' queue. But this would not be good enough to stop social and employment laws that would have to be adopted in exchange for unfettered access to the single market.

The Fresh Start group of Conservative MPs was very sceptical that the EEA arrangement could work in the national interest.

In light of the UK's large trade volumes with other EU member states, it is vital that the UK retain influence of the rules by which the game is played, as well as the body responsible for refereeing those rules. Both these exigencies would become problematic if the UK were to join the EEA. A scenario could be foreseen in which the UK loses its ability to shape laws covering financial as well as employment and social regulation to its advantage. These laws are of less importance to Norway owing to its small financial services industry and high social costs, which are greater than those imposed by the EU.[270]

Nor was there any guarantee that the EEA states would wholly welcome such a large new member. 'The UK's accession would fundamentally alter the composition of the association and the legal requirements necessitated by such a change would be complex and require difficult negotiation.'

If Britain did opt for the EEA as a new relationship, it would be expected to continue to pay a share of the 'sustainable growth' portion of the EU budget, which covers structural, regional and research funds, as an entry fee for the privilege of free access to the single market. Sustainable growth made up 42.9 per cent of the 2012 budget. As Britain would no longer be in the Common Agricultural Policy, there would be no rebate any more to discount its payments. So, based on the 2012 budget, the UK's possible contribution to the EU if it left and arranged its new relationship through the EEA could be as much as 42.9 per cent of its £15 billion gross contribution, or £6.4 billion. Which is only slightly less than the £6.9 billion net payment that the UK actually paid in 2012, allowing for the rebate and the money returned from Brussels in public sector receipts. Another recent estimate put the annual cost for the UK at €2.54 billion. Norway? No way.

So could Britain look to Switzerland for a better model of how to relate to the EU if it broke with Brussels? Like Britain and Norway, the Swiss were founder members of the European Free Trade Association in 1960. They secured a free trade agreement with Brussels for goods in 1972. The government took part in negotiations to join the single market through the EEA along with Norway and launched an application for EU membership in May 1992. But then its voters decided in a close-fought referendum to stay out of the EEA in December 1992. The country was split by 50.3 per cent to 49.7 per cent on a record turnout.[271] What followed was a lengthy renegotiation of Switzerland's relationship with the post-Maastricht EU. It took more than six years of tough talking to get the first batch of seven bilateral agreements, which were signed in June 1999 and entered into force three years later. Two of these agreements were especially difficult to conclude: the free movement of people and transport by road and rail. They were followed by a second group of nine agreements signed in October 2004, one taking Switzerland into the Schengen visa-free travel zone and one taxing savings after the Swiss refused to relinquish banking secrecy. These agreements took even longer to ratify with one, on education, not coming into force until 2010. There are around 200 other technical agreements, some dating back sixty years. The Swiss confirmed their support for the policy of free movement of people in referenda to extend it to the ten new member states in 2004 and again to the Bulgarians and Romanians, making it more open than the UK. They reduced by two-thirds the number of work permits to the citizens of eight former Communist countries in April 2012, using a safeguard clause in the agreements – an ability the UK does not have.

Switzerland withdrew from talks on the free movement of services, however, including financial services, meaning that its access to the single market is limited. Nevertheless, the Swiss people seem to like their unique relationship with Brussels. Just 16 per cent said that they still wanted their country to become a full member of the EU when questioned in a major annual opinion poll in May 2012, while 67 per cent gave their explicit support to continuing with the current arrangement.[272] Under the Swiss system, each new EU law is subject to negotiation before being incorporated. The European Court of Justice does not have oversight of the agreements, which are governed by at least fifteen joint committees of Swiss politicians or civil servants with representatives from the EU institutions. It all sounds a lot more like the kind of relationship that would be acceptable to UK withdrawalists – the return of British sovereignty, case-by-case consideration of EU law and no membership fees for the single market.

Except that, of course, it is not that simple. Like Norway, Switzerland makes 'voluntary' payments to the EU to support the poorest member states, although on a reduced scale. It set out a programme worth 1 billion Swiss francs (around £654 million at 2012 prices) from 2007 to 2012 for projects in the newly joined ten member states, and added a further 181 million francs in 2009 for Romania and 76 million francs for Bulgaria when they joined. Switzerland's contributions to the EU budget for participation in research, Schengen and various agencies were put at 440 million francs a year for the 2007–2013 period, giving an annual cost together with the support for poor EU member states of around 660 million francs. In 2006, the Swiss government carried out a review which looked at the costs of full European Union membership, taking that year's annual contribution of 557 million francs as a baseline. Joining the EEA would take the annual cost to 737 million francs, a 32 per cent increase, it said. Joining the EU would result in a net annual payment of 3.4 billion francs (a six-fold increase) after receipts from Brussels, based on a gross contribution of 4.94 billion francs (around £2.25 billion at the then exchange rate), an increase of 786 per cent on the cost of its current deal. If it can be inferred from this that the gross cost to the UK of a similar arrangement to Switzerland's would be around one-eighth of Britain's current £15 billion gross contribution, the annual cost would be £1.9 billion.

'The Bilateral Agreements should not be over idealised,' said Professor René Schwok and Cenni Najy of the University of

Geneva in evidence to the Commons Foreign Affairs Select Committee in 2012.

> Switzerland is not immune to outside developments and the processes of 'EU-isation'. Since 1988, with every new federal legislation considered, it is mandatory for the Swiss parliament to include a paragraph summarising the EU position on the relevant matter. As a result, this has led to indirect adaptation in that Switzerland adopts numerous legislation of the European Union without conducting formal agreements.

Another paper for the Foreign Affairs Select Committee, this time by the Centre for Swiss Politics at the University of Kent, added:

> In order to make its economy as EU-compatible as possible, the country has adopted a policy of 'voluntary adaptation' whereby Swiss law is aligned with the EU's *acquis communautaire*... Recent research shows that around 55 per cent of the laws passed by the Swiss parliament concern transposition of international, including EU, law. The bilateral treaties and the country's voluntary adaptation have led to Switzerland being much more deeply integrated with the EU than suggested by its formal status as a non-member. Indeed, in certain respects such integration is deeper than that of EU members such as the UK, as the case of Schengen shows.

The Fresh Start group was cautious but not dismissive about the Swiss example of life outside the European Union.

> It is worth noting from the outset that the Switzerland–EU Free Trade Agreement (FTA) is a particularly idiosyncratic model, driven by the particularities of the Swiss economy and Switzerland's relationship with EU Member States. Therefore, when considering this option it is not clear what shape or form a potential UK–EU FTA would take, as the Swiss model is so

unique, and consequently, it is instructive mainly in form, rather than in content.[273]

The group pointed out that the model enjoyed a good level of democratic legitimacy, with key elements from both rounds of bilateral agreements having been accepted by the public in referenda. The group added:

> Moreover, Switzerland does not, unlike EEA members, have to implement EU internal market legislation relating to social and employment law, including the working-time directive and the agency workers directive, however, Switzerland does implement some EU equivalent legislation in the framework of its bilateral deals with the EU. Importantly, and unlike the EEA, Switzerland's accords with the EU do not involve explicit transfers of legal or decision making powers to Brussels or any supranational authority.[274]

Switzerland, however, has no formal say in EU decision-making and many of its laws are based on the adoption of EU measures, for example in product standards and access to procurement markets.

Fresh Start urged a close consideration of the ongoing negotiation for a bilateral deal between Switzerland and the EU for financial services, since it is not only of fundamental importance for Berne but will also be closely watched by the City of London as a pointer to what may happen one day with the EU. Negotiations for a bilateral deal on services foundered in 2003. Most large Swiss providers have set up subsidiaries in the EU but smaller firms that are not able to follow suit are significantly disadvantaged. The status quo on services only allows for selective coverage, for example Switzerland only has the right to provide services for up to ninety working days per year. 'This represents a significant missed opportunity for Swiss firms; indeed, some studies indicate that if the Swiss were to implement the EU's Services Directive, the gains achieved would be significant.'[275]

But an altogether more worrying development is the growing dissatisfaction in Brussels with the EU's relationship with Switzerland. All of the joint committees and bilateral negotiations seem to be getting on eurocrat nerves to the point where the EU is now pushing for a consolidated arrangement, so that EU laws are more automatically accepted – and overseen by the European Court of Justice. This would be a step too far for the Swiss for reasons of national sovereignty, not least because it would practically reconstitute the EEA by the back door. Once again, a national referendum decision (Swiss rejection of the EEA) has upset Brussels and, just as with the Irish votes against the Nice and Lisbon treaties, the EU wants Switzerland to come back with the 'right' answer, one way or another. The European Council issued particularly harsh conclusions in December 2010 which seemed to make clear that the system of Swiss bilateral agreements had come to the end of the road.

> In full respect of the Swiss sovereignty and choices, the Council has come to the conclusion that while the present system of bilateral agreements has worked well in the past, the key challenge for the coming years will be to go beyond that system, which has become complex and unwieldy to manage and has clearly reached its limits.[276]

A cynic might conclude that Brussels was cutting up rough with the Swiss to make the whole bilateral free-trading partnership paradigm a lot less attractive to any potential takers. Who could they have in mind?

In response to growing pressure from Brussels to simplify their relationship, the Swiss government reviewed its options in 2010, looking at whether to join the EU or the EEA, or withdraw altogether. The Swiss Federal Council concluded that 'the bilateral way is currently the most suitable way to ensure the necessary convergence of Switzerland's and the EU's respective interests'.[277] It set up a Swiss–EU working group to discuss with the European Commission 'possible institutional provisions of future agreements between Switzerland and the EU'. The working group is looking at

> dynamically adjusting the agreements to comply with new EU legislation, how to ensure the coherent application and consistent interpretation of future agreements, and the development of an effective dispute procedure. We share these aims with the EU. Any solution must respect the sovereignty of both parties and the efficient operation of their institutions.

The talks continue.

If Britain was to realign itself Swiss-style through a free trade agreement and associated bilateral agreements with the EU, day-to-day management of its affairs would be carried out by European Commission experts in various directorates under the auspices of the European External Action Service – ironically the body set up by the British member of the European Commission to conduct EU foreign policy. An office of ten eurocrats in the EEAS HQ in Brussels oversees the arrangements for Switzerland, Norway, Iceland and Liechtenstein. One senior eurocrat described growing frustration in Brussels with the Swiss model. 'We are not happy with the way we are proceeding,' the eurocrat said.[278]

> We had this proliferation of different agreements, each one with a joint committee... and if one of the two parties refuses, in that case there is not much one can do. There is no dispute settlement mechanism. Therefore, the two start discussing with certain time limits on the incorporation of certain legislation and after this time limit, if nothing has happened, then the only possibility is to start suspending part of the entire agreement... We don't have any way to go to court or to someone who is independent... This

is the kind of thing that in an internal market we cannot allow to happen.

In the case of 'non-harmonised goods', that is to say, products the Swiss want to sell in the EU for which Brussels has no agreed standard, the eurocrat added: 'We cannot have the supreme court of Switzerland deciding if something is compatible or not ... there are rules to be applied and if you decide not to apply these rules, we cannot let you play.' Be prepared to hear many more discussions like this if the UK leaves the EU and tries to forge a Swiss-style bilateral relationship to preserve access to the single market. Or maybe not, given the views of this particular eurocrat from the sharp end of the EU–Switzerland relationship. 'You can imagine, we are not going to repeat this with any other country... You can deduct it from the Council conclusions [of December 2010]. It is not totally spelled out, but there is a sentence that says this way of proceeding has reached its limits.'

While the Swiss have forged their own distinctive relationship with the EU – and are now battling to save it – they have shown both the advantages and the pitfalls of the bilateral method. On the plus side, the costs are far lower than EU member-ship, national sovereignty is much better preserved than under the EU or EEA and they escape the writ of Brussels in a wide range of activities from social and employment laws to farm-ing, fisheries and foreign affairs. There is also the freedom to pursue free trade deals with other international partners. But the flip side of the deal is a constant and difficult negotiation with Brussels over adopting its rules and the complete loss of influence over how those rules are written. Given the govern-ment's strong commitment to remaining in the single market, and the EU's insistence on drawing the boundaries of that market more widely than many British eurosceptics can accept, the EEA would only seem to offer a short-term fall-back posi-tion if the public voted to leave the EU, and nothing better could be negotiated through a bilateral free trade deal. But it would not endure – indeed, the Norwegians themselves seem surprised that it has lasted as long as it has. This can best be explained by Norway's relative wealth and size, combined with a relaxed attitude to globalisation that has created its very pragmatic 'adapt or die' mentality. A Swiss arrangement for the UK would be more acceptable because it seems less like EU-lite and more like a partnership – but growing frustration in Brussels means that it may not be on offer to a secessionist UK.

Another alternative model suggested for a newly independent Britain is that of Turkey's deal which locates it within the EU's customs union while the country prepares for full membership. Turkey shares the common external tariff system set by Brussels for trade from the rest of the world, which essentially gives it one of the EU's four freedoms – the free circulation of its goods – even if it does not yet have free movement of services, capital or people. If the UK sought to copy this model, it like Turkey would have no involvement with the Common Agricultural or Fisheries Policies, nor with common EU defence, security or foreign affairs. Nor would it necessarily pay into the regional funding programme although some kind of quid pro quo for trading rights within the single market in goods would likely be demanded by Brussels. After all, the whole point of this arrangement is to enable Turkey to prepare for membership while it adopts the EU's body of laws, the *acquis communautaire*. To this end it also receives large grants to help with the reforms needed to prepare for EU accession.

On the face of it, there are several potential advantages in the Turkey example from the point of view of disentangling Britain from Brussels. As the Fresh Start group pointed out in its analysis of the relationship:

> The UK would not be obliged to implement EU labour and social laws, leaving it more room for manoeuvre and flexibility when deciding its domestic legislation. It would also gain the

ability to negotiate on behalf of its domestic services sector with third countries independent of the EU, however, the UK's access to the EU's services market would be governed by a new agreement, possibly along the lines of the agreements that Switzerland currently shares with the EU.[279]

Switzerland, of course, has not been able to agree a services agreement with Brussels, forcing some of its biggest companies to create subsidiaries inside the EU. An agreement of some kind on services would be a priority for British negotiators following any vote to leave the EU, given the size of this sector in the UK and its potential for development in Europe.

However, once again there is a democratic deficit question on having to swallow whole the EU's rules on product regulations, state aid and competition in order to take part in the free movement of goods, all of which are refereed by the European Commission. Turkey has no member of the European Commission, MEPs or seat for its ministers at the European Council, leading to the same loss of influence that would be felt in Britain if it switched to the EEA or EFTA. Fresh Start added:

The UK would not be negotiating to join the EU, rather it would be going in the opposite direction. This peculiarity would create significant problems for the UK given that the EU's uniform product regulations would apply to goods in Great Britain's domestic market, regardless of whether or not they were to be exported to the EU. Coupled with this, the UK would to a large extent be losing its ability to influence future possible internal liberalisation of the single market. The single market would not have taken the shape it has today had it not been championed by Baroness Thatcher and it is hard to imagine that the EU would become more liberal if the main proponent of free trade both within and without the bloc were to leave.

In Turkey's situation, Britain would be dependent on Brussels to enforce its international trade rights, without having any formal input into negotiations or formulation of trade policy. That is because the Turkish deal was designed as a temporary measure for a country on a trajectory to join the EU. Turkey has accepted that the EU will negotiate international free trade agreements on its behalf, such as the recent package with South Korea, under intense pressure to get a good deal for the big EU trading nations. Turkey, and by implication Britain if it left the EU and emulated its arrangement, merits barely an afterthought in such deals. In other words, quitting as a full member of the EU but staying inside its customs union would severely curtail one of the biggest supposed advantages of leaving in the first place – the unfettered ability to strike new trade deals around the world. It is for this reason that the UK Independence Party and others advocate a complete break from all forms of associate membership of EU systems. The EU would become the subject of a free trade agreement (FTA) with an independent Britain in much the same way as South Korea thrashed out its own agreement with Brussels. Some sectors, like car manufacturing, would be covered by a tariff waiver for imports and exports, while other sectors, like some sensitive agricultural products, might face restrictions depending on the outcome of FTA talks. This would then leave Britain free to realign itself with the rest of a world that has changed very much since 1973.

Seven

Old Friends

We don't want to be stuck inside a Customs Union that prohibits us from making our own trade deals with the rest of the world – the growing parts of the world. After the renegotiation of a simple free trade deal with the European Union, we would like to see Britain thinking bigger. There is a group of countries out there that represent nearly a third of the population of the globe, where they speak English, have common law, are our real friends in the world. We would like to extend free trade to include the Commonwealth. That is the way forward.
– Nigel Farage

A charismatic former City trader and founder member of the UK Independence Party, Nigel Farage has mastered the art of turning a two-minute speech at the European Parliament into YouTube gold. The UKIP leader notoriously taunted the Belgian President of the European Council, Herman Van Rompuy, as a 'damp rag' that nobody had heard of from a non-country, a tirade of insults that has been viewed more than a million times. If it was meant to garner support for Farage's attempt to become an MP a few months later, however, it failed miserably – he came a poor third. But his party's popularity rose steadily after the 2010 election, reaching as much as 13 per cent in national opinion polls in 2012. While UKIP is never likely to win power, it is having a growing influence over who does win, and how they win. It is putting extreme pressure on the Conservatives to neutralise UKIP's appeal by conceding an in/out referendum on British membership of the European Union. The ultimate goal of UKIP is not to storm to government but to trigger the plebiscite that sees Britain leave the EU. And once that vote is achieved, Farage believes that the argument for taking the final step to withdrawal can be won on the core issue of trade, so often cited by pro-Europeans and eurosceptics alike as the main benefit of membership.

The bulk of Conservative eurosceptic MPs (for which, read the bulk of Conservative MPs) have grouped around a call for a looser relationship between the UK and the EU, with as many powers as possible claimed back – as long as access is preserved to the single market. Many Conservative MPs still believe that the single market can be defined as a basic trading arrangement, even though this is not how it is perceived elsewhere on the continent. To the pro-EU lobby, the wider benefits of the single market with its web of social and employment checks and balances ensure that commerce, competition and prosperity are built upon a solid foundation of fairness. Provision for maternity leave, paid holidays and equal treatment for agency workers represent hard-fought gains that tame the anti-social forces unleashed by market-opening across countries with different standards of living and welfare expectations. To Nigel Farage, the single market is a beguilingly simple phrase for a many-headed monster that is bad for Britain because it is the source of all that bothersome European regulation. 'We have got to argue that keeping us in this innocuous-sounding single market means that our employment legislation will continue to come from Brussels. Our health and safety legislation will continue to come from Brussels,' he told the UKIP conference in September 2012. It is also bad for Britain, in his view, to be shackled to a trading bloc that is in decline. The UK cannot set its own import and export duties or strike international preferential trade agreements because control over customs rules and trade negotiation belongs to the European Commission.

Farage is right that the EU is generally seen in the UK as restrictive rather than enabling. This has been confirmed by many polls, not least the YouGov survey of October 2012 which showed that 25 per cent of Britons agreed with the statement 'For all its faults, the European Union is a pioneering example of the way different countries can work together for mutual benefit' while 52 per cent agreed with 'The EU has failed. It is expensive, inefficient and overbearing. It stops the governments of member states from doing the things they need to do to improve the lives of their citizens.'[280] This YouGov poll also confirmed that a successful renegotiation to exempt Britain from Brussels regulations had become crucial to any campaign to keep the country even partially inside the EU. The fact that such a renegotiation is almost certain to disappoint helps to explain why Britain's europhiles are staring defeat in the face. Only the scale of their loss is now in question, because it is already clear that Britain will play no further part in the closer integration of Europe. To win popular support for clinging on, especially as the club becomes more integrated and more focused on the euro, paradoxically the UK must be excused from more and more of it. Without a successful repatriation, the inevitable in/out referendum will probably be lost. But even with a deal to claim back powers, the general dissatisfaction with the EU shown in poll after poll may not be curable. Britain is sliding to the exit. Can it cope outside?

Britain became a member of the European project, in large part, to secure its own prosperous economic future. There was simply no other option available in the Cold War era with a similar potential to grow trade – globalisation had not even been defined in 1973. But it turned out that, in the very year the UK joined, Europe's post-war economic miracle went into reverse. The recovery boom and the gains of closer cooperation and coordination achieved by the EEC passed their peak at the precise moment that the first contingent of fresh-faced British eurocrats were settling behind their new desks in Brussels.

Economists refer to 1950 to 1973 as the Golden Age of growth in western Europe. From 1973 to 1995 European productivity growth slowed down markedly, although it still outperformed the USA. From 1995 onwards, European growth rates stagnated as those across the pond rose.[281] It is illegal under EU law for Britain to seek new opportunities for growth elsewhere in the world by forging preferential trade agreements unilaterally with other countries. The only way it could do so would be to break with Brussels – and then go into battle with its EU neighbours.

When the UK joined the EEC, it was impossible to foresee that Brazil or India would become consumer societies, let alone China or Russia, with these four nations together adding three billion people to international trade markets. But Farage slipped into glib YouTube two-minute mode when he told his conference of the global trade bonanza that he would like 'after the renegotiation of a simple free trade deal with the European Union'. There is no such thing as a simple free trade deal. They usually take several years to negotiate and years more to come fully into force, even between willing and well-intentioned partners. Free trade deals are in fact never actually free in the sense of completely open borders; there are always particular interests to be safeguarded such as the EU's fierce protection of its farmers from overseas competition by high import taxes on certain products. A British renegotiation with the EU will be nothing like as straightforward as Farage's simple half-sentence suggests. And nor should the importance of trade in Britain's back yard be dismissed lightly – it is the other crucial side of the entire argument. Half of Britain's trade is with fellow EU member states – goods exports to the twenty-six allies totalled £159 billion in 2011.[282] Supporters of continued EU membership warn that Brussels will not take kindly to one of its own (net contributor) member states simply walking away, and therefore would hinder British trade on the continent with new tariffs or other barriers such as hygiene rules. The dilemma for the EU in the event of British withdrawal was summed up by a European academic interviewed for this book:

> Certainly the EU would like to maintain agreements with the UK and find some kind of solution. But in such a negotiation process, what kind of position should the EU take? Should they negotiate terms that are so favourable that also the Germans, the Dutch and others would join you and move in the same direction? Or should they make it so hard towards the UK that the Brits would be even more pissed off and really make the tensions in Europe much higher? For the EU, it is a kind of lose/lose situation.[283]

Should we care? And could it be a win/win for the UK? For many years, the dream of revitalising the 54-nation Commonwealth of Nations as a global trading exchange has seemed like pointless harking back to a bygone age. The organisation was seen as a legacy and hangover from the days of the British Empire when member countries were subjected to rule from London and their resources often exploited for commercial gain. Britain made a choice in 1973 to sacrifice its preferential 'empire' trading deals with Commonwealth countries (largely struck during the protectionist 1930s) in favour of free trade with its European neighbours. The logic behind this choice had become quite clear to policy-makers during the 1960s – trade with the Commonwealth was in sharp decline due to a number of factors, including a big increase in the home-grown production of staples such as wheat and meat, the major Commonwealth nations' own development of their domestic industries and the demise of the Sterling Area following sharp devaluations of the currency.[284]

In the UK accession treaty, the EEC allowed Commonwealth preferences to continue on meat and dairy from New Zealand, and sugar from the Caribbean. A number of the smaller African and Caribbean countries were then included in the EU's aid and preferential trade system, originally set up mainly for French former colonies. As one US academic put it:

> Much of the world's trade expansion was taking place in Western Europe, and the UK saw that it would become necessary to divorce itself from its traditional empire trading partners in order to maintain its economic position as a world leader... This was a pivotal moment in relations between Britain and the Commonwealth, as the UK's desire to formally align itself more closely with Europe and away from its Commonwealths was a clear signal that British interests, for the first time since its empire began in the sixteenth century, were no longer viewed in the context of its wider empire ... the UK's EEC applications were both a signal and a symptom of the end of its once-grand empire.[285]

The year 1973 marked a decisive break from Britain's past and a re-orientation towards a European future.

British exports to Empire countries comprised 49.9 per cent of all its overseas trade in 1938. By 2008, UK exports to the Commonwealth nations were just 8.8 per cent of the total. Britain's imports from its old friends also plummeted during those seventy years from 40.4 to 8.6 per cent.[286] The impact of Britain's definitive orientation towards Europe was felt severely by its most distant partner, New Zealand. This particular Commonwealth realm seemed to fall off the map as far as British traders were concerned. In 1960, 43 per cent of New Zealand's imports came from the UK but this fell to 30 per cent in 1970, 14.5 per cent in 1980 and was down to 2.7 per cent in 2011. Britain was the destination for 36 per cent of New Zealand's exports in 1970 but just 3.2 per cent in 2011.[287] There was a new focus for British merchants now. In the twenty years before accession, the proportion of all UK trade (total of imports and exports) with the original six members of the EEC rose from 13 to 21 per cent. In the twenty years following accession, trade with these six countries more than doubled to

44 per cent.[288] This was hardly surprising given the EU's work to smooth the trade in goods through common standards and rules, as well as that common external tariff to deter competition from outside the club.

But from its peak of 50.9 per cent in – yes – 1973, Europe's share of world merchandise trade fell to 45.4 per cent in 1993 and 37.9 per cent in 2010.[289] The EU nations have become reliant on trading with one another, which is fine during periods of growth but a problem if the EU economy is crisis. In the Mercosur group of nations in South America, 16 per cent of exports are to each other and 84 per cent further afield; in the ASEAN group in South East Asia, 25 per cent of exports are within the region; and in NAFTA in North America, 51 per cent are intra-regional.[290] In the EU meanwhile, 65 per cent of exporting is between member nations. Moreover the EU now finds itself in decline, both in absolute terms and relative to the rest of the world.

Although it has taken unprecedented steps to create a free market covering 500 million people, Europe is getting older and growing less, both economically and demographically, than the rest of the world. The EU had two countries among the world's most populous twenty nations in 2000: Germany in twelfth place with 82.3 million and France in twentieth place with 59.3 million.[291] The Commonwealth had four in the top ten: India in second place with 1.02 billion people; Pakistan seventh with 142.7 million; Bangladesh eighth with 138 million; and Nigeria tenth with 114.7 million. By 2050 there are no current EU countries forecast to be among the world's biggest twenty, although Turkey makes nineteenth place with 97.8 million people. In contrast, India will become the world's most populous country with 1.53 billion inhabitants and the Commonwealth will have four more in the top twenty: Pakistan (fourth), Nigeria (sixth), Bangladesh (seventh) and Uganda (seventeenth). In fact, out of 192 nations, six EU members are forecast to be among the ten biggest drops in national population in the fifty years from 2000 to 2050, led by Italy with a fall of 12.7 million, and followed by Poland (down 5.7 million), Romania (-4.4 million), Spain (-3.4 million), Germany (-3.1 million) and Bulgaria (-2.8 million).

To a europhile, these demographic changes provide even more reason to stick together in the EU. Europeans will only have real clout on the world stage as a coherent bloc. To a eurosceptic, they suggest that Europe's importance as a trading partner for the UK will be even less promising in future than during the 'lost decade' being discussed as a result of the euro crisis. If Britain were to leave the EU, its first port of call would be the so-called Anglosphere (basically, the Commonwealth plus the USA). And this brings us back to the old question of whether the Commonwealth is simply a sepia-tinted relic or something with genuine modern-day economic potential. Reviving the Commonwealth is a central tenet of UK Independence Party policy:

> UKIP will seek to establish a Commonwealth Free Trade Area (CFTA) with the fifty-three other Commonwealth countries. The Commonwealth Business Council estimates that a CFTA would account for more than 20 per cent of all international trade and investment, facilitating annual trade exchanges worth more than $1.8 trillion and direct foreign investment worth about $100bn. Yet the Commonwealth has been shamefully betrayed and neglected by previous governments. Commonwealth nations share a common language, legal and democratic systems, account for a third of the world's population and a quarter of its trade, with the average age of a citizen just twenty-five years. India, for example, will soon become the second largest world economy and Britain should not be tied to the dead political weight of the European Union, but retain its own friendly trading and cultural links.[292]

It is a plausible argument, one made more seductive by the dire straits of the eurozone. But would a Britain free of EU restrictions really be able to transform the Commonwealth organisation to its own long-term trading advantage, especially given the whiff of colonial exploitation which still lingers over Empire-era trading links?

For a long time, Commonwealth meetings seemed more ceremonial than commercial. Its gatherings are known as Commonwealth Heads of Government Meetings (CHOGM for short, popularly characterised as a Cheap Holiday on Government Money). These jamborees are held every two years – in 2002, for instance, it was at a seaside resort in Australia for five days, overshadowed by concern at the presidential election in Zimbabwe and the Commonwealth's own navel-gazing about its purpose in the new century. For journalists assigned to cover the CHOGM, it was a struggle to find something to write about. Nothing much happened. Robert Mugabe ignored it and Yoweri Museveni, the President of Uganda, picked up an award for his country's work reducing Aids, telling the audience during the prize-giving ceremony that this was partly because 'we don't have homosexuals in Uganda'.[293] Apart from anything else, the fact that Museveni was in his twenty-sixth year as Ugandan President in 2012 suggested a certain inertia about the Commonwealth.

All is not lost, however. The Commonwealth has subsequently recognised that its future survival depends on its commercial relevance as a trade facilitator. And recent research suggests that not only is there much untapped potential out there, but that Commonwealth links are already being exploited by member nations with handsome rewards. The Commonwealth Business Council was formed in 1997 to 'act as a bridge for cooperation between business and government, between developed and emerging markets and between large and small businesses'.[294] Despite a slow start, it has become adept at assisting smaller member nations to find trading partners. Things certainly seemed to have improved since the holiday resort atmosphere of the 2002 Australian CHOGM meeting: 'An estimated 1 billion US dollars' worth of new business and investment deals were made on the fringes of the 2009 CHOGM, yielding a significant windfall to the host country, Trinidad and Tobago,' the Royal Commonwealth Society reported.[295]

> The total value of imports into Commonwealth countries was around 2.3 trillion US dollars in 2008 and the total value of exports from Commonwealth countries was around 2.1 trillion US dollars in 2008. About one-sixth of this total trade occurred purely within the Commonwealth, though on average the Commonwealth share of trade for each member state was about a third.

The international trade politics environment has also given Commonwealth links extra impetus. The stalling of the Doha round of World Trade Organization talks, a negotiation process labelled the 'Development Round' which began in 2001 with the aim of liberalising trade barriers to benefit the poorer countries of the world, has led to an explosion of bilateral free trade dealing as countries realised that they would have to fend for themselves. To take New Zealand as one pertinent example, it has struck eight free trade deals since 2001 including with China, Malaysia and Thailand, and is negotiating with India, Japan and Russia. In stark contrast, the European Union does not have free trade agreements with any of these important trading countries.

Many of the world's recent preferential trade deals are between or involve Commonwealth countries – and for good reason. The spontaneous growth in intra-Commonwealth trade was highlighted in research for the Royal Commonwealth Society, which found:

> The proportion of total imports into Commonwealth member states from other Commonwealth members has grown steadily from 11.9 per cent in 1990 to 15.1 per cent in 2008. Similarly, the proportion of the Commonwealth share of exports has grown from 12.8 per cent in 1998 to 17.1 per cent in 2008.

In other words, over the last two decades the importance of Commonwealth members to each other as sources of imports and destinations for exports has grown by around a quarter and third respectively.[296]

It is not enormous, but not bad considering that the biggest Commonwealth trading nation, the UK, is legally bound by its membership of the EU to focus elsewhere.

The analysis for the Royal Commonwealth Society went further. When both trading countries are in the Commonwealth, their imports and exports are worth more in cash terms than trade with a non-Commonwealth nation.

> There is a considerable trade advantage to be found in the Commonwealth. We have found that the value of trade is likely to be a third to a half more between Commonwealth member states compared to pairs of countries where one or both are not Commonwealth members. This effect can be seen even after controlling for a range of other factors that might also explain trade patterns. The data collated here shows that there is a clear relationship between Commonwealth membership and increased trade and investment, but explaining causality remains a challenge. While our regressions do account for factors such as language commonalities, they do not control for other factors which may favourably dispose the Commonwealth to trade and investment – for example, the fact that it encourages multi-party democracy, human rights, the rule of law, good governance, similar legal and administrative systems, an open media and, since 1997, market-orientated economic policies. Without further analysis and a more sophisticated treatment of political, legal and cultural factors, it is impossible to say for sure what impact these factors have.

It does seem as if Britain is missing opportunities in the new century through its inability to conduct preferential trade deals with its old friends. But it has not been a mere spectator to these developments – in fact, the EU prohibition on UK participation in trade agreements has actually had a malign influence on the Commonwealth's own commercial development.

In 2005, meeting on the eve of a CHOGM in Malta, the Commonwealth Business Council's forum issued a report to the heads of government that 'urged that countries that are willing should explore the possibility of establishing a Commonwealth preferential or free trade area. This would be particularly important if the Doha Round of trade negotiations is not successful.'[297] It was a prescient suggestion, given the subsequent failure of the Doha Round to produce any breakthrough to benefit rich or poor countries alike. The heads of government at Malta, with the UK represented at the time by Tony Blair, shot the idea down, however. It underlined that any revival of the Commonwealth would need political commitment at the highest levels and a champion in the British government. Until the reshuffle of September 2012, the coalition administration had such a potential champion: Lord Howell of Guildford, who was Minister of State in the House of Lords for Foreign Office business, the Commonwealth, and International Energy Policy.

Lord Howell has made regular speeches extolling the virtues of the Commonwealth within the bounds of government policy, which, of course, is to stay in the EU, thus prohibiting any UK involvement in a Commonwealth free trade area. After visiting the CHOGM in Perth, Australia, in October 2011, Lord Howell remarked that its business forum was the biggest in Commonwealth history and 'the fact that delegations came from China and Korea, for example, shows a recognition and endorsement of the strength of trade opportunities within the Commonwealth'. He added:

Intra-Commonwealth trade is booming. Trade worth over $3 trillion happens every year in the Commonwealth. Its combined GDP has almost doubled in the last twenty years, while the middle class has expanded by nearly a billion people – representing a huge and growing consumer market... Five of the top ten countries in the world in which to do business are Commonwealth countries, and seventeen of the top twenty countries in which to do business in sub-Saharan Africa are Commonwealth. No wonder the Commonwealth brand is increasingly sought after.[298]

In July 2012 he wrote a blog praising Canada's support of the Commonwealth, 'which most people (but not everybody) realise is one of our best hopes and mainstays in a dangerous world'. It is hard to find a recent speech by a government minister praising the European Union in such glowing terms, or able to talk of 'booming' trade on Britain's doorstep. Nor does the EU routinely organise parallel gatherings alongside its regular summits for businesses from around the world to meet high-placed European entrepreneurs and politicians.

Lord Howell had radical ambitions for the Commonwealth. In 2005, while in opposition, he lamented the public perception of the organisation as a talking shop and a relic. In an article for the *Financial Times*, he wrote:

Yet it is possible we are being blinded by these perceptions from seeing the Commonwealth institution in a different light. It could be that with many of the world's twentieth-century institutions performing so disappointingly, a gap in the global institutional architecture has opened up which the Commonwealth model, if its leaders were ready to adapt it, could fill.

Intra-Commonwealth trade appears to be expanding steadily, as are intra-Commonwealth investment flows. This is hardly surprising, given that thirteen of the world's fastest growing economies are in the Commonwealth and that six of the leading countries in information technology and e-commerce – India, Australia, the UK, Canada, Singapore and Malaysia – are Commonwealth members. Shared legal procedures, lack of language barriers (there are no interpreters at Commonwealth gatherings) and many common business 'habits' make life easier for direct investment flows between members... None of this may amount – at least yet – to the case for a Commonwealth free trade area. But it does suggest a pause for thought as to how this extraordinary network, stretching across regions and embracing a third of the world's population, might, if it were strengthened imaginatively, do a better job than the existing battered international institutions.[299]

He had another bold suggestion which would point the way for Britain to expand Commonwealth influence if it found itself suddenly outside the European Union and looking for new global partners.

Although countries continue to queue up to join the Commonwealth as it is – which must say something for it – the question is whether in its present form it could ever carry enough clout to perform this wider role. A possible way forward might be to offer a much closer association, if not actual membership, to some other important countries outside the existing blocs or uncomfortable within them, but which plainly belong in the 'good guys' camp. The obvious candidate is Japan – a nation that is at last returning to what it terms 'normal country status', engaging actively in world affairs after decades of pacifism. An intimately allied grouping including Japan, India, Australasia and the UK, for a start, would indeed be a network of common wealth, interests and power, able to speak on friendly but firm and equal terms with America and able also to stand up for common values of justice and democracy in a way that no other international institution currently seems capable of doing.

Even if admitting Japan is an ambition too far, the organisation is attracting new members from outside the traditional British dominion, such as Mozambique. Rwanda joined in 2009, with President Kagame saying that he wanted his country 'to be part of the English-speaking world because that would provide more trade, investment and business to Rwanda'.[300] Although the prospect of a comprehensive Commonwealth free trade area is remote, the organisation has global potential and would at least provide a springboard and a starting place for Britain to rediscover some of the international clout that would be lost by withdrawing from the EU.

The theory that Britain's trade with the Commonwealth would flourish if it relaxed its focus on the European Union even has royal approval. Speaking privately and in off-the-cuff remarks to the Commonwealth Business Council in June 2012, the Duke of York, who has acted as a roving trade ambassador for Britain, 'said that Britain had been somewhat distracted from trading with the Commonwealth because of our policy towards working with the European Union'.[301] This was revealed by an MP during a Commons hearing into the future role of the Commonwealth, when Lord Howell was asked whether he shared Prince Andrew's views. 'I do agree with the Duke of York. I was there when he made that statement – it was an excellent speech,' Howell said. The Duke of York speaks from considerable experience of the international trading environment and recent research has shown that this enthusiasm for the Commonwealth should not be dismissed as merely fanciful.

Researchers for the World Economics organisation found in June 2012 that the Commonwealth's share of world GDP had overtaken that of Britain's major partners in Europe. Their researchers plotted real-terms GDP and growth for the eight nations (excluding the UK) which have been members of the EU since 1973, and compared it to the growth rate for Commonwealth countries and also with the seventeen-nation eurozone. They found that the Commonwealth had come from a long way behind to outperform the EU8 in terms of share of world GDP and was poised to do the same with the eurozone. 'Economic growth, in real terms, in the EU has been falling decade upon decade since the 1970s, and more sharply since 1973,' the researchers concluded.[302] 'From 5 per cent or more annual growth in the 1970s, growth in more recent years has averaged only 1 to 2 per cent. In contrast to the EU, economic growth in the Commonwealth has accelerated over the post-1973 period.' Moreover, real-terms average annual growth for the eurozone was forecast to rise by 2.7 per cent from 2012 until 2017 and for the Commonwealth by 7.3 per cent, using International Monetary Fund figures. World Economics concluded:

> Whilst joining the EU may have been a good thing for the UK for a number of reasons, it is clear that in sheer market growth terms, the Commonwealth is proving the more dynamic economic grouping. The potential for future market growth appears very limited in the EU, whereas the potential is still vast in the Commonwealth.

They added that population in the 54-nation Commonwealth is set to grow twice as quickly as in the eurozone up until 2050.

Far from being a relic, the Commonwealth therefore offers real future potential for trade development. While it should not be considered the main reason for the UK to leave the EU, it would certainly provide fertile ground for future free trade agreements if it did, even if the notion of a comprehensive Commonwealth Free Trade Area (CFTA) would remain an incredibly complex task, not least because of the wide range of developed, emerging and stagnant economies to be found in the organisation. A key prize for the UK if it was again able to negotiate its own preferential trade agreements would be a deal with India, which is forecast to overtake Britain and become the fifth largest economy in the world within a decade and the world's largest economy by 2050. Encouragingly, it was a leading Indian entrepreneur who pushed the CFTA idea at the 2005 CHOGM, only to see it buried by Britain, among others. 'Everybody including the United States is signing bilaterals,' said Rahul Bajaj, chief executive of the Bajaj Auto Company in India and co-chair of the Commonwealth Business Council.[303]

> We have a common language, judicial system, free press, we all feel at home in Commonwealth countries. There are three countries, UK, Malta and Cyprus, which are members of the EU. As per their rules they may not be able to join a separate trade agreement. But what about the other fifty countries? All of these can.

The fact that Commonwealth countries are scattered need not be an obstacle, he said.

> If there can be an agreement between China and India, and ASEAN [Association of Southeast Asian Nations] and India, then why not the Commonwealth? Because we are not contiguous? So what has Chile to do with APEC [Asia-Pacific Economic Cooperation], which involves the United States?

The Commonwealth would not be the only option available to Britain if it found itself outside the EU and free to make global trade deals again, of course. The other obvious place to look would be across the Atlantic to North America, where Canada, Mexico and the USA concluded the North American Free Trade Agreement (NAFTA) in 1994. The benefits in terms of increased trade were huge in the following decade, especially as the agreement coincided with the last successful world trade deal, known as the Uruguay Round, to lower tariffs around the globe. Most of NAFTA was a trilateral agreement although the sensitive area of agriculture was thrashed out in three bilateral treaties between the countries. NAFTA's combined GDP now vies with that of the EU as the largest of any trade bloc. And according to some US politicians over the years, notably on the Republican side of the fence, the UK would fit in very well as a member of the arrangement.

It has been a while since Newt Gingrich, as Speaker of the House, caused a stir by writing:

> If, as appears likely, there is a movement in the US Congress, as there has been in the Parliament of Canada, to offer Britain some associate status in the North American Free Trade Agreement, I would support it. Britain must know that she still has friends on the other side of the Atlantic.[304]

The Times called it 'an alluring fantasy'; for *The Economist* it was 'the lifeline Britain's eurosceptics have been waiting for'. It added that

> NAFTA looks like the kind of arrangement that Britain has always wanted the European Union to become – a giant free-trade area linking sovereign countries, without any common body of law, or any notion of developing a common foreign policy... There is just one snag. On joining the European Union, Britain agreed to conduct all trade negotiation under the aegis of the EU. It would be illegal under European law for the British to make a unilateral decision to join NAFTA, even if it were invited to do so. This is an example of the sort of European encroachment on Britain's freedom of action that so vexes the eurosceptics – which only adds to the bitterness of the irony.[305]

The plan was pushed a little further by a Bill in Congress drawn up by Senator Phil Gramm but it was purely symbolic – Britain could not contemplate joining while remaining a member of the EU, where mainstream US opinion especially among Democrat leaders believes it is best located for American strategic interests.

The *Chicago Sun-Times* (then owned by Conrad Black, a

fierce eurosceptic) made some observations that would still hold good today, however, should Britain find itself released from EU legal obligations.

> British workers earn roughly the same as their counterparts in Canada and the United States. British courts are as fair and accessible as any in North America. British accounting and business practices are similar to those here. When Mexico was admitted to NAFTA in 1994, critics predicted dire results. They said that Mexicans eager to work for $15 a day would take the jobs of Americans earning $15 an hour and that many industries here would simply disappear. Instead, the United States has enjoyed its lowest unemployment in fifty years, and Canada is undergoing a financial boom. Mexico has seen the least benefit – a flood of cheap consumer goods imported from the United States helped undermine Mexico's finances for a time – but the economy is improving. While NAFTA is simply reducing trade barriers between the three powers of North America, the European Union is doing much more – devising a continental political body and a code of transnational laws and political rights. British critics say European unity infringes on the sovereignty of member states. NAFTA does no such thing.[306]

A British application to join NAFTA would be logical after a withdrawal from the EU, especially if the departure led to trade recriminations and an urgent search for improved trading relations elsewhere. It would not be a like-for-like switch of allegiance. NAFTA does not require the freedom of movement of workers, so there would be no influx of Mexican plumbers. Instead, as in most free trade agreements, there is a clause for company employees to be assigned under contract, with family members, for defined periods of time. Nor does it require working hour limitations, equal treatment for agency workers or minimum paid holidays as a pre-condition for market entry. And while it has a flag, nobody in North America is forced to display it on their car number plates or encouraged to celebrate 'NAFTA Day'.

There is a whole world out there, of course, one that is growing more rapidly than Europe. China's imports grew by an annual average of 11.5 per cent from 2005 to 2010, according to the World Trade Organization, a performance only eclipsed by India with yearly import growth of 13.5 per cent.[307] In the same period, annual import growth in South and Central America was 9.5 per cent, in Asia it was 6 per cent and in Australia 5.5 per cent. While total world import growth was put at 3 per cent a year, for the European Union it was just 1 per cent. And while the UK would obviously be smaller and have less clout in international trade negotiations on its own, it would not be a minnow. It is the world's tenth largest merchandise exporter, with US$406 billion worth in 2010, a quarter the value of China's and a third the value of the USA's. Britain is the sixth biggest importer of goods, with US$560 billion, behind the US, China, Germany, Japan and France.[308] But when it comes to the trade in commercial services, the UK actually exports more in dollar value than China, 227 billion compared to 170 billion, putting it in third place globally behind the USA and Germany.

Besides trying to revive the Commonwealth as a trading association, UKIP proposes to 'actively pursue trade deals with trade blocs such as the countries in the North American Free Trade Agreement and the Association of Southeast Asian Nations. This will secure trade benefits for all countries concerned.' Famously dismissed by Michael Howard as cranks, gadflies and extremists, and by David Cameron as fruitcakes, loonies and closet racists, how crazy is UKIP's trade policy? It is worth comparing it to the EU's own agenda, as set out in July 2012. 'This year, free trade agreements (FTAs) are within reach with Canada and Singapore,' stated a memo released by the trade directorate of the European Commission.[309]

Both are important precedents for other potential agreements with similar or neighbouring countries. A positive dynamic with other member countries of the Association of South East Asian Nations (ASEAN) would reinforce the EU's position in Asia. On-going FTA negotiations with large emerging economies such as India or the Mercosur countries, albeit being very challenging, are important to prepare for the future. The key question for the EU remains whether we will be able to conclude these agreements within a realistic timetable and at an acceptable level of ambition.

This showed that the European Commission's trade directorate was now fully switched on to the importance of making bilateral trade deals in the post-Doha world. It has a lot of ground to make up, having only implemented one modern non-regional deal, the FTA with South Korea in 2011. And in its own words, the EU's grand plan is to break into NAFTA via a deal with Canada and into ASEAN through a deal with Singapore – both Commonwealth countries with relatively relaxed trading regimes where the gains are large and within reach. Then an attempt should be made to negotiate with India, another Commonwealth giant. Sound familiar?

But that is not all. The EU's own ambitions now go further, the European Commission explained. 'As recent estimates show, deepening relationships between the EU and its key trading partners can contribute significantly to Europe's recovery,' it stated.

If the EU pursues its ambitious external trade agenda, this could boost the EU's GDP by 2 per cent or more than €250 billion. This is equivalent to adding an economy of the size of Austria or Denmark. An ambitious agenda could also help create more than two million jobs across the EU. More than two-thirds of these gains in growth and jobs would materialise through trade agreements with the US and Japan. In July 2012 the European Commission requested the EU member states' approval to open negotiations with Japan. In June 2012, the interim report of the EU-US High Level Working Group on growth and jobs underlined the benefits of a comprehensive trade agreement between the EU and the US. A recommendation should follow later this year on prospects for launching negotiations.

The pinnacle of the EU's ambitions is to open up trade relationships with the other main NAFTA economy, the USA, as well as Japan – the country which one British minister proposed approaching in 2005 to team up with the Commonwealth. The European Commission is finally showing the ambition to do for the EU what UKIP has been calling for the past twenty years for Britain to be able to do.

And to those who believe that tying up free trade deals with allies like the US, Canada, India or Singapore sounds like a pointless yearning for a long-lost imperial past, the EU sets out precisely why it wants to get in there. 'By 2015, 90 per cent of economic growth will be generated outside Europe, with one third in China alone. Hence, tapping into the markets of our key trading partners will play an increasingly significant role for Europe's growth in the future,' the European Commission said in its trade statement.

> To be sustainable, economic recovery will therefore need to be consolidated by stronger links with the new global growth centres... The impact of all on-going and potential negotiations taken together could provide an increase of about 1.2 percentage points of GDP or some €150 billion to the EU economy in the short to medium term. Productivity gains stemming from trade integration further increase the impact of trade agreements by more than half.

The European Commission figures for the benefits of free trade agreements with these major partners should give pause for thought. A preferential trade agreement with the USA would stimulate European GDP by €65 billion, Japan by €43 billion, Canada by €10 billion and India by €3.8 billion, the commission forecast, with further significant productivity gains to follow. As a trading nation, Britain, with 11.5 per cent of all EU exports and 14.5 per cent of EU imports, could expect to benefit disproportionately from this potential windfall.[310] Indeed, EU success in these ambitions would certainly negate a big part of the argument for British withdrawal, namely that the EU is too sclerotic, inward-looking and fundamentally protectionist to open up sufficiently to conclude the kind of free trade deals now under consideration. The European Commission's ambitious plans have given extra weight to one of the main europhile arguments for continued and ever closer UK membership – that the EU is much better placed to conduct the complex and wide-ranging negotiations necessary to lock down a free trade agreement.

But should Britain hold its breath for the Commission trade directorate to deliver? Not if the experience of the last attempt to forge a free trade deal with the USA is anything to go by. That was in 1998, under the direction of the then European Commissioner for trade, the British former Cabinet minister Sir Leon, now Lord, Brittan. It was so controversial with the French that he dared not call it a free trade agreement but rather described it as the New Trans-Atlantic Marketplace (NTM). France, ever keen to protect its farmers from competition, feared that agricultural goods would get dragged into the negotiations, despite repeated promises that they were not even on the table. 'We do not want our American friends to come and stick their noses into the way we organise Europe,' said the then French Finance Minister, one Dominique Strauss-Kahn, who would later become managing director of the International Monetary Fund.[311] French President Jacques Chirac was even more forthright. He accused Leon Brittan of

going off on his own, like a big man, to negotiate a free trade

zone between the United States and Europe without a mandate...
It is absurd, and, I have to say, it is indecent. We have the World
Trade Organization, we all wanted it and we all signed it. And
this is where commercial agreements should be negotiated.

And so the French torpedoed the NTM. Brittan's plan for a
free trade deal with Mercosur, the bloc that represents five
Latin American countries, forecast to have been worth an
annual boost of US$6.2 billion to the EU economy and US$5.1
billion to Mercosur, was similarly thwarted. It would have
been the largest free trade deal in the world. It also fell amid
(mainly French) concerns that it would destabilise the WTO's
multilateral process, and because the EU decided that its main
priority was to concentrate on reform of its Common
Agricultural Policy to deliver growth.

There are still ominous signs that the French in particular
will try and scupper the European Commission's ambitious
trade plans. In the early discussions on a possible EU–Japan
agreement, the French and Germans have identified numerous barriers to trade that they want addressed before a
full-scale negotiation, a move seen as a wrecking tactic by free
trade reformers. They are also demanding that Japan Airlines
commit to buying Airbus planes made by the European EADS
corporation and TGV trains made by the French company
Alstom – although there is no sign of the French buying bullet
trains in return. Another stumbling block for EU free trade
agreements is the European Parliament, which has full rights
of co-decision following the Lisbon Treaty. MEPs have held up
the EU–Colombia and EU–eru deals because of concerns over
human rights issues and want the governments to commit to a
binding timetable to protect human rights, trade unions and the
environment. Meanwhile the USA, with no such qualms, stole a
march for its exporters by completing the ratification of its preferential trade deal with Colombia in May 2012. Free-traders in
the European Parliament believe that trade deals with India,

Japan or the USA could be blocked by a majority of MEPs in protest at the death penalty in those countries, showing how broadly some MEPs believe that trade should be used by the EU to push its human rights agenda. The UK acting unilaterally would not hold up a trade agreement with the USA, India or Japan in protest at the death penalty, and would probably consider that the mutual benefits of a trade agreement with Colombia outweigh human rights issues that were at their most troubling under a previous government.

Meanwhile, in the past decade, Commonwealth countries have been showing Europe the way in how to make international trade deals, often between themselves. Australia, for example, has tied up with Singapore (2003), Thailand (2005), Chile (2009), USA (full implementation for goods in 2015), Malaysia (ratification due in 2013) and, together with New Zealand, struck a deal with the ASEAN group of ten south-east Asian countries (2010). Australian Senator Alan Eggleston, chair of the Senate Foreign Affairs, Defence and Trade References Committee, said:

> I think Australia has lost confidence in the Doha Round so we are doing individual free trade agreements with countries like Malaysia and Singapore. The Commonwealth was really about imperial trade preferences and then you [the UK] joined the Common Market and we started looking around for other places to trade. And we found those places in Asia.[312]

Eggleston thought it would be 'a long road' back for the UK to revive Commonwealth trading links now that most countries are more interested in building up trade relationships in their regions. 'While we would be prepared, I am sure, to trade again with the UK, we have very strong trading links with north Asia in particular,' he said.

> We are also looking west across the Indian Ocean because we feel we are a little bit too dependent on China, which is now our

biggest trading partner. There are countries in the ASEAN group just below China and they have a population of 600 million people... we have very high status with ASEAN. That is a group we can use as a diversifying focus away from China. We have also done a lot of bilaterals in the last ten years.

Australia, one of the largest exporters and importers in its region, is a model for the approach that the UK could take outside the EU. It has pushed ahead with important bilateral trade deals while becoming a preferred partner of the main bloc in the region. Similarly, while the UK would be freed by leaving the EU to pursue new deals around the world, it would be sheer folly for both Britain and the EU to wreck their mutually beneficial trading relationship if Britain withdrew its membership.

Nor are trade deals simple matters to conclude. New Zealand took three years and fifteen rounds of negotiations to clinch its agreement with China, the first such deal by any OECD (Organisation for Economic Co-operation and Development) nation. Phil Goff MP, former leader of the New Zealand Labour Party and the Minister of Foreign Affairs and Trade who signed the deal, believes that the world has moved on from the idea of a Commonwealth Free Trade Area. The model now is for bilateral and so-called plurilateral deals, meaning a focused group agreement like the Trans-Pacific Partnership that the USA began negotiating in 2008 with Chile, New Zealand, Singapore, Brunei, Australia, Vietnam, Peru and Malaysia. Mexico, Canada and Japan are also interested. In other words, a mixture of Commonwealth and other mainly developed countries with the potential for incredibly lucrative trade synergies. Compared to the ambition shown by this initiative, the EU has been off the international pace on trade, its potential hamstrung by the difficulty of agreeing an agenda and negotiating mandate internally that satisfies all twenty-seven member countries.

'For New Zealand, the fastest growing area of trade development is in the Asia-Pacific,' said Goff.[313]

If you look at the rest of the Commonwealth, it is largely in the developing world. And they are each looking at their own areas. If they are in Latin America, they are looking at the concept of a Latin American trade agreement. If they are in Africa it is part of the African Union grouping. I don't think there is a realistic option of saying 'take the Commonwealth as an entity', I don't see there is a basis of a coherent trading bloc.

Goff believes that the Doha global deal is still worth pursuing because it would reduce a huge number of trade barriers, including many of the agricultural tariffs that protect European farmers from produce from the developing world. In the meantime, bilaterals and group agreements are the way to go.

New Zealand is negotiating a free trade agreement at the moment with Russia. We are still the only western country with a free trade-agreement with China. We are negotiating a free trade agreement with India, but it is a tough one. It is one of the great ironies – we have got a free trade agreement with China, with which we have a totally different historical relationship. And we don't have one with India with whom we share the English language, British-style institutions and Commonwealth ties.

India's desire to protect home-grown industries from potentially destructive foreign competition has made it reluctant to commit to the kind of reciprocal trade-opening deals that developed countries want to do.

New Zealand's experience as a trade agreement pioneer has many lessons for the UK, should Britain return to the international trading network as an independent player. The plurilateral model of the Trans-Pacific Partnership shows how countries of different sizes and strengths can retain their goals in a tough trading environment. Phil Goff added:

One reason why we are doing it that way, if I was to be perfectly frank, is that if we were negotiating solely with the US, they would screw us down as they did in the free trade-agreement with Australia. The [US] dairy-lobby is incredibly powerful and they would try to do with dairy what they did with sugar in Australia and exclude it, carve it out. Because this is plurilateral and the rules apply as much to our dairy going into the United States in the future as it would to their produce going into other countries like Vietnam and potentially Japan, they want a high quality agreement. So we had a far better prospect of getting a more advantageous trading relationship with the United States as part of a plurilateral agreement than we would have in a straight bilateral arrangement.

Here is the real model for the UK's future trading relationship outside the EU – forget romantic notions of a Commonwealth Free Trade Area and focus on the most advantageous relationships with individual nations and new groupings where each player has something to gain. Post-EU Britain has a lot to learn from its old friends in the Commonwealth such as Australia and New Zealand, and one thing they have learnt the hard way following Britain's decision to turn its focus away from them in 1973 is that there should be no hankering after a lost world when there are far better modern deals to be done with the likes of China, Japan and some South American countries, as well as nations like Malaysia, Singapore and Canada where a shared Commonwealth identity is an extra benefit rather than a guiding principle for a modern trading relationship.

This is precisely the view of a former senior member of the Commonwealth based on many years' involvement in trade diplomacy. Ransford Smith, Jamaica's former envoy to the World Trade Organization and Deputy Secretary-General (Economic) of the Commonwealth from 2006 until 2012, believes that there are too many hurdles to overcome for a comprehensive Commonwealth Free Trade Agreement. Most of its countries are still developing the infrastructure, production and administrative systems necessary to compete internationally. 'Arrangements that might raise the cost of supply of imports because they are sourced through the Commonwealth when they could be sourced cheaper elsewhere are not going to help anyone, the real objective of these countries is to trade with the most competitive source and build the capacity to trade,' Smith said.[314]

> So the important thing is not really building trade within the Commonwealth, it is building trade for the Commonwealth. If the Commonwealth focuses on building the supply side of its members then all boats will be lifted. It is about transforming more Commonwealth countries into the Singapores and Malaysias and doing that does not mean those countries should become more closely interlinked with the UK... it is a little too far-fetched to believe you are going to re-orient those economies.

Smith's advice to Britain, should it find itself withdrawing from the EU as a result of a referendum decision to leave, would be to stay as engaged as possible with the single market and not to consider the Commonwealth or North America as a panacea.

> You have to find another way, but that way is not to replace the EU relationship which must continue substantially, it is to top up the relationship to replace what has been lost... that way the Commonwealth and NAFTA can be options seen in a realistic perspective, not as alternatives to but as important potential supplements to a different kind of EU relationship.

If the UK were to leave the EU, it simply would not have any choice but to try and negotiate a new trading framework with its former allies, as well as with Commonwealth countries and other nations in NAFTA, ASEAN and elsewhere. The most important single relationship would still be with the European Union, currently the partner for around half of British trade.

Even with the distortion of the so-called Rotterdam/Antwerp effect, that is to say the merchandise that features in the figures as EU trade even though it is en route to farther-flung destinations via European ports, the EU is still the UK's most important trading partner by far.

What would a new trading relationship with the EU look like? It would be similar to being a full member, but without decision-making rights, if the Norway model of the European Economic Area is followed. If not, then it will probably look something like a cross between the Swiss model of bilateral agreements, and the all-encompassing single treaty example of the EU's one and only modern fully functioning non-regional free trade deal – the agreement in force since July 2011 with South Korea. After a phasing-in period, this will provide almost unfettered access to each other's markets, give or take a few sensitive areas. The overseeing body of the South Korea deal is a trade committee of fifteen members, five from each side and five neutrals, along with six specialised committees of experts in particular fields: trade in goods, sanitary and phytosanitary, customs, trade in services, sustainable development, and outward processing zones. There are also seven sectoral working groups. All told, that is quite some reduction in bureaucratic scale from the UK's current arrangement overseen by the European Commission and its 36,687 staff. The European Court of Justice (ECJ) would no longer have jurisdiction over the UK. Instead, under the South Korea–EU model, there is a system of consultations to resolve disputes and failing that, matters are brought before a three-person arbitration panel, made up of members of the trade committee and chaired by one of the independents. Again, that is quite a reduction in scale from the ECJ with its 1,954 staff and annual budget of €348.3 million.

There is always the possibility that the EU could play hardball over trade with the UK out of anger at being dumped by such a prominent and wealthy member. If the 'Brexit' turns sour, the trade relationship could revert to the common denominator on market access, which could trigger a trade war between the two sides. The relationship would then be based on the general rules of the World Trade Organization, which would not mean exorbitant new import taxes for all British exporters, but some sectors would suffer. Cars would face a 10 per cent import duty, for example, which would hit British-based manufacturers hard if applied by Brussels. But if applied reciprocally by London, as it surely would be in a trade war, that would not go down well with European car-manufacturers, especially German high-end car-makers, which would find their prices in Britain shooting up – especially as non-EU car imports into the UK currently attract VAT, which could well be extended to imports from former EU allies following a British exit in a further escalation of trade recriminations. Sources at Mercedes, for example, are very concerned about the potential rise in border tax that could follow a British withdrawal and are bound to put pressure on the German government to safeguard their business in the UK by pushing for tariff reductions or waivers. Renault would probably follow suit in France. After all the years of free trade between the UK and the EU, the reality of commerce and market forces is likely to impel a much lower import duty on cars than the WTO benchmark.

Common sense could prevail once emotions have calmed about a British EU exit and lead to a mutually beneficial trading arrangement, especially given the UK's huge trade deficit with the EU in goods, meaning that the continent would have a lot more to lose in any trade war than Britain. In the three months to July 2012, UK exports to its main EU trade partner, Germany, were £7.7 billion and imports £13 billion, suggesting that Germany will want to keep the UK as a preferential partner on favourable terms in the eventuality of a British withdrawal from the EU.[315] But this is by no means certain – a period of huge disruption is likely to follow any British vote to quit Brussels before a new trading framework is settled.

It would mean swapping the certainty of close EU ties for a leap into the unpredictable waters of old-fashioned trade empire-building in a modern world much changed from pre-globalisation 1973. Nigel Farage and UKIP are also out of step with this fast-changing world in hankering after a Commonwealth Free Trade Agreement, if they believe that it could be negotiated to cover most or all of the fifty-four member nations. But they are right to point to the potential advantages to be gained from an independent trade mandate, with the inevitable loss of clout to some extent compensated by the greater ease and relevance of negotiations. Surprisingly, it is old friends from the Commonwealth who have the most to teach their former colonising power about the way trade agreements work in the post-Doha world. But the other side of the coin will also be a European Union without the liberalising influence of the UK at the heart of its own decision-making process, relieving pressure to continue market-opening in areas such as financial and other services where far too little progress has yet been made, even with Britain on the inside.

EIGHT

Independent Britain

One of the things that I find quite astonishing is the inability of this country and, particularly, of its media to recognise the staggering achievements of the European Union... The first and perhaps greatest achievement is that now, on the anniversary of the First World War, we cannot imagine another war in western Europe. It is simply beyond the understanding of our children and grandchildren to think of another war between Britain, Germany, France and Italy... The second great achievement was to help bring the whole of central and much of eastern Europe back to democracy after the collapse of the Soviet Union... The third achievement is much more recent and of great importance. The European Union – to an extraordinary extent which is hardly recognised at all in our country – has undertaken the burden of being a very good neighbour indeed to countries much poorer than itself. The EU is the greatest giver of aid in the world, and by a substantial margin. The EU has gone out of its way to help bring democracy, and training in democracy, not just to central and eastern Europe but far beyond it as well... I do not know why we fail to recognise these staggering achievements of which we are a part, though a diminishing part. I should therefore like to say, loud and clear, that anything that makes the development of our relationship with the continent of Europe more difficult will not be helpful in meeting some of the most crucial problems in the world.

– Baroness Williams of Crosby[316]

By withdrawing from the European Union, Britain would regain a whole host of positive and enabling freedoms that are denied to us by EU membership. Britain would take back control over its own destiny, defence, economy, foreign relations, environment, transport, fishing, farming and market controls – to name but a few.

– David Campbell Bannerman[317]

There can be few bigger gulfs in British politics than the one between Shirley Williams, the Liberal Democrat peer and lifelong cheerleader for the European cause who quit the Labour Party partly because of its opposition to British EEC membership in the early 1980s, and David Campbell Bannerman, Member of the European Parliament, campaigner for British withdrawal and one-time deputy leader of UKIP who defected to the Conservatives in 2011 accusing his old party of 'shouting from the sidelines'. The EU's strongest supporters, like Williams, are aghast that its achievements are not better recognised in the UK, and see the idea of leaving as an affront. On the other hand, the EU's biggest detractors, like Campbell Bannerman, are driven to near madness by its apparently unstoppable momentum towards a superstate that squashes national sovereignty. In between their resolute positions at either end of the spectrum of British responses to Brussels lies a vast and complex tapestry of pros and cons of the European Union. Many areas of British life have been touched and some have been transformed during the forty years of membership, all of which would have to be rethought and many of them reconfigured in the event of a Brexit. Incredibly, while the general subject of EU membership is widely debated, there is almost no analysis as to what withdrawal would really mean. That is partly because the agenda has been captured by the extremes and partly because the issues are so complicated and overlapping. This chapter considers ten areas, from climate change to jobs, and fishing to financial services, all likely to be hot topics for debate during the next British in/out referendum – and none as straightforward for either the In or Out camps as at first they might appear.

Jobs
The case for EU membership: 3.5 million British jobs depend on the EU.

The case against EU membership: Jobs involved in trade with the EU do not necessarily require British membership; Jobs lost as a result of EU withdrawal would eventually be replaced as trade expanded elsewhere.

An oft-quoted claim, repeated in May 2012 by Nick Clegg, the Deputy Prime Minister, is that '3.5 million British jobs depend on the EU economy'.[318] The assertion features prominently on the website of the pro-EU European Movement under the section headed *The EU creates jobs* ('3.5 million jobs are linked, directly and indirectly, to the export of goods and services to the EU').[319] The figure can trace its roots to the former pressure group Britain in Europe, which campaigned for Britain to join the euro. Back in December 2001, the group's director said: 'The EU takes well over half of our trade. Up to 3.5 million British jobs depend on that trade' (although here 'up to' was used to enable a high-sounding figure to be more safely claimed).[320] Where does the true figure lie, is it somewhere 'up to 3.5 million'? Are the jobs 'linked, directly and indirectly' to EU membership? How many, actually, are linked directly?

The 3.5 million jobs figure, despite being repeated by senior ministers today as if contemporary fact, originates from two pieces of research commissioned by Britain in Europe and published in early 2000. The first, by the European Institute at South Bank University, said that exports to the EU generated direct employment of 2.53 million jobs in British industry and supply chains, while the secondary impact of spending on British goods and services arising from revenue generated by exporting to the EU supported 'indirect employment effects' amounting to 917,000 jobs.[321] The report stated: 'The aim of the present investigation is not an overall evaluation of EU membership, but rather an estimate of the employment effects that result from the exports of goods and services from the UK to the EU.' The researchers used export figures from 1997, when trade with the EU (then fourteen member states besides the UK) made up 55.8 per cent of British goods exports (it had fallen to 53.1 per cent in 2011 for twenty-six member states) and 34.4 per cent of British services exports (it was 39.2 per cent in 2010).[322] One key variable in the researchers' calculations (the import component of exports) was taken from 1990, which was the best available figure at the time. The data behind the headline jobs figures still being used today are therefore rather out of date.

The second analysis led to some extravagant job claims. Research by the National Institute for Economic and Social Research was scooped ahead of its scheduled launch by a newspaper which said that it showed eight million jobs would be in jeopardy if Britain left the EU. Martin Weale, director of the NIESR, accused Britain in Europe of leaking the report. 'The report does not state, and it is untrue, that eight million jobs would be put in jeopardy by withdrawal (from the EU),' the NIESR said in a statement. 'Although a large number of jobs are now connected to EU exports and the income they generate, it is not the case that many of these would be lost permanently if Britain was to leave the EU.'[323] Weale called the eight million jobs claim 'pure Goebbels. In many years of academic research I cannot recall such a wilful distortion of the facts.'[324] The eight million figure came from a modelling exercise in the research paper.

In fact, the NIESR calculated that about 2.7 million British jobs, around 10 per cent of the national total, were directly related to the goods and services sold to the EU, while a further

500,000 were supported by other sources of demand for firms which derive much of their activity from exporting to Europe. That made 3.2 million jobs dependent on trade with the EU. The report added: 'As the experience of the 1960s indicates, there is no reason why being outside the EU should necessarily involve mass unemployment, although living standards would probably be slightly lower... exports to the rest of the EU would not fall to zero if the UK were to leave the EU.' Some level of trade would continue, after all, even in the case of an acrimonious British departure. The report concluded that living standards would be affected by withdrawal, with gross national income declining after twenty years by 1.5 per cent and output by 2 per cent. As for job losses in the event of British withdrawal from Brussels, around 175,000 would be lost after three years, but these would be reabsorbed at lower wage levels in the longer term, the report estimated.

One of the NIESR authors, Nigel Pain, had this to say about the EU jobs controversy in the institute's annual report:

Over the past thirty years the British economy has become increasingly integrated with that of the other EU members. Detailed estimates from input-output tables suggest that up to 3.2 million UK jobs are now associated directly with exports of goods and services to other EU countries. This has given rise to popular concern that some of these jobs might be at risk if Britain were to leave the Union. Opponents of membership on the other hand argue that many of the benefits flowing from the increasingly integrated European Economic Area might still be available even if the UK were to withdraw... In conjunction with the potential gains from withdrawing from the Common Agricultural Policy and no longer paying net fiscal contributions to the EU, there is a case that withdrawal from the EU might actually offer net economic benefits.

One of the authors of the South Bank research, Professor Iain

Begg, said in 2011 that he would not expect mass redundancies if Britain withdrew from the EU, again on the assumption that there would be some kind of deal to continue with trade, even if the UK was no longer involved in setting the rules in Brussels.[325] He added that the cost–benefit balance calculation of UK membership was probably negligible. 'If anyone tried to do it completely objectively, you would probably find that the economic plus or minus is very small.' Nigel Pain of the NIESR added that EU membership was more important for foreign investment in the UK than for jobs.

> The size of national economies has to be viewed as partially determined by the degree of integration with Europe. This does not necessarily mean that the number of jobs in the economy is similarly affected. In an economy such as the UK with flexible real wages, trade and direct investment might ultimately be expected to affect only the types of jobs available rather than the quantity.[326]

The overall number of jobs lost if Britain left the EU was forecast to be negligible in two sets of independent research commissioned by the pro-euro campaign Britain in Europe. Even in the case of a complete breakdown in preferential trading negotiations between the UK and the EU, some activity would continue under the basic World Trade Organization rules. The main impact would be on the types of jobs in the new British economy, which, after a disruptive period of higher unemployment, would almost certainly be lower paid. As the NIESR put it: 'Higher unemployment would put downward pressure on wages and prices so that those losing their jobs as a consequence of trade and investment shocks could price themselves back into work.' Leaving the EU will create job market turbulence and realignment but probably not permanent contraction even if British negotiators fail in their top post-EU priority of retaining full access to the single market.

Climate Change and Energy

The case for EU membership: Only the EU acting as a strong bloc can ensure global and continental action to adopt binding targets for emissions cuts and the use of renewables. The EU's emissions trading scheme not only leads the world by showing how greenhouse gas can be reduced through market forces but it is also cleaning up Europe, and its profits will develop green technologies like carbon capture and storage. EU coordination is vital to secure a stable future energy supply for the continent.

The case against EU membership: The EU has been ineffective in international climate negotiations; its emissions trading scheme has largely failed so far; environmental targets push up energy and travel bills as well as food prices in the developing world when farmers switch to biofuel production. The UK has its own tough emissions targets anyway.

Britain was instrumental in creating the EU's climate change targets with Tony Blair's support in the European Council and Lord Stern's advice to the European Commission. The UK's own Climate Change Act of 2008 – the world's first long-term legally binding national framework – set a reduction target of 34 per cent in carbon emissions by 2020, on the way to a mandatory 80 per cent cut in 2050 compared to 1990 levels. The British government also adopted a Renewables Obligation to generate 15 per cent of energy from renewable sources by 2020. This is lower than the EU headline goal but in line with the national target agreed with Brussels in 2009. At the EU level, resistance from Poland is hampering further binding target-setting. The economic downturn caused a drop in emissions of 1.8 per cent globally in 2009 as industry contracted. But polluting returned to normal in 2010 with a 6.7 per cent annual rise, led by a 15.5 per cent increase in China and a 12.8 per cent rise in Russia.[327] The original aim of climate campaigners, of keeping the global temperature rise to below two degrees Celsius, compared to pre-industrial levels, seems unlikely to be met. Lord Stern has warned of serious consequences if the world continues on a 'business as usual' path. 'According to the [Intergovernmental Panel on Climate Change's] projections, such a path... would mean around a 50 per cent chance of a rise in global average temperature of more than four degrees Celsius by 2100,' he said.[328] 'Such warming would disrupt the lives and livelihoods of hundreds of millions of people across the planet, leading to widespread mass migration and conflict. That is a risk any sane person would seek to drastically reduce.'

While it is important that Europe plays its part, the Copenhagen climate summit of 2009 highlighted the reluctance to sign up to binding emissions targets of China, with a quarter of world emissions, and the USA, with a fifth, as well as key developing countries like Brazil and India. An EU official present at the summit disputed the impression that these powers concluded a deal without any European involvement but added: 'The basic point is that, as a bloc, we are sinking in influence – but would the UK have more influence on its own?'[329] Britain has been a driving force inside the EU for climate targets, and while it will continue to push for a 30 per cent emissions cut, the coalition government has shifted to a less affirmative approach. David Cameron decided not to attend the inconclusive Rio+20 summit in June 2012, the Treasury has offered tax breaks for natural gas production and nuclear energy is being promoted as a low-carbon option in dramatic contrast to Germany's decision to phase out atomic power. The coalition has secretly lobbied in Brussels for an end to renewables targets.[330] Whatever action the EU decides to take in future, China, the USA and Russia seem impervious to its example of self-imposed mandatory targets. They are also hostile to developments like the extension in 2012 of the EU's emissions trading scheme to all airlines that fly into European airspace. If the UK left the EU, this would open up the possibility of opting out of the emissions trading scheme or its application to overseas airlines, possibly attracting more business to Britain. Leaving the EU would also give the UK the option to exempt heavy-emitting British power stations from the large combustion plant directive of 2001, which will see 11gigawatts (GW) of UK generating capacity closed down in 2015, although it is hard to see any British government taking this retrograde step for emissions. The Conservative Fresh Start group warned:

> The UK currently has around 97GW of generation capacity covering an estimated peak demand of 57.1GW. However, of this only 64.1GW of generation capacity is 'base load' or reliable for peak periods, this currently gives the UK a spare peak time capacity of 13 per cent. However, as a result of the removal of large plants from production the base load is predicted to fall to 46.8GW. Unless measures are taken, this could leave the UK with very little or no peak time generation cover, potentially leading to blackouts.[331]

Fresh Start also suggested that EU renewable targets hampered the development of shale gas exploitation through fracking, the controversial process of blasting large amounts of water, sand and chemicals into layers of shale rock deep underground to release trapped natural gas. It was temporarily suspended in the UK after causing minor earthquakes in Lancashire in 2011. 'Although shale gas will clearly contribute to carbon emission reductions, it is not a renewable energy source. Nonetheless, an energy source that could reduce energy costs, contribute to lower carbon emissions, and improve UK energy security deserves further exploration,' the group said.[332] 'Over the past five years, the US, which did not sign the Kyoto protocol and does not have binding carbon reduction targets, has cut carbon dioxide emissions by 450m tonnes, a feat the chief economist at the International Energy Agency accredits to its shale boom.'

With the EU's energy commissioner, Gunter Oettinger, saying that he is 'personally in favour' of a higher binding target on renewables for 2030, a clash with the UK seems likely if current government policy continues and Britain remains in the EU.[333] Another source of friction could be the estimated cost of Oettinger's main priority during his five-year term, the completion of a pan-European integrated energy market. The commissioner has set a target date of 2015 and called for overall energy infrastructure investments of €1 trillion. It is a price tag for continental capacity-building that seems impossibly high and will be a big call on structural funds in future budgets.

The EU's environment commissioner, Janez Potočnik of Slovenia, is 'almost certainly' going to propose legislation on shale gas extraction in 2013, following a public consultation. His spokesman said: 'We are surrounded by risks in our society but we need energy. We need to manufacture things. So what you try to do is limit those risks and take as many prevention measures as you possibly can.' In an era when there are increasing UK government fears that green measures are stifling economic recovery, Potočnik remains determined that the European Commission will enforce and uphold world-leading environmental standards. 'When someone talks about the cost of doing something, you should ask about the cost of not doing it,' he said.[334] Expensive environmental regulations will continue to be set by Brussels and withdrawing from the EU would reduce the pressure for Britain to follow suit and increase the temptation to relegate the green agenda at a time when critics argue it is sometimes an expensive luxury. On the other hand, the EU will continue to pump vast sums of money into environmental research, such as carbon capture and storage, with two British projects in the running for EU grants of €337 million each in 2012. British ambitions to become a world leader in this and other green technologies will be much more expensive to fund unilaterally.

Investment

The case for staying in the EU: As a member state, Britain attracts more foreign direct investment (FDI) and international company headquarters because of its position as a gateway for overseas companies to access the single market of 500 million people.

The case for leaving the EU: Foreign companies invest in the UK primarily because of its flexible employment laws, lower business taxes and the attraction of established centres of expertise such as the City of London.

The UK was the leading destination in Europe for foreign direct investment (FDI) in 2011, with an influx of US$53.9 billion according to the UN World Investment Report, an increase of 7 per cent that put Britain second in the world behind the US and ahead of Hong Kong and France. In the year to March 2012, FDI created or safeguarded 112,659 jobs from 1,406 projects, according to UK Trade and Investment (UKTI). The number of jobs attributed to FDI increased by 19 per cent on the previous year with companies from fifty-eight countries investing in the UK, up from fifty-four countries. The UK was also ranked as the primary FDI location in Europe by the *Financial Times*, through its fDi Intelligence Report 2012. What is hard to know for certain is how much of this investment flowing into Britain was dependent upon its membership of the European Union. Almost half of investors surveyed for UKTI in 2010 said that a factor in their decision to plough money into the British economy was the ability to serve the European market from a base in an English-speaking country.[335] But EU access was not given as the most important factor in their decision, with 90 per cent of respondents saying that their top motivation was servicing the UK market. Being close to customers and being able to access centres of expertise were also among the reasons given.

Several researchers have claimed that the formation of the

eurozone led to a modest drop in investment coming into the UK in the immediate aftermath of monetary union. One paper in the *Journal of Common Market Studies* in 2011 went as far as to suggest that investment from the US could be as much as 15 per cent lower than if the UK had joined the single currency.[336] But given the chaos in the eurozone since then, any assessment of the impact of not joining the euro would surely present a different picture now. The NIESR study of 2004 estimated that, twenty years after UK withdrawal from the EU, the stock of inward investment could be one-third lower for manufacturing and 10 per cent less for services. This would leave the UK GDP 2.25 per cent lower than otherwise expected, it said. But the Department for Business, Innovation and Skills remains uncertain as to what will happen to investment if Britain leaves the EU, as it showed in an internal restricted paper:

> Analysing foreign direct investment is complex as motives for investment vary from company to company. Access to the single market might be important for a horizontal [i.e. carrying out the same business as in the home country] but not necessarily for a vertical investor [i.e. production fragmented in different countries]. Similarly the single market may matter less for a technology seeking rather than a technology exploiting venture... Surveys suggest that access to the single market is not the sole reason for choosing the UK as a destination for investment. Being a global hub, having a good established business network, the English language and good international linkages were all cited as factors.

While it remains hard to tell just how important a role EU membership plays in attracting inward investment to Britain, one of the most important conditions for investors is stability – which covers many factors from the regulatory and fiscal environment to government, politics and the exchange rate. Stability would be in short supply, however, in the immediate aftermath of a decision to quit the European Union. It could take many years to establish reliable new market relationships, not to mention the potential for chaos in domestic politics and the macroeconomic environment. This could have a similarly disruptive effect on FDI as the banking and economic crisis of 2008 did. FDI peaked in 2007 in the UK at £196 billion, halved in 2008 and was down to £46 billion in 2010, slipping behind Belgium and Germany in Europe.[337] The UK seems to be bouncing back, but investment is attracted to growth, another factor in short supply across Europe. FDI would only recover properly once the UK's post-EU arrangements with all international partners were back on a solid footing.

Financial Services

The case for staying in the EU: The financial services market in Europe has not yet reached its true potential and only membership will ensure full access for British-based banks, funds and insurers. A strong British voice is needed at the table during discussions on often hostile proposed laws.

The case for leaving the EU: In the aftermath of the economic crisis, Brussels is churning out regulations that will emasculate the City of London and reduce its competitiveness, whether Britain is in the room or not. It is time to focus on markets elsewhere.

Britain has a 70 per cent market share of financial services in Europe and yet its control over the rules for the sector is diminishing – more and more regulation and supervision is being driven by the countries of the eurozone. At the time of writing, the balance of powers in the EU lay delicately between seventeen countries inside the single currency and the ten other EU states, including the UK, not in the euro (although three of the 'Outs', Bulgaria, Latvia and Lithuania, have pegged their currencies to it). From 2014, a change in voting weights agreed in the Lisbon Treaty will give the eurozone members an unbeatable qualified majority should they choose to vote together to push through measures. While Greece might leave the euro, and Britain and Denmark have opt-outs, all the others with the probable exception of Sweden are likely to join one day. In other words, the chips are being stacked against Britain getting its way on legislation, and on supervisory disputes, that bear upon an industry where it is a world leader. Most London-based banks and other financial companies believe that Britain should do all it can to maximise its leverage in Brussels and maintain a seat at the table to influence as far as possible the sector it knows best. 'I don't see that leaving makes it any easier, it will become more complex,' said Chris Cummings, CEO of TheCityUK, an organisation that promotes the City. 'We need to decide as a nation if we are part of Europe or not and to commit to the project if we are. The mixed signals that we are sending out damage our negotiating ability with other European member states.'

But while many banks forecast a drift away of staff and commercial activity from the City to Frankfurt or Paris if British voters decide to leave the EU, big European banks that employ hundreds of staff in London are likely to come under pressure to quit London whether or not the UK leaves the EU. That is because the likes of Deutsche Bank and BNP Paribas have their main wholesale activities for products like derivatives in London while using their retail branches in Europe to underwrite this. The proposed new supervisor at the European Central Bank (ECB) in Frankfurt could well insist that the entire operation is carried out within the jurisdiction of the planned eurozone banking union, forcing them to relocate away from the City. The ECB has already made a statement of its intent – not on banks but on clearing houses, another key part of City life. An ECB policy paper in 2011 demanded that clearing houses should be based in the eurozone if they handle more than 5 per cent of the market in a euro-denominated financial product. The British government immediately took the ECB to the European Court of Justice to protect the City, otherwise the ECB demands would force a partial relocation away from the City of LCH Clearnet, one of the world's largest clearing houses, which processes most of the share trading on the London Stock Exchange and operates a derivatives clearing service. As the *Financial Times* reported: 'British diplomats have long feared that Paris was leading attempts to rig market regulations in a bid to shift the centre of gravity for financial services from the City to the continent.'[338]

Could the City be better off, or at least undamaged, by a British departure from the EU? There are two schools of thought for what happens to the City in the event of a Brexit. One is the conventional wisdom that global companies, which chose London partly because it is the world's largest trading centre for the euro and has access to the single market, would relocate partially or mainly inside the EU. The other is that we have heard all this before at the launch of the euro in 2000, when there was a lot of paranoia fuelled by claims that the new currency would mean the demise of the City. It proved to be far from the case, with twice as many euros traded in London in 2012 as in the whole of the rest of the eurozone. Says one senior City figure:

> It is possible that London, being outside the EU, could still survive as an offshore financial centre in the way that Singapore is a major centre or Hong Kong is outside mainstream China. It is not clear if being outside would be the death knell for London, but it would certainly not be as beneficial as being on the inside.[339]

TheCityUK analysed the sources of the £61 billion tax take from the financial services industry in 2008–9 and identified three main groups in terms of who might stay or go if Britain quit the EU: the largest was the 'hard to impossible to leave'

category of domestic financial services providers, which generated £35 to 41 billion in tax; the second group were 'sticky
but not unmovable', mostly major international banks, who
contributed £17 to 22 billion in tax; the third category, with
'lowest hurdles to departure', consisted of highly paid foreign
nationals and international finance firms headquartered in the
City out of convenience, contributing £3 billion. 'We found that
the internationally mobile cohort accounts for up to £25 billion
of the tax take to the Treasury,' said Chris Cummings.

> The reason why these firms stay is not because of the domes-
> tic market of 63 million but because they want access to the
> European market of 440 million. Once an institution from
> the US, China or Japan decide they want to be in Europe, the
> question is, where is the best place to be based. That comes down
> to a fight between Paris, Frankfurt and London. The time zone,
> language, skills base and cluster factor of all these firms here
> benefit the City. There also needs to be a settlement currency –
> that could be sterling but mostly it is going to be the euro, so we
> need to be inside the trading bloc. If we are outside we have less
> capacity and liquidity.

TheCityUK believes Britain is better off staying inside the single
market for financial services and this is 'nothing to do with
politics, simply the money', based on research of the factors
that keep international companies in the UK. It also believes
that full EU membership and participation in decision-making
is important for the future of the sector:

> We have heard from many in businesses in the member states
> that they want the UK to be at the table because we provide the
> liberal economics view that other member states do not bring
> with them. It is not part of their culture. If we were outside the
> EU, we would have to renegotiate a right of access based on
> market access treaties, trying to have something akin to the

World Trade Organisation's Most Favoured Nation Status. Of course, it is a perfectly logical thing to talk about but, in my view, if we have just left that trading bloc, trying to then re-enter on grounds at least equal as we enjoyed would be hard because inevitably individuals would be bruised.

The UK's financial sector is set for a challenging period vis-à-vis Brussels whether voters decide to keep the country fully engaged in the EU or not. British officials and MEPs have been able to restrain the more aggressive and punitive nature of EU legislation on financial services from their positions inside the system. As senior MEP Sharon Bowles, who chairs the European Parliament economic and monetary affairs committee, told the Liberal Democrat conference in 2012:

> Whether fairly or not, and it is probably a bit of both, the rest of Europe blames the City for the financial crisis and its consequences... Just as everyone now wants to be tough on big banks that made epic mistakes, so too the rest of Europe wants to be tough on a big financial centre and its regulators, that could and did spread risk through the single market to them.

There is no escape, in the EU or out, given the move towards a global regulatory environment where all players increasingly have to follow international standards such as the Basel Accords on banking and G20 agreements on issues like tax havens. But despite the welter of new EU regulations spawned by the economic crisis and designed to curb the industry, from bankers' pay to institutional capital requirements, leaving the EU causes the greater headache for the City because of the uncertainty of Britain's future relationship with the continent and the loss of any kind of control over its future actions.

Transport
The case for staying in the EU: Low-cost airlines rely on internal

EU liberalisation measures to operate cheap flights to the continent; the EU's ambitious transport White Paper will transform European travel by 2050 into a fully integrated low-carbon system that facilitates more trade and tourism.

The case for leaving the EU: Foreign lorries could be charged to use British roads, while 60-tonne 'superlorries' could be permanently blocked and a centralised Common European Transport Area avoided.

Aviation safety and diversity, in particular the achievement of low-cost airlines in bringing affordable travel to millions of people, are inconvenient success stories for those who believe that nothing good ever came of the European Union. The question faced in an in/out referendum looking to the future would be whether these achievements are so entrenched that they would still be available to passengers if Britain voted to leave the EU. The answer is that they probably would be, but not without a period of turbulence that would present British negotiators with tough challenges to try and cling on to the status quo in the aviation sector. The withdrawalist MEP David Campbell Bannerman has suggested that there are many benefits to be had in transport from leaving the EU, including:

> Britain could end EU moves to centralise control of transport within a Common European Transport Area and to force 'super-lorries' onto UK roads (60 tonne trucks at 82 feet long). Britain could require foreign lorries to pay a Swiss-style vignette to use British roads (illegal under EU rules), enforce British safety standards on vehicles, hold down rail prices, liberalise ports regulation and take back national control of aviation safety.[340]

These arguments do not bear much scrutiny. Transport is one field where the EU can claim to have made great strides, largely because this is a policy area which by definition requires impeccable international safety standards and seamless cross-border cooperation.

The spectre of 'superlorries' being forced onto British roads is a classic scare story based on a report written in 2009 for the European Commission which supported the use of LHVs (longer, heavier vehicles). The British government carried out its own review which reported in 2011 and allowed an extension of lorries by up to two further metres but no extra weight-carrying capacity. 'In 2006, DfT commissioned research into the potential effects of longer, heavier vehicles (LHVs) including longer semi-trailers,' the report said.

> The research completed in 2008 and highlighted a number of drawbacks that make the introduction of significantly longer and heavier vehicles (i.e. typically 25.25 metres long) – those beyond the existing limits of 18.75 metres length and 44 tonnes gross vehicle weight (GVW) – impractical on either a permanent or a trial basis in the UK. Consequently, the Government has ruled out the introduction of this type of LHV for the foreseeable future.[341]

Although the European Commission did produce a report on LHVs, it decided to leave the decision on whether to allow longer or heavier trucks onto roads entirely in national hands. So while Sweden and Finland decided to authorise LHVs, and the Dutch, Danish and Germans are holding trials, the UK government has ruled them out.

The UK does not need to leave the EU to be able to charge foreign lorries a Swiss-style vignette tax to use British roads, as it is not illegal under EU rules. Distance-based charges or vignettes for trucks are used in at least nine EU member nations already, including Austria, France and Germany. Moreover the Swiss charges apply equally to local as well as foreign lorries. If they did not, the EU would seek redress for discrimination against its hauliers from the twenty-seven member states. 'If the UK, in the event that it was outside the EU, decided to introduce legislation which discriminates against foreigners, it would expose itself to the risk of countervailing measures from the EU member states, which could end up being very costly for British hauliers,' a source at the European Commission transport directorate said. The UK has not made use of its ability to charge lorries to use its roads partly because of resistance from the domestic haulage industry, which would also have to pay the tax.

In answer to Campbell Bannerman's other claims, roadworthiness testing is covered by an EU directive which applies a minimum standard, allowing national flexibility to increase test frequency and items covered, while certain categories of vehicles can be exempted. There is no EU legislation which regulates prices for rail tickets or freight services. The oversight of aviation safety in British airspace remains under national competence but the UK authorities decided several decades ago to follow common rules on aviation safety at international and European level, as a condition for mutual recognition by other states.

What would become of the low-cost airlines if Britain left the EU? EasyJet, the Luton-based carrier, is worried about the prospect. Only EU-based companies can operate inside the area, which explains why no American low-cost airlines have broken into the market. (The US is similarly restrictive about who operates flights in its jurisdiction). 'For us, being part of the EU "open skies" agreement enables us as a British-based business to operate across all its states,' said Paul Moore, easyJet's communications director.[342]

> If that was to be taken away, I suspect we might end up with two companies – easyJet inside Europe and easyJet with a separate air licence for the UK. One does not want to imagine how complicated that would be. We have got a relatively simple business model at the moment and any change that would require

us to split into separate companies would pose potentially quite significant issues.

The EU is developing the European Common Aviation Area (ECAA), a series of bilateral agreements with ten neighbouring countries including Norway, Iceland and Albania, to allow any company from participating countries to fly anywhere inside the common zone. Switzerland and Turkey are keen to join but the fact they are still outside shows that it would not necessarily be straightforward for UK operators following a 'Brexit'. Should the UK vote in a referendum to leave the EU, a top priority would be to negotiate staying inside the ECAA to preserve the range of air travel options – and low prices – currently enjoyed.

Farming

The case for staying in the EU: British farmers need to remain in the same regime of subsidies, tariffs and production standards as their continental peers or risk losing market share to them; losing access to the single market would damage exports.

The case for leaving the EU: Britain would stop subsidising European competitors, save billions of pounds of taxpayers' money and be free to modernise British farm support; cutting regulation would help bring down costs to the consumer.

At first glance, the case for leaving the European Union's expensive and complicated system of agricultural protection seems unanswerable. The EU has reformed its Common Agricultural Policy over the years to refocus on direct payments to farmers and on rewards for environmental measures, rather than bulk buying to prop up sales, but farming still accounted for 40 per cent of the EU budget in 2012. That amounted to £4.74 billion of the UK's annual gross contribution to Brussels, of which £3.3 billion was returned back and shared between nearly 200,000 farmers in the UK. It means that the net yearly amount given by the British government to other European farmers was £1.44 billion (or nearly £4 million a day). UKIP policy seems simple and sensible – pay British farmers the same amount in subsidies that they currently receive from the EU and then 'use labelling and advertising campaigns to promote British produce and fairer food prices. This will replace the need for many subsidies.'[343] In his pamphlet on leaving the EU, Campbell Bannerman said: 'Food prices are increased through requirements to take in expensive French agricultural produce and by the undermining of British farming. The cost of excessive red tape also feeds through to consumer prices across the board, and a reduction in red tape will bring price cuts over time.'[344] Among other irritations, leaving the EU would relieve farmers of the expensive requirement to electronically identify (EID) their sheep; it would also protect beef farmers from the proposed EU free trade agreement with the Mercosur countries of South America which, if agreed, is likely to see cheap beef exports threaten to put many domestic producers out of business. On top of all that, another reform of the CAP is under way and due to be completed by 2014 with proposals to raise the amount of direct payments given to farmers for environmental reasons to 30 per cent; forcing farmers to grow at least three crops on their land 'to move away from destructive monocultures'; and ordering farmers to leave 7 per cent of all farmland uncultivated to allow wildlife to develop.

The Environment, Food and Rural Affairs Select Committee of MPs warned that the changes would reduce food production and harm the environment. Anne McIntosh MP, the chair, said:

The Commission's proposals to green the CAP would hurt UK farmers, consumers and our countryside. They will reduce food security by taking land out of production and are likely to impact badly on our environment. It is a nonsense to think that farmers from Finland to Sicily should be tied to the same narrow prescriptive rules. One-size-fits-all regulation cannot work across the range of environments found in Europe.

Britain has consistently pushed for fundamental reform of the EU's farming system but time after time the reforms have disappointed, not least because the UK's larger farms require a different approach to the smaller and more traditional continental model. Surely, as with fisheries management, it would be better to withdraw from the EU and its CAP and develop a proper BAP?

The picture, of course, is more complicated than it seems at first glance. The primary reason why British farmers are extremely wary of jumping on the UKIP bandwagon is another by-product of UK European policy over the years – the simple mistrust of politicians' promises and reassurances. 'It is completely unrealistic in the current financial climate or in a future scenario to assume that the UK government would continue to provide financial support to UK farmers at the same level as the CAP,' said Tom Hind, director of corporate affairs at the National Farmers Union. 'UK policy under different governments has been to reduce direct payments to farmers.' Such a move would not only leave farmers worse off but also at a competitive disadvantage to their heavily subsidised continental rivals.

> We would like to maintain fair and equal treatment. The UK is a net importer of farm goods from the EU, therefore if we reduce the level of support to farmers in the UK because of a unilateral decision we would put our farms at a massive competitive disadvantage. We would want cast-iron and credible assurances that the interests of UK farmers would be protected and treated on the same basis as competitors in the EU.

Unwittingly, Hind went to the heart of the problem with trusting politicians' promises in his echo of Cameron's unmet 'cast-iron' guarantee of a referendum on the Lisbon Treaty.

Farmers know that despite all the form-filling and other red tape, they would probably receive less cash support outside the EU. Besides this, any farmers exporting to countries in the EU would still have to meet the Union's sanitary and phytosanitary (plant health) requirements, without the UK being able to sit on the committees that determine the standards. The importance of being part of the single market's system of setting and enforcing hygiene requirements was shown after the BSE crisis, when France initially refused to accept British beef following the partial lifting of the three-year ban and only agreed to take it three more years later in 2002 after it was taken to the European Court of Justice. Many Commonwealth countries including Australia, Canada, India and Pakistan are still refusing to take British beef products on sanitary grounds.

UKIP farm policy could have adverse effects on British farmers. Unless handled carefully, a more liberalised independent UK food regime could let in cheap foreign exports that put domestic farmers out of business. The UKIP approach of an aggressive labelling policy would promote high-quality British produce. But if a free trade agreement was struck with Mercosur by either the EU or a non-EU Britain, South American meat reared with lower environmental or animal welfare standards could undercut and undermine the home-grown alternative. One of UKIP's aims is to reduce the cost of the weekly shop and families on a tight budget are not always likely to be too fussy about livestock conditions in Brazil when confronted with cheaper meat alongside well-labelled but more expensive British fare.

The reason why Britain's exporting farmers would still want access to the EU's single market under equal terms with their competitors becomes clear after a look at the tariffs applied to non-EU produce by Brussels. The tariff rate for bovine carcases or half carcases is 12.8 per cent plus €176.8 per 100kg. For ovine carcases and half carcases the rate is 12.8 per cent plus €171.3 per 100kg. While the UK is a net importer of beef and pork from the EU, it has a thriving sheep meat export industry thanks to production costs which are lower than in France. But export quality lambs from the UK would face a total level of duty close to 40 per cent under the EU's common external tariff, as currently applied to countries like the USA. Clearly, there would be nothing that French farmers would relish more than for the EU, having bid farewell to the UK, to slap these kinds of taxes on British sheep meat. All this means that British negotiators will face a tough job, in the event of a referendum decision to leave the EU, to achieve a free trade agreement between Britain and the EU which keeps tariffs to a minimum, with the status quo being the ideal situation for exporting farmers. Any new system of tariffs will also see EU-sourced produce rise in price for British consumers.

Moreover, as in most other sectors, Britain's departure from the EU would remove a liberalising voice from around the table in Brussels, albeit CAP reform has been extremely hard fought and painfully slow over the years. The farming issue boils down to big savings for the taxpayer and potential reductions at the checkout on the weekly shop for consumers, versus a likely twin assault on the livelihoods of British farmers through lower government subsidies and less protection from global competition. Ironically, a referendum vote to claim back British sovereignty from Brussels will probably mean that more imports are needed to make up for the eventual reduction in UK farming capacity, even as consumers benefit.

Immigration

The case for staying in the EU: Member states of the EU provide a rich source of labour when the British economy needs it, and when it does not, many go back home. The quid pro quo is the right for British citizens to live and work freely across Europe.

The case for leaving the EU: Britain would regain full control over who crosses its borders to live, study and work. The UK would save on the cost of welfare payments to EU migrants if it restricted entry and that would free up more jobs for British workers.

The right of all EU citizens to travel freely to other member states for up to three months at a time and indefinitely if they have a job or declare themselves self-employed is one of the 'four freedoms' that underpin the single market. A million Brits were resident in other EU nations in 2010, including many retirees in Spain who were able to receive their UK pension through the local post office or bank. On the other hand, 27 per cent of net immigration into the UK is from EU nationals whom the government is powerless to stop at the border.[345] The embarrassing under-estimation of the numbers of eastern Europeans thought likely to settle in the UK, after Poland joined with nine other countries in 2004, fuelled a backlash against the freedom of movement that led to temporary restrictions on Bulgarians and Romanians after their countries joined in 2007. They will only enjoy the same freedoms from 2014. But this did not satisfy some critics on the right who believe that regaining full control over immigration is one of the key benefits of leaving the EU. The problem with this approach is that any measures brought in by Britain after withdrawal are likely to be reciprocated. Although the UK has not joined the Schengen system of passport-free travel on the continent, it has opted into the Dublin Convention, an EU system to return asylum-seekers to the country where they first entered the Schengen zone (often a southern border country such as Italy or Greece), which benefits Britain as a popular destination country.

Britain only has the power to control non-EU immigration, which is why there are different queues at airports and ports for EU and non-EU arrivals, a system criticised by supporters of the Commonwealth for discriminating against travellers who often have family ties but must go through a visa application process. The British population has surged in recent years with some of the blame put on the EU free movement system. This led the coalition government to carry out the first analysis of welfare benefit recipients by national origin, published in January 2012, which found that working-age benefits were claimed by 5.5 million Britons and 371,000 non-UK nationals, of whom 113,300 were from the EU and EEA (i.e. Norway, Iceland and Liechtenstein, who have the same rights as EU nationals), meaning that 31 per cent of foreign claimants of benefits (mainly Jobseeker's Allowance and incapacity benefits) were Europeans. EU nations were the source of six of the top twenty foreign claimants by origin, a list topped by Pakistan, Somalia and India, with Ireland in fourth place, Poland in seventh and Portugal in ninth.[346] Clearly Europe is not the main source of immigrant benefit claims in the UK and any calculation of the value should bear in mind the reciprocal access to benefits for British migrants in EU countries – the same goes for access to healthcare with the European Health Insurance Card, which provides basic free treatment.

'Leaving the EU will empower Britain to adopt a more balanced and more tightly controlled immigration policy, similar to the Australian visa-based system,' said Campbell Bannerman, who argues that leaving the EU will mean better controls over 'criminal elements' coming into the UK.

This visa system could set down the number of visas available according to UK needs and the ability of public services, housing and infrastructure on a very crowded island to cope. It is likely that certain EU nation states will enjoy visa waiver schemes (in reality there is less need for visas with nations with comparative economic profiles such as France, Germany and Holland, the biggest inflows have been from former Communist states).[347]

While not impossible legally (the USA excludes Bulgarians and Romanians from its visa waiver programme) British relations with its neighbours could be strained by selective visa waivers. Moreover, the stricter the system applied for Europeans to settle and work in the UK, the more difficult it will become in turn for Brits aboard. If Britons were treated like Americans or Australians by the authorities in Spain, for example, it would be much harder to meet requirements for work visas. Non-EU nationals have to complete much more paperwork to qualify for residency in EU countries, often including criminal record checks and certificates of tax status, a bureaucratic challenge that extends to many things currently taken for granted, such as the mutual driving licence recognition between EU countries whereas non-EU residents in Spain have to take lessons and pass the country's driving test.

Do EU immigrants take British jobs? Overall UK unemployment did rise shortly after the 2004 accession of ten new member states and the arrival of the notorious Polish plumber and his eastern European colleagues, but a direct link is hard to prove. An OECD report concluded that

> an increase in the share of immigrants in the labour force increases unemployment of natives, but this impact is temporary and vanishes between four and nine years after the shock. Beyond this transitory period, the level of the share of immigrants in the labour force does not influence significantly natives' unemployment.

Open Europe, in a study on the freedom of movement, said that

> as [eastern European] migrants are overwhelmingly concentrated in low-skilled sectors, their impact on the native UK population is likely to be concentrated in this section of the labour market. It could be argued that UK natives might have filled these lower skilled jobs following unemployment, had they not already been taken up by [migrants], or that younger workers have faced greater barriers to entering the labour market.[348]

But it added that job creation was not stifled 'as over a long time frame total UK employment has increased'.

The failure to end the long-term UK structural unemployment level of 1.5 million people was a British problem and not necessarily the fault of immigrants, Open Europe concluded.

> The UK economy had a good record in creating jobs but these have tended to be filled by EU and non-EU migrants even as the number of UK natives employed decreased. UK-born unemployment has remained stubbornly over 1.5 million for most of the last decade, despite at least 3 million jobs being created.

Chris Grayling, Employment Minister in 2010, seemed to concur with the Open Europe conclusion when he said: 'You could argue that immigration filled the economic gap that allowed us as a country to ignore deeper problems within our own society... Businesses brought in people while we ignored the opportunity to motivate our own citizens – many of whom remain stuck in a welfare dependency trap.'[349] The overall conclusion must be that managed immigration is better for Britain than open borders, but that imposing new restrictions on arrivals from the EU could well be counterproductive. Queues at arrival points will be longer under a system which offers visa-free access to selected European countries only, while Brits who want to live and work on the continent will find that the baffling bureaucracy of other countries only gets worse the more that Britain attempts to insulate itself from the world.

Fishing

The case for staying in the EU: After years of mismanagement, the Common Fisheries Policy is finally being revamped to end the discarding of unwanted caught fish and devolve some powers back to national authorities.

The case for leaving the EU: Britain could assume full control over its territorial waters, which extend to 200 nautical miles from the coast, and implement a sustainable fishing policy based on scientific advice rather than the political priorities responsible for unrealistic quotas that are destroying fish stocks.

Rapacious over-fishing and the hugely wasteful dumping at sea of around a million tonnes of dead or dying edible fish every year have rightly brought the EU's Common Fisheries Policy into complete disrepute. Species that were once plentiful have all but disappeared from European waters as, year-in and year-out, the annual setting of quotas carried out each December in Brussels has flagrantly ignored scientific advice and continued to allow the over-exploitation of the seas. The final catch allowances are set by politicians from the EU nations, with moves towards ten-year plans for individual species often cynically delayed by member states. Cod, blue-fin tuna and anchovy have almost been fished to extinction, while half of all fish caught in the North Sea are thrown back by fishermen because of strict quotas on what can be landed or to make room for more lucrative fish on the boat within their total allowable catch. While the size of the fleet is in long-term decline, with Britain having 6,763 fishing vessels in 2007 compared to 8,458 ten years earlier, campaign groups argue for a 40 per cent cut in the EU's 90,000 vessels. The European Commission has said that 88 per cent of EU stocks are over-fished, compared with only 25 per cent worldwide.[350] In 2008, 93 per cent of cod was caught before the fish were mature enough to reproduce, but then even higher quotas were set by ministers for the following year. Given the industrial scale of mismanagement, it is hardly surprising that fishing is one policy area repeatedly subject to British demands for a return of national sovereignty. Leaving the EU would give Britain legal control back over its territorial waters, known as the Exclusive Economic Zone, stretching out for 200 nautical miles. While it sounds extremely tempting, once again things are rather more complicated.

One of the troubles with fish is that they do not observe international boundaries. Mackerel for example start off in the Bay of Biscay, pass through British and Irish waters on their way towards Iceland, then swim back down through Norwegian territory and again into British waters on their return journey. Reciprocal agreements with other jurisdictions and in international waters through several international bodies are the order of the day – and this would become the task of British negotiators rather than the European Commission in the event of leaving the EU. Some argue that the UK might as well remain inside the EU because it would give British ministers a seat at the more powerful European table where decisions are made that affect stock levels for everyone in the North Atlantic and North Sea. But the power to manage national waters would bring real benefits such as enabling the UK to ban so-called discards and follow scientific advice on annual catch limits to rebuild stocks, as Norway did with great success, but which the EU routinely ignores.

A glimmer of hope for the future of fishing has emerged at the EU level, however, with proposals in 2011 to phase out discards, moving to an all-out ban in 2016, combined with more devolved national management. The rethink followed intense campaigning, including by the chef Hugh Fearnley-Whittingstall. But at the time of writing, the negotiations were delicately poised. Members of the European Commission were seeking to water down the regionalisation proposals, with fingers being pointed at the French Commissioner, Michel Barnier, for wanting to retain as much central control as possible. The reason? Hand back powers from the Common Fisheries Policy and, the next thing you know, member states will want more control over farming – and the Common Agricultural Policy remains as sacred to Paris as the rebate is to the British. Before fishing policy is considered as a reason to leave the EU by the UK, it would make sense to see how the latest reform of the CFP pans out by the final deadline of 1 January 2014, although the prospect of truly radical reform is receding.

Education

The case for staying in the EU: British university undergraduates can study in any EU member state for the same course fees as a national of that country, often also receiving maintenance grants.

The case for leaving the EU: British universities can charge much higher international fees for students from the EU who at the moment pay UK fee rates.

Universities across the EU are increasingly introducing undergraduate courses in English to attract British students put off by the steep rise in course fees, which saw domestic institutions able to charge up to £9,000 a year from 2012. Universities in Denmark and Sweden do not charge undergraduates for tuition while those in the Netherlands have a much lower fee, with the University of Maastricht, for example, staging a recruitment drive for British students for courses priced at €1,771 a year. The impact of the changing rate of British course fees on student mobility has yet to be fully felt, with the latest OECD figures dating from 2009 and showing only 22,000 UK students studying full-time in the EU (as opposed to spending just a year abroad as part of their UK-based course), a figure which has the potential to rise sharply. The numbers of EU students in British institutions had been rising, from 125,045 in the 2009–10 academic year to 130,120 in 2010–11. After the steep rise in fees, new entrants from the EU in 2012 were down by 13.7 per cent, according to an initial assessment by the Universities and Colleges Admissions Service.[351] Nevertheless, Britain imports many more students from the EU than it exports, a fact which has led eurosceptics to point out that there would be a large net income gain if UK institutions were able to charge full international fees. With classroom-based degrees costing one third more for non-EU students and medical courses three times as much, there could be a considerable windfall for UK universities in the event of British EU withdrawal – provided that the higher fees did not in turn put the European students off from coming to the UK in the first place. EU countries could also then apply international rates to British students, reducing their appeal, although in many cases they would still be cheaper than the UK fee – Maastricht University's tuition costs for non-EU students are €8,500 a year.

The EU's level playing field for undergraduate fees also means that EU students can access government-subsidised support from the Student Loan Company. But the recovery of these loans is causing growing concern. The amount of money owed by European graduates increased from £167 million in 2009 to £239 million in 2012, with those classed as 'in arrears' or 'not currently repaying – further information being sought' owing approximately £75 million. Loans would no longer have to be provided from the SLC to EU students if the UK withdrew from the Union.

Despite fears to the contrary, a British departure from the EU need not bring an end to Erasmus, a popular scheme for student and staff placements in European universities. Erasmus provides grants for undergraduate placements of three to twelve months. Almost 200,000 British students have been abroad on the Erasmus programme since it began in 1987, with 12,833 receiving an average monthly allowance of just under €400 each from the EU in 2010–11. British universities accept around twice as many students as they send to Europe, a total of 24,474 in 2010–11. But several non-EU countries have already joined Erasmus by paying a membership fee, including Turkey and Switzerland. So Britain could continue its involvement in the scheme from outside the EU.

Peace

The case for staying in the EU: Membership of the EU has kept the peace between historic foes who warred for centuries, earning the organisation the Nobel Peace Prize; their economic cooperation and interdependency will prevent future conflict; Britain's support is vital.

The case for leaving the EU: The peace was primarily kept by NATO, which the UK has no intention of leaving; it depends in future upon liberal democracies thriving across Europe, not on British membership of the EU.

When EEC negotiators arrived to broker the agreement that ended the brief Slovenian war of independence in 1991, one of those present, a Luxembourg Foreign Minister by the unfortunate name of Jacques Poos, famously declared that 'the hour of Europe has dawned'. It hadn't, sadly, and it eventually took NATO bombs and American diplomacy to bring the bloody Yugoslav conflict to an end four years later following the deaths of more than 100,000 people. While Ronald Reagan and Margaret Thatcher arguably did more to encourage Solidarity to break the stranglehold of Communism in Poland than Gaston Thorn or Jacques Delors, the Brussels-based club has, however, succeeded in its primary objective of keeping the peace between France and Germany, who have fought each other three times since 1870 with increasingly terrible consequences. Liberal democracies tend not to go to war with each other, and the EU has also acted to help entrench democracy in the former dictatorships and downtrodden nations of southern, central and eastern Europe as they have emerged from darkness. The job is not yet done, with Bosnia and Kosovo still mired in tense stand-offs with Serbia on the EU's borders, and Cyprus remaining divided in a frozen conflict with Turkey despite the island's EU membership. The ongoing need for Brussels to act as a bulwark for democratic values even inside the EU was demonstrated as recently as 2011, following the Hungarian government's changes to the constitution which led to legal action from the European Commission in an attempt to preserve key freedoms for the central bank, judiciary and the media.

Five reasons were given for the award of the Nobel Peace Prize to the EU in 2012: Franco-German reconciliation after the Second World War; support for new democracies in Greece, Portugal and Spain in the 1980s; support for former Communist states in the 1990s; modernisation of Turkey; and peace-building in the western Balkans. What would British withdrawal mean for the peace project? Would it trigger a resurgence of nationalism so strong that the EU fractured into independent, aggressive and warring nation states? Given the enormous sums of money transferred within the EU from the rich countries to the poor, it seems unlikely that any of the newer members where democracy is most fragile would follow Britain's example and walk away, forfeiting all those billions of euros. The biggest recent danger to the peace among and within member states has, in fact, been the increasingly bitter struggle to save the euro, a self-inflicted torment that will unfold with or without UK membership of the EU. Britain has not initiated armed conflict in mainland Europe since the fourth Anglo-Dutch War of 1780. It will never be the instigator of continental war again. The EU has nothing to fear from an independent Britain apart from the withdrawal of its membership fee, its liberalising influence and a certain loss of prestige. It will not trigger a stampede towards the exit door. While the leaders of France, Germany and Italy constantly have to claim the irreversibility of the single currency and the solidarity of the eurozone to maintain the confidence of the markets in their own economies, there is no such urgency to appease financiers by keeping a recalcitrant nation like Britain in the EU. The UK will continue to support the European Union from the outside, to team up on important foreign policy campaigns such as sanctions on Iran or Syria, and to pursue its bilateral defence partnership with France, the EU's only other significant military power, which is already taking place outside the Brussels structures.

The study of costs and benefits by the Centre for Economic Policy Research published in 2008 managed a parting shot at those who maintain that the greatest achievement of the

European Union was not trade or a rise in GDP but a guarantee of peace for more than sixty years.

> However plausible this view may have seemed to a generation that had lived through two world wars, it ignores another political factor that, on its own, would almost certainly have made for West European cooperation even in the absence of economic integration efforts, namely the Cold War. The threat of a communist take-over (particularly felt in the 1950s in countries such as France and Italy), would surely have made otherwise querulous nations close ranks, all the more so given America's pre-eminent role in aiding and cajoling its much poorer and weaker European partners. Peace in post-war Europe owes almost certainly much more to Stalin (and Eisenhower) than it does to Monnet or Schuman.[352]

While this tends to belittle the EU's core achievement of binding France and Germany together through economic and political structures, beginning with the Coal and Steel Community of 1952, the Cold War did cause western European nations to unite in defence of their borders through NATO. Europeans often choose to overlook the American role in repairing and unifying the western part of the continent through the post-war European Recovery Programme, known as the Marshall Plan, which pumped 5 per cent of US GDP (then $13 billion) into rebuilding seventeen European countries. The US was a strong agitator for British membership of the EEC at a time when war with the Soviet Union was a possibility. Today the US focus is on maintaining Turkey on a western path and the UK has played a key role in keeping Ankara's membership dreams alive. The loss of such a powerful supporter for Turkish entry into the EU could be the main long-term threat to European peace that arises from a British withdrawal. It would kill off any lingering hopes of full membership for Turkey and EU diplomats would be well advised to offer a viable form of associate membership or watch Turkey drift into forming a rival power bloc in the east as its economic strength grows.

Reactions to the Nobel Peace Prize in October 2012 spoke volumes about the way the EU has become viewed around Europe. In the corridors of the European Commission headquarters in Brussels there were high-fives between eurocrats who at last felt vindicated, while in the major continental capitals there was relief at a much-needed boost in a time of economic and institutional turmoil. Chancellor Angela Merkel convened an immediate press conference and called it 'a wonderful decision'. In the UK there was mostly derision and scorn. Britain could not quite bring itself to share Europe's proud moment, with not a peep out of senior government ministers in London despite fulsome statements of self-congratulation around the continent. The UK felt less than ever part of the club amid growing signs that a parting of the ways was becoming inevitable – just two days later the Sunday newspapers splashed with reports of another Cabinet minister who would vote to leave the EU unless powers were returned to Westminster. It showed again that the EU's achievements were too easily overlooked in the UK, lost among the myriad annoyances that had sapped enthusiasm for a noble cause. Much in the same way as Brussels is fond of creating and awarding its own prizes, the Nobel medal was used by the EU to validate its existence, justify its methods and inspire further integration. The ailing octogenarian Helmut Kohl celebrated by saying: 'I am proud and I wish for God's blessing for us on our further path to a united Europe.' If only the prize could have been seen as the cue to shift focus away from vainglorious projects – attempts to conquer space or create a European Public Prosecutor – and instead consolidate the twin founding goals of peace and prosperity, Britain and the EU might then have been able to rebuild their common ground. But even a Nobel Peace Prize could not salvage the relationship.

For some people, the decision on whether to give Britain another forty years of EU membership will be made on gut feeling. Years of political strife, unwanted changes to national life and adverse media coverage have seemingly created an unstoppable momentum towards British exit. At the same time, most of our European allies are hurtling away from us, fixated on plans to save the single currency. Many voters, however, even if they come to the same conclusion, will at least want to know a little more about the true impact of departing – and indeed of staying in. Neither the dwindling band of Britain's pro-Europeans nor the growing ranks of withdrawalists have yet produced balanced, comprehensive and detailed manifestos for their respective causes. In her speech to the House of Lords in March 2011, Baroness Williams invoked three great achievements of the EU – peace, democracy in central and eastern Europe and aid to poorer countries. While undoubtedly very important, they all seemed rather remote from the day-to-day concerns of a country mired in recession and a continent facing its worst unemployment crisis for a generation. Peace, as incredible as it may seem to the generation that lived through the war and its immediate aftermath, has been banked and taken for granted by those looking for more immediate benefits from the EU membership fee. Peace, moreover, no longer requires UK membership. Williams went on to suggest several reasons for continued British involvement – climate change and energy security, international organised crime and relationships with China and India – all of which the EU can and will help with. But again, they seemed somewhat distant from daily concerns, reflecting the pro-Europeans' persistent failure to mount a convincing argument for continuing in the club they cherish so dearly.

Each voter will have his or her own reasons for wanting to stick with Brussels or withdraw from the European project. It could be the progressive pooling of sovereignty, explored in Chapters 1 and 2, or the economic balance sheet after consideration of what the EU does with the £32 million a day it receives from Britain, as discussed in Chapter 3. It could be concern at the seemingly unstoppable momentum towards ever closer union, seen through the prism of forty years of developments that were mainly not foreseen by the last British voters to cast their ballot on the EEC in 1975. Here is where the overlapping layers of EU benefits, obligations and responsibilities come into play. What relative level of importance should be given to low-cost airfares, the ease of retiring abroad, the waste of a million tonnes of fish every year, the many billions of pounds redistributed to Spain and Greece, or the importance of keeping Turkey facing west? How to balance the prospect of 'more Europe' outlined in Chapter 4 with the potential for trade as a non-aligned nation covered in Chapter 7? Only the kind of intense national debate spurred by a referendum campaign could really explore and weigh all these issues – if it manages to avoid becoming a proxy vote on the government of the day. There are aspects of EU influence that are widely appreciated, sometimes unwittingly, and there are others that have caused such annoyance that many find the idea of another forty years' membership intolerable. The youngest person eligible to vote in the 1975 referendum was over fifty-five years of age by the end of 2012. Around thirty-four million British voters have not had a direct democratic say on the European question. Referenda are, quite rightly, highly exceptional in British democratic life. But the EU, because of the way its measures bind future parliaments to such a range of impacts like no kind of Westminster-made law, is uniquely appropriate to be judged by this rare mechanism.

NINE

Looking Back

The European Union is not just some sort of deal to be reduced to the lowest common denominator. It is a precious thing. It is about our history, our values, our shared identity and our joint place in the world... I believe in the European Union. I'm a Unionist head, heart and soul. I believe that Britain, France, Germany and Spain are stronger together than they would ever be apart... I am not just proud of the Union because it is useful. I am proud because it shapes and strengthens us all.
– David Cameron*
*Not exactly what he said

The year is 2023. Queen Elizabeth is in the seventy-first year of her record-breaking reign, Romeo Beckham has been chosen for the England football team and the British government has just applied to join the North American Free Trade Agreement. Looking back on the recent history of Britain's tumultuous and dysfunctional relationship with its closest neighbours in Europe, it is remarkable just how clear it seems from this distance that the UK was drifting inexorably away from Brussels for years before the final moment of departure. Fifty years on from Britain joining the club of European nations, there would be no golden anniversary celebration. The EU referendum of 2017 brought an end to British membership of an organisation that it had effectively been leaving ever since John Major declared 'Game, set and match' over the Maastricht

Treaty. He kept the country out of the currency that would eventually define the closer European Federation proposed by European Commission President José Manuel Barroso in 2014 and which, frankly, scared most British voters rigid. On the other hand, continental irritation at Britain's growing insularity, which first surfaced after David Cameron's wielding of his veto in December 2011, grew into open animosity as his government sought to use the Federation treaty negotiation to try and claw back as much control as it could from Brussels. Time and again British diplomats were treated to table-banging harangues from eurocrats and eurozone politicians who refused to concede unilateral powers to one country for the purpose of, as they saw it, distorting the single market in its favour by allowing derogations from hard-fought social protections. Brussels breathed a collective sigh of relief when British attempts to repatriate powers had to be halted for the 2015 general election campaign but it just proved a brief respite in the country's drift towards the exit door.

David Cameron, of course, could never quite bring himself to say the quotation attributed to him at the start of this chapter. While he believed that British membership of the EU was in the national interest, his overriding feeling about the European question was the fervent desire that it would just go away. What Cameron actually said, back in February 2012, was a passionate defence of the United Kingdom, rather than the European Union, in the context of the looming Scottish independence referendum. Here are his actual words, from a speech he gave in Edinburgh, opposing the push for Scotland's independence:

> The United Kingdom is not just some sort of deal, to be reduced to the lowest common denominator. It is a precious thing. It is about our history, our values, our shared identity and our joint place in the world... I believe in the United Kingdom. I'm a Unionist head, heart and soul. I believe that England, Scotland, Wales and Northern Ireland are stronger together than they

would ever be apart… I am not just proud of the Union because it is useful. I am proud because it shapes and strengthens us all.[353]

Cameron's passionate defence of the UK exuded a depth of feeling in every sentence that neither he nor most other leading British politicians of his era could ever truly evoke about Brussels. The pro-Europeans had become apologetic pragmatists, forced to admit that the EU was far from perfect, but would have to be invented if it did not exist to protect against rather abstract fears such as climate change, an energy crisis or China. It was not a very exciting or convincing argument for continued British membership. Scotland, in comparison, really seemed to matter to Cameron. 'It is time to speak out, whatever the consequences, because something very special is in danger,' he continued in his defence of the United Kingdom against secessionist Scots. 'To me, this is not some issue of policy or strategy or calculation… Our shared home is under threat and everyone who cares about it needs to speak out.' Brussels had probably never been referred to in Britain as 'precious' and it was rarely considered 'very special'. It was, in fact, more of a 'policy or strategy or calculation' than something to be proud of. Voting on Scotland's future touched the soul. Voting to stay in the EU was like holding a referendum on the Inland Revenue. Or, as an adviser to European Council President Herman Van Rompuy put it:

> The campaign for a British referendum has been driven largely by eurosceptics, mainly because they think they would have an advantage in a referendum given the overwhelming hostility of the press which has made a lot of people think the EU is the equivalent to the bubonic plague. And if you have a referendum on the bubonic plague, people are largely against it.[354]

It sounded about right. It also sounded like an admission of defeat.

There was another echo of the Scotland campaign in the British debate about its future relationship with Brussels. In the run-up to the EU referendum which eventually came in 2017, Brussels agreed to return some powers to London after the government's renegotiation of Britain's terms of membership. Likewise, Scotland was promised control over extra responsibilities by Cameron should it vote to stay in the UK. The choice for the Scottish people was therefore not the status quo, but it was between complete withdrawal and an enhanced devolution settlement. This was one factor seen as cementing the majority in favour of staying in the UK, despite warnings from Alex Salmond, the First Minister and leader of the Scottish National Party, that it was itself an echo of an earlier empty promise. During the 1979 referendum campaign on Scottish devolution, a senior Conservative had said that a better Scottish Assembly would result, which then failed to materialise during the next eighteen years of Tory rule in Westminster. 'What's the old saying? "Fool me once, shame on you; fool me twice, shame on me?" Scotland, I don't believe, will be fooled twice,' said Salmond, in response to Cameron's offer of extra devolution.[355] In the Scottish context, Salmond's argument failed to resonate because Edinburgh had, eventually, won full parliament status from Westminster (admittedly the Scots had to wait for a Labour government first). In the EU context, the promise of a renegotiation to enhance UK power had also been tried before – but with only limited success.

The attempted refashioning of Britain's accession terms under the government of Harold Wilson proved so ineffective that it was rarely mentioned once it had served its purpose – as the springboard for the 'In' campaign during the 1975 referendum on EEC membership. The ten-month talks led by Foreign Secretary James Callaghan produced a better deal for New Zealand's farmers in terms of guaranteed European imports and 'further reviews' of the Common Agricultural Policy, a pledge on contribution discounts which proved so unsatisfactory that Margaret Thatcher later fought for five years to secure a permanent rebate, confirmation of zero-rating for VAT on some items, and the removal of the threat of a fixed exchange rate for the pound. Voters were reminded of it during the 2017 campaign as a salutary lesson not to believe in the reassurances of the latest government programme to repatriate powers. It felt like history was repeating itself when the recent redrawing of Britain's EU deal was similarly dismissed as a political ploy and, as one historian noted of Callaghan's efforts, 'a largely, though not wholly, cosmetic membership renegotiation… Those huge and vexing questions of the Common Agricultural Policy and Britain's contribution to the Community Budget were barely scratched.'[356] As in 1975, so it was again in 2017. To borrow a phrase: fool me twice, shame on me.

The Conservatives went into the 2015 general election promising a referendum within two years on a renegotiated relationship with the EU. Party managers reasoned that they had little choice, given Cameron's pledges in 2012 and the need to do something to neutralise votes for UKIP that were sapping Tory support. The Liberal Democrats decided that they could not ditch another policy so in 2015 they stuck with the 2010 manifesto promise of an in/out referendum to settle the matter, from the standpoint of campaigning to stay in. The party's commitment to the EU had been underscored by the deal to send Nick Clegg to Brussels as the next British member of the European Commission when Baroness Ashton's term ended in October 2014. Clegg was usurped as Lib Dem leader by his party colleagues when poll ratings hit an all-time low in the run-up to the 2014 party conference, which was personally painful but professionally perfect timing for his nomination as Commissioner. He landed the trade portfolio and was soon able to make a strong argument for staying in the EU from the midst of the potentially lucrative free trade agreements that he was in charge of negotiating with the United States and Japan. Ultimately, French wrecking tactics on these deals made a much more powerful argument for Britain to go it alone.

Ed Miliband, the Labour leader, desperately wanted to avoid making a promise for an EU referendum in the party's manifesto for the 2015 election but events would conspire against him. With both the Conservatives and Liberal Democrats clearly committed to an in/out referendum in the next parliament, the pledge was added at the very last minute to Labour's own manifesto after a heated internal debate. This was won by those who said that Miliband could neither be left out of the stampede to offer the public a democratic say over Britain's European future, nor could he afford to be left on the spot when he was forced to spell out his policy during the party leaders' televised debates. Labour Party managers also argued that it would not be politically attractive for an incoming Labour government to make one of their first acts the repeal of the EU Act of 2011, which provided for a referendum on any future transfer of Westminster power to Brussels. With coalition negotiations on repatriating powers as part of a new EU treaty well under way by the time of the 2015 election, a referendum of some kind was inevitable. Miliband was persuaded by the argument that the only winnable referendum on the EU was an in/out vote, so he decided to make the public vote on the European Federation treaty all-or-nothing. It was a fateful move. Miliband narrowly won the 2015 general election and it soon became clear that Europe would overshadow the parliament.

The government's information leaflet to voters in 2017 was an uncanny repeat of Wilson's own leaflet in 1975, which declared that

> the Government, after long, hard negotiations, are recommending to the British people that we should remain a member of the European Community... We do not pretend, and never have pretended, that we got everything we wanted in these negotiations. But we did get big and significant improvements on the previous terms. We confidently believe that these better terms can give Britain a New Deal in Europe.[357]

The Wilson leaflet went on to extol changes in the CAP (the ones that primarily benefited New Zealand) with the promise that 'this is not the end of improvements in the Market's food policy. There will be further reviews. Britain, as a member, will be able to seek further changes to our advantage'; it talked up the new funding arrangements by declaring that 'under the previous terms, Britain's contribution to the Common Market budget imposed too heavy a burden on us. The new terms ensure that Britain will pay a fairer share'; and it added that 'we have also maintained our freedom to pursue our own policies on taxation and on industry'. The eurosceptics of 2017 warned that the latest renegotiation would carry as much weight in the long term as Wilson's deal – which was soon forgotten, eclipsed by French resistance to farm policy reform, constant battles to win and retain the rebate, and constant attempts in Brussels to take control of taxation and other issues.

In 2017, the European Federation treaty created a directly elected European Commission President, whose greater democratic legitimacy would also give him or her a more prominent say in national life, and at the same time trigger a run-off between the final two candidates like the US presidential election. It also established a powerful European Commission Vice President for Economic, Financial and Monetary Affairs, dubbed the Euro Chancellor by the British media, with new powers to coordinate national budgets and veto tax and spending plans. The member state was left with the power to decide how to re-arrange tax or spending to bring its budget into line, but the transfer of ultimate fiscal sovereignty was too much for several countries besides Britain to accept. That was the main reason why the treaty also proposed a more formalised second-tier membership. This was essentially for countries that had ruled out the euro – the UK, Czech Republic, Denmark and Sweden – and soon became known as Membership Lite. It was the EU's final offer to the laggards, with minimal interference from the Euro Chancellor, and an extra concession with Britain in mind. The Lites would

be able to choose whether or not to opt in to future social legislation on a case-by-case basis, much in the same way that already
applied for justice and home affairs measures for the UK. The
Lites would continue to have full access to the single market
and a role in making legislation, provided that they accepted
all employment and environmental laws, kept paying towards
structural funds, withdrew their MEPs from committees relevant
to the eurozone and took part in common foreign policy and in
a 'greener' Common Agricultural Policy.

After the unsatisfactory attempt to reform the Common
Fisheries Policy in 2013, another concession offered to the UK
was autonomy over its territorial waters. This meant that, for
200 nautical miles from the coast, Britain could set catch limits in
line with scientific guidance, overcoming a fundamental flaw
in the EU method that had devastated fish stocks. The European
Commission refused to let go of its mandate to negotiate
international fisheries agreements, however. And with fishing
representing a fraction of national GDP and financial services
unaffected by the renegotiation, the option of withdrawing
altogether from Brussels divided the City. Many banking and
insurance companies warned that their profits and therefore
jobs in the capital would suffer from leaving the EU, triggering a
drop in GDP and a potentially precipitous fall in London house
prices. Funnily enough, the voting public took a somewhat
perverse delight in casting their ballots against the interests of
high finance. House price falls in London were not so widely
feared across the nation as a whole, it seemed, where bricks
and mortar values had been in decline for years. There were
even those who foresaw a rebalancing of the British economy
away from an excessive reliance on the City. The long credit
crunch had caused a surge in micro-finance organisations while
the High Street banks hoarded resources and starved entrepreneurs. It meant that the 'Big Banks Back Brussels' campaign
gave small and medium-sized businesses – that were already fed
up with EU red tape – another reason to vote for withdrawal.

The anti-EU side hammered Brussels for being undemocratic. The pro-unionists hit back that this was a bit rich coming from a country with a hereditary head of state, a largely appointed and partially hereditary upper chamber, and an archaic first-past-the-post voting system for the lower house that – irony of ironies – denied any national representation to the main EU withdrawalist party. UKIP, moreover, owed much of its success to European elections, especially those of 2014, where it only narrowly missed out on winning first place in votes and MEPs. For every clapped-out politician sent to Brussels, a dozen were sent to the House of Lords, the unionists said. The withdrawalists countered that it was far better to have UK laws debated and decided by elected MPs at Westminster, rather than the EU system where all laws originate at the undemocratic European Commission. Ah yes, said the unionists, but MPs rarely propose laws either. They all emanate from the government's programme and are mostly drafted by unelected civil servants anyway. And just as laws in the UK followed a democratic mandate of the general election, so the EU was being reformed to have a legislative programme set by the most popular political group, in this case the Socialists, who made the biggest gains in the 2014 European Parliament election – an outcome which for the first time also dictated the political stripe of the next European Commission President. Brussels was getting more democratic, not less, which would continue with the plan for a directly elected European Commission President. It just so happened that this EU democratic evolution was another development met largely with suspicion in the UK because it felt like more power was being accrued in Brussels. Although the EU had long been bashed for its lack of democratic legitimacy, the prospect of an elected powerful President ironically contributed to the British withdrawal vote.

There had been a lively tussle between the top three centre-left candidates for Commission President: German MEP and European Parliament President Martin Schulz, the French former European Commissioner and retired World Trade Organization chief Pascal Lamy and the Danish Prime Minister Helle Thorning-Schmidt, who was Britain's preferred pick of the trio given her more sceptical credentials (and her link to the UK through her marriage to the son of Lord Kinnock). In the end it came down to the Dane's vision of a 'green growth recovery' against the Frenchman's push to strengthen the European Commission as a continental powerbase with its own tax-raising powers. In a move that hammered another nail in the British membership coffin, Lamy took the crown with his 'son of Delors' programme for ever closer union. Would a Thorning-Schmidt victory, or the choice of any other candidate as Commission President, have changed the course of British history? Probably not, given the deep public disenchantment with the European Union and the way that the previous incumbent, José Manuel Barroso, who was the most Anglo-friendly Commission President of all time, had failed to win the country round to the EU or push through deep liberalising reforms. The Commission never gave up on a Europe of all twenty-seven members and successfully resisted the French plan for an avant-garde of a federal eurozone with its own parliament, although the eurozone did get its own budget.

The signs that the British public would vote in favour of leaving the EU, when finally given the chance to have their say, had been there from many opinion polls over the years. In August 2012, a survey by Canadian pollsters Angus Reid recorded that 46 per cent would vote to leave against 29 per cent for staying in, while 54 per cent said that forty years of British EU membership had a negative effect on the country with 33 per cent saying it was positive.[358] Populus in June 2012 found that just over one-third, 36 per cent, replied 'Yes' to the question 'Do you want the UK to remain in the European Union, keeping open the option of joining the more integrated eurozone?' with 44 per cent saying 'No' and 19 per cent 'Don't Know'; an ICM poll in October 2011 recorded 49 per cent support for leaving the EU against 40 per cent who would vote in a referendum to stay in.[359] Lord Mandelson portrayed a May 2012 poll for Policy Network as showing that 'two-thirds (67 per cent) of people support staying in the European Union' during a keynote speech on Britain and the EU.[360] But what the poll actually found was that, according to the Policy Network website,

> 36 per cent of people think Britain should stay in the EU but only as a member of a free trade area, 18 per cent as we currently are but with no further integration, and 14 per cent of people say the UK should stay in the EU and play a full role in any further integration. A third think Britain should leave.

In other words, besides the one-third who wanted Britain to leave, almost half of Mandelson's 67 per cent of EU supporters wanted simply a free trade arrangement, something not on offer from Brussels and which could only be made possible by leaving; 18 per cent wanted the preferred Cameron option of in but without any deeper integration; and only 14 per cent favoured the real pro-European option of ever closer union. It was devastating confirmation of the defeat of the British europhiles.

Critics said that Mandelson's presentation fitted a pattern of partial pro-EU presentation that followed a direct line all the way from Edward Heath's 'no loss of essential national sovereignty', contributing over the years to widespread mistrust of the European project and its proponents. Buried in the Policy Network research and not mentioned by Mandelson in his speech was a question which asked British voters: 'Which of these nations would you say Britain has most in common with culturally, politically and economically?' Respondents had five countries to choose from. Just 2 per cent went for India, while 10 per cent chose Germany and 11 per cent France. But the top two countries by a mile were Australia on 28 per cent and the United States with 49 per cent support.[361] It was as if the last forty years of European integration had never happened. Once again, the defeat of the europhiles was plain to see – or would have been, if the results had not been buried at the time. It was yet more evidence that the pro-Europeans had lost the argument in Britain.

Many other reasons were suggested for the decision to break with Brussels. By 2017, the British economy was at last performing strongly again, while the continent had become indelibly associated with over-regulation and economic stagnation. This was the total reverse of the situation for the previous European referendum in 1975. The pro-EU campaign of 2017, led by the former Foreign Secretary David Miliband on a cross-party basis but with little support from the Conservatives, was never able to shake off suspicions over what exactly the next forty years of EU membership would hold, given the multitude of unexpected developments that followed the 1975 vote. There was also the release of years of pent-up anger over the failure of previous governments to grant referenda, notably David Cameron's non-ferrous 'cast-iron guarantee' of a vote on the Lisbon Treaty. As British negotiators struggled to win concessions in the European Federation treaty negotiations of 2014–16, critics looked again at Cameron's refusal to push for a retrospective referendum on Lisbon back in 2009–10. Pursuing such a referendum would have strengthened Britain's arm enormously by showing that the government was really serious about recasting the UK's relationship. The decision to avoid one began to look more like a desire not to upset the apple cart in Brussels. Joining forces in the coalition with the Liberal Democrats meant that Cameron would probably have been stopped from carrying out a referendum threat on Lisbon – but his swift climb-down upon the treaty's ratification months before the coalition forming seemed to show his true appetite for a fight over the EU.

By the time the EU referendum came round in 2017, Cameron

had in any case reconciled himself to a period of reflection on the back benches under the new Tory leader. Boris Johnson claimed the top job in the messy aftermath of the close-fought 2015 election when Cameron, who was always blamed by a section of the Conservative Party for not being able to win outright in 2010, had the rug pulled under him from the right soon after the defeat. Johnson proceeded to use his own extensive honeymoon period to campaign vigorously for departure from the European Union, bringing the issues to life with remarks such as 'Voting to leave Brussels will cause your wife to have bigger breasts and increase your chances of owning a BMW M3'. He proved an energetic and formidable leader of the 'Out' camp, especially given the lacklustre pleading of the Labour government for an 'In' vote, which Johnson painted as a self-interested attempt not to have to deal with the fall-out of withdrawal. In the event, the referendum was a close-run thing, with Britain voting by 51.4 per cent to 48.6 per cent against the treaty and to leave the EU on a 54 per cent turnout. In other words, only around a quarter of the voting-age population actually cast a ballot to withdraw.

Of all the EU nations, Germany was the most distressed to see Britain leave. It had long appreciated the role played by UK ministers and officials in fighting for liberalisation and reform in Brussels and the Brexit left Berlin at the mercy of a powerful and protectionist 'southern alliance' headed by France and including Italy, Spain, Portugal and Greece. Angela Merkel made several public appeals to British leaders to stand up to the europhobes, like the one she made to David Cameron in November 2012: 'I want a strong Britain in the EU... When you are somewhere alone in a seven-billion-strong global population, I don't think it is good for Britain. I believe you can be very happy on an island, but being alone in this world doesn't make you any happier.'[362] Britain's exit gave both Spain and Poland a boost in the EU pecking order which made their sorrow at seeing a good friend leave somewhat more bearable. The more progressive northern states such as Finland, Sweden and the Netherlands were also devastated but felt powerless to prevent the inexorable ballet of British departure that traced its first steps back to Maastricht. This had been reluctantly observed by the influential Finnish Europe Minister, Alexander Stubb, an Anglophile married to a British lawyer:

> I think Britain is, voluntarily, by its own will, putting itself in the margins. We see it in foreign policy, we see it in economic policy, we see it linked to the single currency. And I, as someone who advocates the single market and free trade, find that very unfortunate. It is almost as if the boat is pulling away and one of our best friends is somehow saying 'bye-bye' and there is not really that much we can do about it.[363]

As was the case when Norway rejected EU membership in 1972, all the British officials working in the EU institutions were allowed to keep their jobs. Britain's seventy-three Members of the European Parliament were suspended shortly after the referendum, but happily were still able to receive their €95,482 salary for as long as the UK contributed to the EU budget. This was also the case for the Commissioner. Nick Clegg joined the 'Yes' campaign from the comfort of his €243,336-a-year job in Brussels (an increase of €75,000 a year on his salary as Deputy Prime Minister), and safe in the knowledge of his €52,013-a-year Commission pension and €16,709-a-year European Parliament pension from his time as an MEP. He ended up serving his full five-year term because the referendum decision of 2017 to withdraw was not completely enacted until 2020. The European Commission had threatened to take the UK to the European Court of Justice if it left straight away – and stopped paying – before the completion of the seven-year budget that began in 2014. The row over when the UK would stop sending its membership fee to Brussels and the level of payments it would continue to make for access to the single market became

London's biggest bargaining chip in the negotiation over the new arrangement to govern the relationship between the UK and EU.

Although it could have ignored the ECJ, the UK government felt obliged to keep up the proportion of its payments that went towards structural funds during the talks on the new relationship – but it only wanted to contribute to those countries with a GDP of 90 per cent of the EU average or less. With the European Commission insisting upon full UK payments until 2020, the government eventually agreed because it was concerned that the money issue would poison the entire negotiation. It was intended as an act of good faith but the EU felt it had to be dragged out of Britain and it satisfied neither side fully. A Norway-style new relationship in the European Economic Area was ruled out by the UK government on the grounds of democratic accountability, even though it was the best way to ensure access to the single market. Brussels refused to offer a Swiss-style system of numerous treaties covering different aspects of the relationship, and insisted on one all-encompassing framework document which included the automatic updating of technical market standards, governed by a small number of committees, which both sides decided to call the UK/EU free trade agreement (FTA). It took the full two years provided for in the Lisbon Treaty to complete the process.

A breakdown of the referendum verdict showed that the newly independent UK was also a divided country. Scotland and Wales both voted in favour of staying in the EU, which revived the moribund Scottish Nationalist Party from its doldrum years following the referendum vote to stay in the UK. It reignited the campaign for Scottish independence. Opinion polls showed that the 60–40 referendum majority for keeping Scotland in the UK was almost reversed following the UK's withdrawal vote from the EU – a decision seen north of the border as foisted upon them by English and Northern Irish voters. The SNP, ejected in 2015, swept back to power in Holyrood in 2019, and continue to press strongly for the independence vote to be rerun. In Wales, the independence movement was also reinvigorated, despite Westminster promises to keep regional spending at the same level as enjoyed under the EU's structural funds regime. In 2007–13, £1.9 billion went from Brussels to Wales from the EU budget and was topped up with national match-funding to make a grand total of £3.3 billion.[364] While the majority of pro-EU voters in Wales was only narrow, Plaid Cymru benefited from the feeling of injustice and was revived from third place in the 2015 Welsh Assembly elections to a strong second behind Labour in 2019.

The EU referendum vote of 2017 was seen as a defeat of the Miliband government and acted like an earthquake in domestic politics. There were immediate calls for a vote of no confidence in the Labour administration which soon proved too powerful to resist, especially when the Conservative-sympathising press, in triumphant mode after the referendum outcome, followed up with huge pressure on the government. Labour held firm and won the no-confidence vote a fortnight after the referendum with the support of most of the small Liberal Democrat contingent in the House of Commons. But Labour's poll ratings never recovered. It was as fatally damaged as the administration of John Major after the ERM debacle in 1992, and would eventually lose the next general election to deliver the keys of 10 Downing Street to Boris Johnson. Unkind observers remarked that, since David Miliband had been in charge of the 'Yes' campaign for the EU referendum, an opportunity presented to him by his brother's narrow victory in the Labour leadership contest, then some kind of karmic circle had been completed when the younger Miliband's premiership was fatally blighted by the EU result. But the older Miliband's political career was also left in tatters.

The government of the day bore the brunt of the hurricane which hit the British economy and especially the City after the referendum decision to leave the EU. Shares lost a fifth of their value and the pound took a dive, as did London house prices after several large European banks, and later a dozen giant international banks, pulled hundreds of jobs from the City. Some switched their headquarters to Paris or Frankfurt, while others beefed up continental outposts until staff there outnumbered those in London. The European Central Bank had lost no time in renewing its ruling that clearing houses should be based in the eurozone if they handled more than 5 per cent of the market in euro-denominated financial products, forcing the main London clearing house to reconstitute its Paris office as the new EU head-quarters. None of these institutions withdrew completely from London, and the City slowly recovered its poise although it never regained the twin peaks of activity and turnover seen in 2008 and again, following the long road to recovery, in 2016.

While London had a torrid time in the aftermath of with-drawal, the rest of the country fared better in comparison. It took eighteen months for the final shape of Britain's free trade agreement with Brussels to be negotiated and another six months for final ratification by the other EU member nations. The work consumed the government, with a special ministe-rial team almost equivalent in size to the Cabinet assigned to oversee the talks, sector by sector and policy by policy, with the main goal to preserve the status quo on open access to the single market. There had never been so many British civil serv-ants assigned full time to the Belgian capital.

The negotiations were led on behalf of the EU by a team from the European Council but began in a state of extreme suspicion and high farce – the UK had long been scheduled to take over the six-month rotating presidency of the EU on 1 July 2017, just weeks after the referendum. This role was still quite substantial, despite the creation of the permanent European Council President in 2009, first held by Herman Van Rompuy, because the member state was expected to provide ministers to chair all the regular meetings of member state ministers in departmental sectors from agriculture to transport. Although the UK government had been gamely preparing for this task alongside the referendum campaign, the French under their new conservative President immediately offered to take over the EU presidency from Britain with just a month to spare. Paris was the only capital in a position to jump in at such short notice and the UK government reluctantly had little option but to agree. The French took on the role with the relish of the school swot volunteering for extra homework.

France's noble gesture 'in Europe's hour of need' helped the new President to head off popular demands for a referendum on the European Federation treaty, which was ratified instead – and to the great relief of Brussels, which fully expected a 'Non' from a French referendum – by a vote of the National Assembly and Senate. But the British debate had triggered powerful referendum calls across Europe even before the Brexit, just as it did when Tony Blair made his U-turn in 2004 to announce a popular vote on the ill-fated constitution. While the document was passed, narrowly, by plebiscites in Germany, Ireland and Luxembourg, the EU was plunged into further crisis by rejections of the treaty in Denmark, the Netherlands, Sweden and Portugal during the remainder of 2017. These countries did not need the British example to reject Brussels and all her works – eurosceptic feelings of animosity had been building for years. There was seemingly no way back from the large 'No' votes especially in the first two cases, and the reasons were so varied from country to country that the pro-treaty governments eventually agreed to coordinate all-or-nothing referenda 'after a period of reflection' the following year. They would be on the straight choice between the treaty or EU exit. Brussels had a habit of refusing to take 'No' for an answer in referenda, which had already been rerun twice in Ireland and once in Denmark until the 'right' answer was delivered. In June 2018, the high stakes ploy worked – in three of the four cases. The Swedes reasoned that they were little affected by the treaty because of their effective opt-out from the single currency and, unlike the UK, decided to take up the 'Membership Lite' option already adopted by the Czechs. The Portuguese counted up all the euros handed to them by the EU over the years (€60.7 billion up until 2011 in structural funds alone) and all the euros still to come and switched to 'Yes'. The Netherlands saw the economic turmoil caused in the UK by voting to quit and, by the slimmest margin, decided to stay in after a divisive and bad-tempered debate which marked the defeat of the populist Geert Wilders, who tried to use the 'No' campaign to relaunch his political career. But the Danish could not be shifted. Denmark was the only other country to follow the UK out of the EU rather than accept a formalised second-tier membership alongside the European Federation.

There had been growing indications for years that the government would face a tough time reaching its free trade agreement with the EU. Radosław Sikorski, the Polish Foreign Secretary, had reflected growing impatience with Britain back in 2011 when he had some double-edged words of praise for the UK:

> Britain, you have given the Union its common language. The single market was largely your brilliant idea. A British commissioner runs our diplomacy. You could lead Europe on defence. You are an indispensable link across the Atlantic. On the other hand, the eurozone's collapse would hugely harm your economy. Also, your total sovereign, corporate and household debt exceeds 400 per cent of GDP. Are you sure markets will always favour you? We would prefer you in but if you cannot join, please allow us to forge ahead and please start explaining to your people that European decisions are not Brussels diktats but agreements in which you have freely participated.[365]

His warnings grew stronger. In September 2012 he told the UK government:

> Please don't expect us to help you to wreck or paralyse the EU. Don't underestimate our determination not to return to the

politics of the twentieth century. You were not occupied. Most of us on the continent were. We'll do almost anything to prevent it happening again. Europe's leaders will step up integration to make the euro work. We believe the euro will survive, because it is in members' interests for it to survive.[366]

In October 2012, Lord Mandelson warned: 'What is clear to me from my visits to Brussels and other national capitals is that our European partners are losing interest in us.'[367] A leading German magazine dismissed the British as Statler and Waldorf, the two old duffers in *The Muppet Show*, who just complain about the rest of the cast from their balcony.[368] *The Times* headlined the story 'British are the Muppets of Europe, say Germans' although readers were quick to point out that Statler and Waldorf were actually spectators of *The Muppet Show*. In fact, as puppets themselves, everybody was a Muppet. It just about summed up the state of play in the EU at the time, only a week after it received its Nobel Prize for Peace and was struggling to reach agreement on who would accept the award.

The French, having taken over the EU presidency from the British following the vote to leave, became deeply involved in the free trade agreement talks which soon ran into the sand. Since the UK would no longer be paying into the Common Agricultural Policy, Paris wanted compensation in the form of tariffs on British farm exports into the EU's common customs area. British negotiators pointed out that this would be a double whammy for farmers, who would no longer have the same protections or subsidies themselves. The French retorted that British voters should have thought of that before deciding to quit the EU. The situation was defused when most of the technical issues were handed to officials but the key question remained – would Britain be able to retain general access to the single market and on what terms? A complicated deal on market entry for goods emerged which involved Britain agreeing to continue paying towards the structural development funds of the poorest EU states, those with a GDP of 90 per cent or less below the average. This would cost around £20 billion over the next seven-year budget, from 2021 until 2028, more than many were expecting but actually a bargain considering the market involvement it bought. Gross membership costs after the rebate would have exceeded £100 billion during the same period, so this was roughly one-fifth of the full subscription, but one-third of the anticipated net contribution. A full FTA deal on services was not possible, however, again because of French resistance to open access for UK financial services. Trade in services had to be negotiated on a bilateral basis between Britain and individual EU member states, a process still ongoing four years after the formal departure date. The system is due to be reviewed in 2027–8 when the next seven-year budget is drawn up. Britain was able to negotiate a bilateral operational agreement with Europol and other policing and security systems in the same way as Switzerland but had to buy its way back into various other EU schemes where it was keen to remain, notably the European Common Aviation Area to allow British airlines full access to the continent and the Erasmus scheme for student exchanges. This piled on extra expense but withdrawalists accepted it all as 'the price of freedom'. And so, as best it could, the UK bought its way back into the single market that it helped to create.

By deciding to leave the EU, the UK had forfeited its place in the room when any future decisions were made about trading rules in the European Union. But public opinion seemed reconciled to this, given that British officials did not sit in the US Congress or China's State Council to influence their internal trade rules either. The situation that Britain ended up in was curiously like that created for the Channel Islands in 1972 ahead of UK accession – participation in the single market for goods but not directly for services, with none of the requirements to earmark a proportion of VAT for Brussels or pay into an outdated system of farm protectionism and other grand projects like the €20 billion Galileo satellite navigation system, which by 2023 was fully fifteen years behind schedule. Apart from the automatic acceptance of changes to EU technical market rules, Britain had her sovereignty back and Parliament found itself surprised at the additional workload attached to new responsibilities in trade, transport, agriculture, environmental protection, regional funding and fisheries. As part of the settlement, Westminster agreed to 'take account' of all Brussels legislation when it made its own laws – it was not a binding commitment but it was supposed to act as a first defence against a trade war developing if Britain was accused of abusing its single market privileges. Tensions which rose throughout the year were supposed to be relieved by an annual EU–UK summit which in reality only provided an opportunity for recriminations whipped up by the media on both sides of the Channel. London began talks on joining the North American Free Trade Agreement after President Ryan himself offered to convert it to a North Atlantic deal. But, in an era of slow but inexorable decline for Europe in global economic terms, the divorced partners recognised that they still needed each other. Since there was no possibility of uprooting the British Isles and floating off closer to the United States, Canada or Mexico, the UK had no option but to try and stay as closely intertwined as possible with its continental partners on numerous levels. The familiar pattern of frequent arguments, muddles and joint initiatives that has always marked Britain's relationship with the continent continued unabated. It was not *adieu*. It was *au revoir*, Europe.

Endnotes

1   http://europa.eu/legislation_summaries/institutional_affairs/treaties/treaties_eec_en.htm

2   Peter Hennessy, *The Prime Minister*, 2nd edn (London: Penguin Books, 2001), p. 173.

3   http://www.churchill-society-london.org.uk/astonish.html

4   David Reynolds, *The Origins of the Cold War in Europe: International Perspectives* (New Haven, CT: Yale University Press, 1994), p. 13.

5   http://www.europarl.europa.eu/summits/lis1_en.htm

6   http://www.consilium.europa.eu/uedocs/cms_Data/docs/pressdata/en/ec/132270.pdf

7   'Europe, is it the end of the project?' *The Hands Lecture*, 4 May 2012.

8   'Major claims green shoots of economic recovery are appearing', *Sunday Times*, 16 September 2012.

9   http://www.policy-network.net/news_detail.aspx?ID=3942

10 Edward Heath, *Travels: People and Places in My Life* (London: Sidgwick & Jackson, 1977), p. 31.

11 Ibid., p. 29.

12 Ibid. p. 115.

13 'Observer – Europe', *ft.com*, 18 July 2005.

14 http://www.harvard-digital.co.uk/euro/pamphlet.htm

15 Harold Macmillan, 'Britain, the Commonwealth and Europe', in *Britain and Europe in Ten Speeches* (London: UK Office of the European Parliament, 2010), p. 7.

16 Ibid.

17 Margaret Thatcher, *The Path to Power* (London: HarperCollins, 1995), p. 211.

18 'Why I'm right behind Tony Blair', *The Guardian*, 26 April 2004.

19 Hugo Young, *This Blessed Plot*, 2nd edn (London: Papermac, 1999), pp. 246–7.

20 Ibid., p. 223.

21 'Britain and the battle over European Union', *The Guardian*, 11 December 2011.

22 Hugo Young, *This Blessed Plot.*, p. 247.

23 Ibid., pp. 247–8.

24 'A Letter to The Times', *Document*, BBC Radio 4, 3 February 2000.

25 http://law-uk.info/2012/06/bulmer-v-bollinger-1974-2-all-er-1226/

26   http://www.harvard-digital.co.uk/euro/pamphlet.htm

27   Stephen Wall, *A Stranger in Europe* (Oxford: Oxford University Press, 2008) p. 61.

28   Ibid., p. 49.

29   Hansard, HL Deb, 7 June 1993, vol. 546, col. 562.

30   'Eurovision Song Contest is the real union of Europe', *The Telegraph* online, 25 May 2012.

31   Private interview.

32   http://www.europedia.moussis.eu/books/Book_2/6/20/03/05/index.tkl?all=1&pos=294

33   http://www.margaretthatcher.org/document/107332

34   http://www.margaretthatcher.org/archive/Bruges.asp

35   Hansard, HC Deb, 30 October 1990, vol. 178, col. 873.

36   Ian Bache and Stephen George, *Politics in the European Union*, 2nd edn (Oxford: Oxford University Press, 2006), p. 160.

37   http://eur-lex.europa.eu/LexUriServ/LexUriServ.do?uri=CELEX:41981X0919:EN:HTML

38   'UK rejects federal Europe move', *Financial Times*, 18 June 1991.

39   http://www.eurofound.europa.eu/areas/industrialrelations/dictionary/definitions/subsidiarity.htm

40   'Prime Minister Major signals end of Thatcher line on the EC', *The Times*, 12 March 1991.

41   Hansard, HC Deb, 11 March 1975, vol. 888, cols 304–17.

42   Hansard, HC Deb, 20 November 1991, vol. 199, cols 290–98.

43   Helmut Kohl, speech at Bertelsmann Forum, Bonn, 3 April 1992.

44   Bruges Group, *The European Court of Justice: Judges or Policy Makers?* (London: Bruges Group, 1990).

45   'UKIP's hard work has handed Europe more power', *Mail Online*, 10 May 2010.

46   'Minister fights hours limit', *The Guardian*, 8 March 1995, p. 9.

47   John Rentoul, *Tony Blair: Prime Minister* (London: Little, Brown and Company, 2001), p. 84.

48   'Tony Blair's speech to the European Parliament', *The Guardian* online, 23 June 2005.

49   http://www.bbc.co.uk/news/special/politics97/news/05/0505/cook.shtml

50   'Blair keeps Britain's euro flame alive', *Reuters News*, 2 October 2002.

51   Clare Short, *An Honourable Deception? New Labour, Iraq and the Misuse of Power*, (London: Free Press, 2004), pp. 124–5.

52   Hansard, HC Deb, 27 October 1997, vol. 299, col. 588.

53   Anthony Seldon, *Blair Unbound*, (London: Simon & Schuster, 2007), p. 205.

54   Peter Hennessy, *The Prime Minister*, 2nd edn (London: Penguin Books, 2001), p. 269.

55   David Blunkett, *The Blunkett Tapes* (London: Bloomsbury, 2006), p. 511.

56   Stephen Wall, *A Stranger in Europe*, p. 181.

57   Ibid., p. 172.

58   http://european-convention.eu.int/pdf/lknen.pdf

59   'The European Convention', *International Herald Tribune*, 27 December 2001.

60   'The future Europe takes form', *International Herald Tribune*, 3 September 2002.

61   'Ministers play down eurosceptic fears over EU treaty', *Financial Times*, 14 May 2003.

62   Peter Hain on *The Politics Show*, BBC1, 18 May 2003.

63   'EU concern over Blair referendum', *Financial Times*, 19 April 2004.

64   Hansard, HC Deb, 12 March 2007, vol. 458, col. 25.

65   'Brown under pressure to call EU referendum', *Daily Telegraph*, 27 June 2007.

66   'If they treat us like babies we may throw their EU pet toy out of pram', *Irish Examiner*, 24 October 2007.

67   'Cameron: I'll give you EU vote', *The Sun*, 26 September 2007.

68   Hansard, HC Deb, 3 July 2007, vol. 462, col. 803.

69   'Ministers seek to enliven Ecofin meetings', *Financial Times* online, 6 April 2006.

70   'Now EU bans plastic bags', *Daily Express* online, 26 March 2012.

71   http://ec.europa.eu/civil_service/docs/europa_sp2_bs_nat_x_grade_en.pdf

72   'French disappearing from GCSE classrooms', *The Guardian* online, 27 August 2009.

73   Figures provided by European Commission Directorate for Inter-Institutional Relations and Administration for this book.

74   'Back in the saddle again', *The Economist*, 5 September 2009.

75   'Merkel tells Tory leader to stick with EPP partners', *The Times*, 16 December 2005.

76   'Czech leader signs Lisbon Treaty as Tories concede defeat over referendum', *The Times*, 3 November 2009.

77   http://www.brugesgroup.com/eu/cameron-is-breaking-his-pledge-to-hold-a-lisbon-referendum.html?keyword=23

78   'Cameron's crusade for UK rights', *The Sun*, 12 January 2011.

79   *The Conservative Manifesto 2010*, p. 114.

80   *The Coalition: Our Programme for Government*, p. 19.

81   Ibid., p. 19.

82   'Cameron: We will use debt crisis to reshape Europe', *The Times*, 14 November 2011.

83   http://www.number10.gov.uk/news/lord-mayors-banquet/

84   'Cameron in crosshairs over future of Europe', *The Times*, 8 December 2011.

85   Ibid.

86   http://ukconstitutionallaw.org/2012/01/19/paul-yowell-eu-act-2011-law-and-politics/

87   http://www.economist.com/blogs/bagehot/2011/12/britain-and-eu-0

88   'Liam Fox: No more waiting – we must renegotiate our position', *Daily Telegraph*, 30 June 2012.

89   'Cameron opens door to EU referendum', *The Times*, 1 July 2012.

90   'Audit due on EU legislation impact', *Press Association*, 12 July 2012.

91   'David Cameron: I'll never campaign to take us out of Europe', *Daily Telegraph*, interview, 18 July 2012.

92   http://europa.eu/rapid/pressReleasesAction.do?reference=SPEECH/12/596

93   'Cameron anger at £280m for EU's new gilded cage', *The Times*, 25 June 2011.

94 'EU spends £9 million on 13 orchestras', *The Telegraph* online, 18 March 2012.
95 'EU's £2 million bananas fritter', *The Sun*, p. 13.
96 http://ec.europa.eu/budget/library/biblio/documents/fin_fwk0713/COM2012_184final_en.pdf
97 Hansard, HC Deb, 9 December 2005, vol. 440, col. 1564.
98 Ibid.
99 Ibid.
100 *European Union Finances 2012*, HM Treasury, Cm 8405, p. 14.
101 House of Commons Library, SN/EP/864, 28 October 2010.
102 http://ec.europa.eu/budget/library/biblio/publications/2011/fin_report/fin_report_11_en.pdf
103 Graeme Leach, *EU Membership: What's the Bottom Line?* (London: Institute of Directors, 2000), p. 5.
104 http://europa.eu/legislation_summaries/regional_policy/provisions_and_instruments/l60014_en.htm
105 Figures provided by European Commission Regional Policy Directorate for this book.
106 'Help for poorer neighbours designing a transfer union to save the euro', *Spiegel Online International*, 6 September 2011.
107 http://www.communities.gov.uk/newsstories/planningandbuilding/1822690
108 'Italy repays £307 million to EU after road project "mafia corruption" exposed', *The Telegraph* online, 5 July 2012.
109 Ibid.
110 Open Europe, *More for Less: Making the EU's Farm Policy Work for Growth and the Environment* (London: Open Europe, 2012) p. 18.
111 HC Written Answers, 26 January 2009, Col. 42W.
112 Open Europe, *More for Less: Making the EU's Farm Policy Work for Growth and the Environment*, p. 17.
113 Ibid.
114 Department for International Development, *Business Plan 2012–15*, 31 May 2012, p. 14.
115 http://eur-lex.europa.eu/LexUriServ/LexUriServ.do?uri=OJ:L:2012:056:0001:0556:EN:PDF
116 Open Europe, *The Rise of the EU Quangos* (London: Open Europe, 2012), p. 5.
117 http://ec.europa.eu/dgs/secretariat_general/evaluation/docs/decentralised_agencies_2009_part1_en.pdf
118 'Campaign calls for end to MEP travelling circus', *The Times*, 11 February 2011.
119 Committee of Experts, *Conceptual Basis for a House of European History* (Brussels: European Parliament, 2008)
120 http://www.brusselsmuseums.be/en/museum/110-parlamentarium
121 *Official Journal of the European Union*, 29 February 2012, p. 119, http://eur-lex.europa.eu/LexUriServ/LexUriServ.do?uri=OJ:L:2012:056:0001:0556:EN:PDF
122 Ibid., p. 505.
123 European Parliament press release, 11 November 2011.
124 Report A7-0120/2012 European Parliament Committee on Budgetary Control, 10 April 2012.

125 'We need to invest in a European identity', *EU Observer*, 3 March 2012.

126 'A prize that's out of this world', *Watford Observer*, 17 February 2012.

127 Antonio Tajani, 'Leading Europe beyond the crisis', keynote address by Commissioner for Industry and Entrepreneurship, 19 April 2012.

128 'Head of top space company becomes latest WikiLeaks victim after speaking out', *The Times*, 19 January 2011.

129 'Spending on Europe's satellite navigation system is still spiralling', *The Times*, 4 November 2010.

130 http://www.openeurope.org.uk/Content/Documents/PDFs/galileo2010.pdf

131 'Project blighted from the start by bad decisions', *The Times*, 8 December 2011, p. 6.

132 Barry Eichengreen and Andrea Boltho, *The Economic Impact of European Integration* (London: Centre for Economic Policy Research, 2008).

133 Polish Ministry of Regional Development, 'Evaluation of benefits to the EU-15 countries resulting from the implementation of Cohesion Policy in the Visegrad Group countries' (Warsaw, 2011), http://www.ewaluacja.gov.pl/Documents/Final_report_EU-15_V4.pdf

134 Brian Hindley and Martin Howe, *Better Off Out?*, 2nd edn (London: Institute of Economic Affairs, 2000), http://www.iea.org.uk/sites/default/files/publications/files/upldbook33pdf.pdf

135 Graeme Leach, *EU Membership: What's the Bottom Line?* (London: Institute of Directors, 2000).

136 NIESR annual report 2000.

137 Ian Milne, *A Cost Too Far?* (London: Civitas, 2004), p. 17.

138 Ilzkovitz, Dierx, Kovacs and Sousa, *Steps Towards a Deeper Economic Integration: The Internal Market in the 21st Century* (European Economics Papers 271, 2007).

139 Restricted internal document, *The Single Market: Benefits Realised and Potential*, Department for Business, Industry and Skills, p. 11.

140 L. Alan Winters, *Britain in Europe: A Survey of Quantitative Trade Studies* (London: Centre for Economic Policy Research, 1986).

141 Open Europe, *Still out of Control?*, 2nd edn (London: Open Europe, 2010), p. 1.

142 http://www.decc.gov.uk/assets/decc/77_20090423091800_e_@@_euclimateenergypackage.pdf

143 http://blogs.ec.europa.eu/ECintheUK/tag/eu-cost/

144 http://ec.europa.eu/public_opinion/archives/eb/eb71/eb71_uk_en_exec.pdf

145 'The tide is turning against EU bureaucracy', *The Telegraph*, 7 May 2012.

146 Hansard, HC Deb, 6 September 2011, vol. 532, col. 609w.

147 Straathof, Linders, Lejour, Moehlmann, *The Internal Market and the Dutch Economy* (The Hague: Netherlands Bureau for Economic Policy Analysis, 2008) p. 70.

148 European Commission, *20 Years of the European Single Market*, October 2012, p. 13.

149 'The EU has no vision of where we are heading', *Spiegel Online International*, 2 September 2010.

150 Ibid.

151 'Merkel's EU concessions, Germany can't always say no', *Spiegel Online International*, 2 July 2012.

152 'Germany and Europe: a very federal formula', *Financial Times*, 10 February 2012.

153 'Shaking things up in the EU', *Spiegel Online International*, 12 January 2012.

154 Ibid.

155 'We certainly don't want to divide Europe', *Spiegel Online International*, 25 June 2012.

156 'German minister favours referendum on Europe constitution', *Agence France Presse*, 11 August 2012.

157 José Manuel Barroso in conversation with author.

158 'Europe needs democratic rejuvenation', *Wall Street Journal*, 8 February 2012.

159 http://bruxelles.blogs.liberation.fr/coulisses/2010/06/helmut-schmidt-se-paye-merkel-barroso-van-rompuy-et-ashton.html

160 'Britain is left out of talks on the EU's future', *The Times*, 21 June 2012.

161 http://www.auswaertiges-amt.de/cae/servlet/contentblob/626338/publicationFile/171838/120918-Abschlussbericht-Zukunftsgruppe.pdf; jsessionid=1F767FE5F9375713C394E0A32009C8B8

162 'A look behind the news', *Agence Europe*, 3 August 2012.

163 http://europa.eu/rapid/pressReleasesAction.do?reference=SPEECH/12/596

164 http://eur-lex.europa.eu/LexUriServ/LexUriServ.do?uri=OJ:C:2008:115:0047:0199:EN:PDF

165 *The Coalition: Our Programme for Government*, p. 19.

166 'Quiet diplomacy will get our voice heard', *The Times*, 17 December 2009.

167 'EU wins new powers at UN, transforming global body', *EU Observer*, 3 May 2011.

168 'Hague declares war on EU foreign service,' *The Times*, 24 May 2011.

169 Ibid.

170 Special Group on Public Service Numbers and Expenditure Programmes.

171 'Insight: EU foreign policy chief Ashton stays out of the spotlight', *Reuters*, 22 May 2012.

172 'MEPs welcome first special representative for human rights', *New Europe*, 26 July 2012.

173 Official Journal, EU 2012 Budget, p. 544.

174 Foreign Ministry of Finland press release, 9 March 2010; http://www.finlandcoe.fr/public/default.aspx?contentid=199709&nodeid=38770&contentlan=2&culture=en-US

175 'Foreign Minister Stubb and Swedish Foreign Minister Carl Bildt propose establishment of the European Institute of Peace', press release, Foreign Ministry of Finland, http://themediateur.eu/index.php/about-european-institute-of-peace.

176 'Deutsche Macht fürchte ich heute weniger als deutsche Untätigkeit', Deutsche Gesellschaft für Auswärtige Politik, 28 November 2011, https://dgap.org/de/node/20029.

177 'Prime Minister Donald Tusk sums up the Presidency in the European Parliament', http://pl2011.eu/en/content/prime-minister-donald-tusk-sums-presidency-european-parliament

178 'Renewables: EREC presses for 45 per cent by 2030', *Europolitics Energy*, 13 June 2012.
179 'UK opposes a 2030 renewable energy target', *The Guardian*, 11 March 2012.
180 'FYROM – the name issue', statement by Hellenic Republic Ministry of Foreign Affairs, February 2010.
181 'Turkey in 2030: The Future Demographic', Euromonitor International report, 24 March 2004.
182 'World Population to 2300', United Nations Department of Economic and Social Affairs, 2004.
183 'Turkey: 25 years in EU's waiting room', *Deutsche Welle*, 14 April 2012.
184 Abdullah Gül, interview with *Süddeutsche Zeitung*, 16 October 2010.
185 'Turkish OECD veto causes a stir', *Austria Today*, 6 June 2011.
186 'Remarks by President Obama at student roundtable in Turkey', US State Department press release, 7 April 2009.
187 Home Office Migration Advisory Committee Report, December 2008.
188 'Turkey may be waiting at Europe's door for 20 more years', *The Times*, 16 October 2006.
189 Mario Monti, *A New Strategy for the Single Market*, 9 May 2010, p. 2.
190 Ibid. p. 20.
191 'Sweden unveils plan to slash corporate tax rates', *The Local*, 13 September 2012.
192 *Project Europe 2030 Challenges and Opportunities*, p. 13.
193 Ibid, p. 17.
194 Ibid.
195 'Ex German Finance Minister favours joint eurozone debt', *Reuters*, 11 August 2012.
196 Fresh Start, *Options for Change Green Paper*, July 2012, p. 2.
197 'It's time to reclaim powers from EU, urges new Iron Lady', *Daily Express*, 6 January 2012.
198 Hansard, HC Deb, 18 September 2012, vol. 550, col. 244WH.
199 'Thatcher and Carter: the not-so-special relationship', *Daily Telegraph*, 6 February 2010.
200 Second prime ministerial debate, Sky, 22 April 2010.
201 'Britain must rethink ties with Europe, says Hague', *The Times*, 10 September 2011.
202 Hansard, HC Deb, 24 October 2011, vol. 534, col. 27.
203 '"Take power back from EU", says Sir John Major', *The Independent*, 9 October 2011.
204 'Impact assessment on proposal for a regulation laying down common provisions on the European Regional Development Fund... and the Cohesion Fund', European Commission, p. 17.
205 *Off Target: The Case for Bringing Regional Policy Back Home*, Open Europe, January 2012, p. 9.
206 Ibid., p. 3.
207 Fresh Start Project, *Options for Change Green Paper*, p. 49.
208 'Impact assessment', European Commission, October 2011, p. 14.
209 http://www.eurotreaties.com/maastrichtec.pdf
210 'European Funding', *File on 4*, BBC Radio 4, 17 July 2012.
211 Ibid.

212 'What David Cameron really thinks of Nicolas Sarkozy', *Daily Telegraph*, 9 December 2011.
213 'Gordon Brown and Nicolas Sarkozy attempt a reconciliation', *The Times*, 10 December 2009.
214 Open Europe, *Continental Shift: Safeguarding the UK's Financial Trade in a Changing Europe*, December 2011, p. 7.
215 http://www.comres.co.uk/polls/Open_Europe_Final_tables_14th_December11.pdf
216 Fresh Start, *Options for Change Green Paper*, pp. 154 and 159.
217 *Time's Up! The Case against the EU's 48-hour Working Week*, Open Europe, March 2009, pp. 4–5.
218 'NHS pays £20,000 a week for a doctor', *Sunday Telegraph*, 17 March 2012.
219 Fresh Start, *Options for Change Green Paper*, p. 129.
220 European Commission, press release IP11/1121, 29 September 2011.
221 Department for Trade and Industry, *Compendium of Regulatory Impact Assessments*, April 2004.
222 *Time's Up! The Case against the EU's 48-hour Working Week*, Open Europe, March 2009, p. 4.
223 'Stroppy unions put Brown on the spot', *Daily Mail*, 23 September 2008.
224 'The tide is turning against EU bureaucracy', *Daily Telegraph*, 7 May 2012.
225 'Business secretary and employment minister both pledge "concerted attack" on EU employment regulations', *hrmagazine.co.uk*, 7 March 2012.
226 'EU talks to end working time opt-out fail', *Financial Times*, 29 April 2009, p. 4.
227 Open Europe, *Top 100 Regulations*.
228 Fresh Start, *Options for Change Green Paper*, p. 131.
229 'The tide is turning against EU bureaucracy; Britain is no longer a lone voice in the push for deregulation and a flexible labour market', *Daily Telegraph*, 8 May 2012, p. 20.
230 Ibid.
231 'Davos day two', *The Times* online, 26 January 2012.
232 Open Europe, *Repatriating EU Social Policy*, pp. 21–2.
233 *Options for Change*, p. 140.
234 Interview for this book.
235 'Cameron idea to repatriate laws is complete non-starter', *EU Observer*, 13 February 2012.
236 *Options for Change*, p. 141.
237 Hansard, HC Deb, 15 Oct 2012, vol. 551, col. 35.
238 https://www.europol.europa.eu/content/page/history-149
239 Europol Annual Report, 2008.
240 'Ex-MI5 chief urges Cameron to defy party on European Union crime policies', *The Observer*, 26 August 2012.
241 'A review of the UK's extradition arrangements', *Home Office*, 30 September 2011, p. 462.
242 'How Europe is working for Wales' by Peter Hain, *Western Mail*, 22 October 2001.
243 'European justice demands the glory of British liberty', *The Guardian*, 5 February 2002.
244 'Stop condemning Britons to sham justice abroad', *The Times*, 22 June 2011.

245 Council of the European Union note: Proposed subject for discussion at the experts' meeting on the application of the Framework Decision on the European arrest warrant on 17 July 2007 – the proportionality principle, 9 July 2007.

246 'A review of the UK's extradition arrangements', *Home Office*, 30 September 2011, p. 462.

247 'Repatriate powers on crime and policing, say Conservative MPs', *Daily Telegraph*, 6 February 2012.

248 'Ex-MI5 chief urges Cameron to defy party on European Union crime policies', *The Observer*, 26 August 2012.

249 Hansard, HC Deb, 23 March 2003, vol. 402, cols 194–5.

250 'The EU Debate', *File on 4*, BBC Radio 4, 8 August 2012.

251 'We won't get fooled again, PM', *The Sun*, 10 July 2012.

252 'The EU Debate', *File on 4*, BBC Radio 4, 8 August 2012.

253 'Claw back Euro powers? £2.50 says you can't', *The Times*, 28 October 2011.

254 'Britain should pick-and-mix over Europe instead of apeing Norway', *Daily Telegraph*, 10 July 2012.

255 'France: autistic Tories have castrated UK in Europe', *The Guardian*, 4 November 2009, p. 1.

256 'Hollande prepares for Berlin clash – and fires a warning shot across the Channel', *The Times*, 8 May 2012.

257 'Europe Restructured? The eurozone crisis and its aftermath', *The Times* online, 6 June 2012.

258 'Budget leak in Berlin sparks complaint by government', *Irish Times*, 18 November 2011.

259 'Europe Restructured? The eurozone crisis and its aftermath', *The Times* online, 6 June 2012.

260 Jean-Claude Piris, *The Future of Europe* (Cambridge: Cambridge University Press, 2012), p. 146.

261 Ibid., p. 147.

262 Andrew Duff, *On Governing Europe* (London: Policy Network and ALDE, 2012), p. 68.

263 'Let's take back Britain's powers from the European Union, and let's do it now', *Daily Telegraph*, 17 November 2011.

264 'EU countries criticised for cutting aid budgets', *Public Service Europe*, 4 April 2012.

265 OECD short-term labour market statistics.

266 Private interview for this book.

267 'Nei-rekord i Oslo' (No-record in Oslo), *Nationen*, 10 April 2012.

268 Private interview for this book.

269 http://trade.ec.europa.eu/doclib/docs/2006/september/tradoc_113429.pdf

270 *Fresh Start, Options for Change Green Paper*, pp. 31–2.

271 http://www.admin.ch/ch/f/pore/va/19921206/can388.html

272 http://www.mistrend.ch/articles/SOPHIA%20_2012_Hebdo.pdf

273 *Fresh Start, Options for Change Green Paper*, p. 32.

274 Ibid., p. 33.

275 Ibid., p. 34.

276 Council conclusions on EU relations with EFTA countries, 14 December 2010.

277 Statement by the Integration Office FDFA/FDEA, 14 December 2010.

278   Private interview for this book.
279   *Fresh Start, Options for Change Green Paper*, p. 36.
280   Peter Kellner, *Worried Nationalists, Pragmatic Nationalists and Progressive Internationalists: Who Might Win a British Referendum on Europe?* (European Council on Foreign Relations, 2012).
281   Nicholas Crafts, 'Fifty Years of Economic Growth in Western Europe', *World Economics*, vol. 5, no. 2, April–June 2004.
282   http://www.ons.gov.uk/ons/dcp171778_275476.pdf
283   Private interview for this book.
284   Nicholas Fram, 'Decolonization, the Commonwealth, and British Trade 1945–2004', Stanford University, 17 May 2006.
285   Ibid., p. 20–21.
286   Ibid., p. 11, and Royal Commonwealth Society, 'Trading Places: The Commonwealth Effect Re-visited', 30 September 2010.
287   http://www.teara.govt.nz/en/overseas-trade-policy/4
288   Henry Overman and Alan Winters, 'North and South', *CentrePiece*, Winter 2004.
289   http://www.wto.org/english/res_e/statis_e/its2011_e/its11_world_trade_dev_e.pdf
290   'World trade developments 2010', World Trade Organization, 2011.
291   'World Population to 2300', United Nations Department of Economic and Social Affairs, 2004.
292   Foreign Affairs and International Trade, UKIP website, 12 April 2010.
293   'Ugandan president says nation winning fight against AIDS because it has no homosexuals', *Associated Press*, 3 March 2002.
294   http://www.cbcglobal.org/about/origins-of-cbc
295   'Trading Places: The Commonwealth Effect Re-visited', Royal Commonwealth Society, 30 September 2010, p. 4.
296   Ibid., p. 9.
297   Communiqué and Report to Heads of Government (CHOGM), Commonwealth Business Forum, 24 November 2005.
298   Lord Howell, 'Commonwealth: A Force for Good across the World', speech to the Royal Over-Seas League, 10 November 2011.
299   'How the Commonwealth can regain its relevance', *Financial Times*, 24 November 2005, p. 21.
300   Mohan Kaul, 'Global Growth and the Commonwealth', Commonwealth Business Council, September 2010.
301   Foreign Affairs Select Committee, Oral Evidence, 12 June 2012, Q169.
302   http://www.worldeconomics.com/papers/Commonwealth_Growth_Monitor_0e53b963-bce5-4ba1-9cab-333cedaab048.paper
303   'Commonwealth nations consider free trade pact', *Inter Press Service*, 24 November 2005.
304   'Letter from America – Gingrich warns Europe against the euro', *The Times*, 21 April 1998.
305   'Gingrich's mirage', *The Economist*, 25 April 1998.
306   'New accent for NAFTA? Gingrich raises possibility that Britain could join trade group', *Chicago Sun-Times*, 29 April 1998.
307   http://www.wto.org/english/res_e/statis_e/its2011_e/its11_world_trade_dev_e.pdf
308   Ibid.
309   http://trade.ec.europa.eu/doclib/docs/2012/july/tradoc_149828.pdf

310   http://epp.eurostat.ec.europa.eu/portal/page/portal/international_trade/
       data/main_tables

311   'France keeps up barrage against Brittan trade plan', *Reuters*, 31 March
       1998.

312   Interview for this book.

313   Interview for this book.

314   Interview for this book.

315   http://www.ons.gov.uk/ons/dcp171778_278439.pdf

316   Hansard, HL Deb, 22 March 2011, vol. 726, cols 625–6.

317   David Campbell Bannerman, *The Ultimate Plan B: A Positive Vision of
       an Independent Britain outside the European Union* (Cambridge: David
       Campbell Bannerman, 2011), p. 14.

318   http://www.dpm.cabinetoffice.gov.uk/news/deputy-prime-minister-nick-
       clegg-visits-berlin

319   http://www.euromove.org.uk/index.php?id=7280

320   'The case for joining the euro', *BBC Online News*, 17 December 2001.

321   'UK Jobs Dependent on the EU', Brian Ardy, Iain Begg and Dermot
       Hodson, South Bank University, 2000.

322   http://www.ons.gov.uk/ons/publications/re-reference-tables.
       html?edition=tcm%3A77-250820

323   'No big job losses if UK quits EU, NIESR says', *Reuters News*, 18
       February 2000.

324   'Pro-euro group "acted like Goebbels" to distort figures', *The Times*, 19
       February 2000, p. 2.

325   'What happens to the economy if we pull out of the EU?', *Channel 4
       FactCheck*, 31 October 2011.

326   http://www.niesr.ac.uk/pdf/annual%20report/AR-2000.PDF

327   'Global carbon emissions rise is far bigger than previous estimates', *The
       Guardian*, 21 June 2012.

328   'Worst ever carbon emissions leave climate on the brink', *The Guardian*,
       29 May 2011.

329   Private interview.

330   'UK opposes a 2030 renewable energy target', *The Guardian*, 11 March
       2012.

331   *Fresh Start, Options for Change Green Paper*, p. 180.

332   Ibid., p. 179.

333   'Oettinger considering binding renewables targets for after 2020',
       Agence Europe, 7 June 2012. 334 'Tories warned by EU against stifling
       green agenda', *The Guardian* online, 5 October 2012.

335   Restricted internal paper for Department for Business, Innovation &
       Skills, p. 24.

336   Ibid., p. 24.

337   'Capital collapse: Britain no longer the money capital of Europe, says
       UN', *The Guardian*, 27 July 2011, p. 25.

338   'Britain to sue ECB over threat to City', *ft.com*, 14 September 2011.

339   Private interview.

340   David Campbell Bannerman.

341   'Government proposes longer lorries to help cut carbon', *Central Office
       of Information*, 30 March 2011.

342   Interview for this book.

343   http://www.ukip.org/content/ukip-policies/1452-food-farming-and-the-countryside-ukip-policy
344   David Campbell Bannerman, *The Ultimate Plan B: A Positive Vision of an Independent Britain outside the European Union* (Cambridge: David Campbell Bannerman, 2011), p. 19.
345   Stephen Booth, Christopher Howarth and Vincent Scarpetta, *Tread Carefully: The Impact and Management of EU Free Movement and Immigration Policy* (London: Open Europe, 2012), p. 17.
346   'Nationality at Point of National Insurance Number Registration of DWP Benefit Claimants', Department for Work and Pensions, January 2012.
347   David Campbell Bannerman, *The Ultimate Plan B: A Positive Vision of an Independent Britain outside the European Union* (Cambridge: David Campbell Bannerman, 2011), p. 17.
348   Booth, Howarth and Scarpetta, *Tread Carefully*, p. 26.
349   http://www.dwp.gov.uk/newsroom/ministers-speeches/2010/17-11-10.shtml
350   'We've got it all wrong says EU as it prepares to toss fishing strategy overboard', *The Times*, 23 April 2009, pp. 16–17.
351   http://www.ucas.ac.uk/about_us/media_enquiries/media_releases/2012/20120823
352   Barry Eichengreen and Andrea Boltho, *The Economic Impact of European Integration* (London: Centre for Economic Policy Research, 2008) p. 43.
353   'PM offers to devolve more powers to Scotland', *The Times* online, 16 February 2012.
354   Private interview for this book.
355   'Cameron makes Scots an offer', *Financial Times*, 17 February 2012, p. 2.
356   Peter Hennessy, *The Prime Minister*, 2nd edn (London: Penguin Books, 2001), p. 366.
357   http://www.harvard-digital.co.uk/euro/pamphlet.htm
358   http://www.angus-reid.com/polls/46221/animosity-towards-european-union-continues-in-britain/
359   'EU referendum: poll shows 49% would vote for UK withdrawal', *The Guardian*, 24 October 2011.
360   'Europe, is it the end of the project?', The Hands Lecture, 4 May 2012.
361   http://www.policy-network.net/uploads/media/17/7907.pdf
362   'Angela Merkel warns David Cameron over talk of EU exit', *The Times*, 8 November 2012.
363   'Cameron says Britain isn't waving bye-bye to EU', *Reuters*, 19 October 2012.
364   http://wefo.wales.gov.uk/programmes/?lang=en
365   'Deutsche Macht fürchte ich heute weniger als deutsche Untätigkeit', Deutsche Gesellschaft für Auswärtige Politik, 28 November 2011, https://dgap.org/de/node/20029.
366   'Seven EU myths you should never believe', *The Times*, 25 September 2012.
367   'Mandelson says UK foot-stomping is sabotaging relations with the EU', *The Guardian*, 17 October 2012.
368   'British are the Muppets of Europe, say Germans', *The Times*, 17 October 2012.

Appendix

Britain's EU contributions, rebate and receipts
All figures in £million

Year	Gross total	Rebate	Gross contribution	Public sector receipts	Net contribution
1973	181	n/a	181	79	102
1974	181	n/a	181	150	31
1975	342	n/a	342	398	-56
1976	463	n/a	463	296	167
1977	737	n/a	737	368	369
1978	1,348	n/a	1,348	526	822
1979	1,606	n/a	1,606	659	947
1980	1,767	98	1,669	963	706
1981	2,174	693	1,481	1,084	397
1982	2,863	1,019	1,844	1,238	606
1983	2,976	807	2,169	1,522	647
1984	3,204	528	2,676	2,020	656
1985	3,940	227	3,713	1,905	1,808
1986	4,493	1,701	2,792	2,220	572
1987	5,202	1,153	4,049	2,328	1,721
1988	5,138	1,594	3,544	2,182	1,362
1989	5,585	1,154	4,431	2,116	2,315
1990	6,355	1,697	4,658	2,183	2,475
1991	5,807	2,497	3,309	2,765	544
1992	6,738	1,881	4,857	2,827	2,030
1993	7,985	2,539	5,446	3,291	2,155
1994	7,189	1,726	5,463	3,253	2,211
1995	8,889	1,207	7,682	3,665	4,017
1996	9,133	2,412	6,721	4,373	2,348
1997	7,991	1,733	6,258	4,661	1,597
1998	10,090	1,378	8,712	4,115	4,597
1999	10,287	3,171	7,117	3,479	3,638
2000	10,517	2,085	8,433	4,241	4,192

2001	9,379	4,560	4,819	3,430	1,389
2002	9,439	3,099	6,340	3,201	3,139
2003	10,966	3,559	7,407	3,728	3,679
2004	10,895	3,593	7,302	4,294	3,008
2005	12,567	3,656	8,911	5,329	3,581
2006	12,426	3,569	8,857	4,948	3,909
2007	12,456	3,523	8,933	4,332	4,601
2008	12,653	4,862	7,791	4,497	3,294
2009	14,129	5,392	8,737	4,401	4,336
2010	15,197	3,047	12,150	4,775	7,375
2011	15,357	3,143	12,214	4,112	8,102
2012	15,021	3,172	11,849	4,954	6,895
Total	283,667	76,474	207,193	110,909	96,284

Notes: 2012 figures are provisional; rebate column includes ad hoc refunds from 1980 until 1984 and some of the 1985 total when the rebate officially started (total of pure rebate is £73,268 million). Net contribution figure £1 million out in some years due to rounding.

The Pink Book, the United Kingdom Balance of Payments 2012 edition, compiled by the Office for National Statistics, shows that the total amount transferred from the UK to the EU institutions in 2011 was £19.188 billion. This figure is sometimes taken as the taxpayer contribution to the EU but in fact includes private sector as well as public sector payments.

Sources: 'The EU Budget', House of Commons Library Standard Note SN/EP/864; *European Union Finances 2012*, HM Treasury, Cm 8405.

Where the money went – Structural funds
Figures show €million or equivalent

Country (year of joining)	Structural funds received from EU 1976–2011	Amount provided by UK at 11.6 per cent
Spain (1986)	131,388	15,241
Italy (1957)	80,332	9,319
Germany (1957)	73,021	8,470
Greece (1981)	61,739	7,162
Portugal (1986)	60,681	7,039
France (1957)	49,850	5,783
UK (1973)	49,404	5,731
Poland (2004)	36,564	4,241
Ireland (1973)	20,018	2,322
Hungary (2004)	11,646	1,351
Czech Republic (2004)	9,355	1,085
Netherlands (1957)	7,170	832
Belgium (1957)	6,966	808
Slovakia (2004)	4,760	552
Lithuania (2004)	4,648	539
Finland (1995)	4,550	528
Sweden (1995)	4,367	507
Austria (1995)	4,264	495
Denmark (1973)	3,222	374
Romania (2007)	3,192	370
Latvia (2004)	2,686	312
Estonia (2004)	2,068	240
Slovenia (2004)	1,935	224
Bulgaria (2007)	1,571	182
Luxembourg (1957)	425	49
Cyprus (2004)	339	39
Malta (2004)	311	36

Table shows total funding since 1976 or since year of joining for European Regional Development Fund, Cohesion Fund, European Social Fund, European Fund for Rural Development and European Fisheries Fund.

Source: European Commission Regional Policy Directorate (compiled for this book).

Bibliography

Publications

Bache, Ian and George, Stephen, *Politics in the European Union* (Oxford: Oxford University Press, 2006)

Bennett, Chappell, Reed and Sriskandarajah, *Trading Places: The Commonwealth Effect Re-visited* (London: Royal Commonwealth Society, 2010)

Blunkett, David, *The Blunkett Tapes* (London: Bloomsbury, 2006)

Booth, Howarth, Persson and Scarpetta, *Continental Shift: Safeguarding the UK's Financial Trade in a Changing Europe* (London: Open Europe, 2011)

Booth, Howarth and Scarpetta, *Tread Carefully: The Impact and Management of EU Free Movement and Immigration Policy* (London: Open Europe, 2012)

Campbell Bannerman, David, *The Ultimate Plan B: A Positive Vision of an Independent Britain outside the European Union* (Cambridge: David Campbell Bannerman, 2011)

Crafts, Nicholas, 'Fifty Years of Economic Growth in Western Europe', *World Economics*, vol. 5, no. 2 (2004).

Duff, Andrew, *On Governing Europe* (London: Policy Network and ALDE, 2012)

EEA Review Committee, The, *Utenfor og Innenfor (Outside and Inside)* (Oslo: Norwegian Ministry of Foreign Affairs, 2012)

Eichengreen, Barry and Boltho, Angela, *The Economic Impact of European Integration* (London: Centre for Economic Policy Research, 2008)

Fram, Nicholas, 'Decolonization, the Commonwealth, and British Trade 1945–2004' (PhD thesis, Stanford University, 2006)

Fresh Start Project, *Options for Change Green Paper: Renegotiating the UK's Relationship with the EU* (London: 2012)

Gaskell, Sarah and Persson, Mats, *Still Out of Control?*, 2nd edn (London: Open Europe, 2010)

Heath, Edward, *Travels: People and Places in My Life* (London: Sidgwick & Jackson, 1977)

Hennessy, Peter, *The Prime Minister: The Office and Its Holders since 1945*, 2nd edn (London: Penguin Books, 2001)

Hindley, Brian and Howe, Martin, *Better Off Out?*, 2nd edn (London: Institute of Economic Affairs, 2000)

Howarth, Kullman and Swidlicki, *More for Less: Making the EU's Farm Policy Work for Growth and the Environment* (London: Open Europe, 2012)

Ilzkovitz, Dierx, Kovacs and Sousa, *Steps towards a Deeper Economic Integration: The Internal Market in the 21st Century* (European Economics Papers 271, 2007).

Jenkins, Roy, *Churchill* (London: Macmillan, 2001)

Kellner, Peter, *Worried Nationalists, Pragmatic Nationalists and Progressive Internationalists: Who Might Win a British Referendum on Europe?* (London: European Council on Foreign Relations, 2012)

Leach, Graeme, *EU Membership, What's the Bottom Line?* (London: Institute of Directors, 2000)

Milne, Ian, *A Cost Too Far?* (London: Civitas, 2004)

Monti, Mario, *A New Strategy for the Single Market* (Brussels: European Commission, 2010)

Open Europe, *The Rise of the EU Quangos* (London: Open Europe, 2012)

Persson, Gaskell and Booth, *Time's Up! The Case against the EU's 48-hour Working Week* (London: Open Europe, 2009)

Piris, Jean-Claude, *The Future of Europe* (Cambridge, Cambridge University Press, 2012)

Rennie, David, *The Continent or the Open Sea: Does Britain have a European Future?* (London: Centre for European Reform, 2012)

Rentoul, John, *Tony Blair: Prime Minister* (London: Little, Brown and Company, 2001)

Reynolds, David, *The Origins of the Cold War in Europe: International Perspectives* (New Haven, CT: Yale University Press, 1994)

Seldon, Anthony with Peter Snowdon and Daniel Collings, *Blair Unbound* (London: Simon & Schuster, 2007)

Short, Clare, *An Honourable Deception? New Labour, Iraq and the Misuse of Power* (London: Free Press, 2004)

Straathof, Linders, Lejour and Moehlmann, *The Internal Market and the Dutch Economy* (The Hague: Netherlands Bureau for Economic Policy Analysis, 2008)

Swidlicki, Ruparel, Persson and Howarth, *Off Target: The Case for Bringing Regional Policy Back Home* (London: Open Europe, 2012)

Thatcher, Margaret, *The Path to Power* (London: HarperCollins, 1995)

Wall, Stephen, *A Stranger in Europe* (Oxford: Oxford University Press, 2008)

Winters, L. Alan, *Britain in Europe: A Survey of Quantitative Trade Studies* (London: Centre for Economic Policy Research, 1986)

Young, Hugo, *This Blessed Plot: Britain and Europe from Churchill to Blair*, 2nd edn (London: Papermac, 1999)

Broadcasts

'A Letter to *The Times*', *Document*, BBC Radio 4, 3 February 2000

'European Funding', *File on 4*, BBC Radio 4, 17 July 2012
'The EU Debate', *File on 4*, BBC Radio 4, 8 August 2012
The Politics Show, BBC1, 18 May 2003

Index

Also available from Biteback

GREEKONOMICS
Vicky Pryce

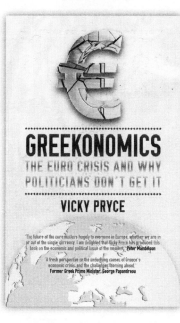

"The future of the euro matters hugely to everyone in Europe, whether we are in or out of the single currency. I am delighted that Vicky Pryce has produced this book on the economic and political issue of the moment." PETER MANDELSON

"A fresh perspective on the underlying causes of Greece's economic crisis, and the challenges looming ahead."
FORMER GREEK PRIME MINISTER, GEORGE PAPANDREOU

"I am delighted Vicky Pryce has used her experience to give her own perspective on the eurozone crisis." ALISTAIR DARLING

304pp paperback, £12.99
Available from all good bookshops or order from
www.bitebackpublishing.com